FILM IS

FILM IS

the international free cinema

Stephen Dwoskin

The Overlook Press

Woodstock, New York

© Stephen Dwoskin 1975

First published in the United
States in 1975 by the Overlook
Press, Lewis Hollow Road
Woodstock, New York 12498

ISBN 0-87951-036-6

Library of Congress
Catalog Number 75-7685

Printed by The Studley Press Inc.

To independent film-makers

Contents

Illustrations appear between pages 256 and 257

Acknowledgements

I would like to take this opportunity to thank all the film-makers. I would also like to express thanks for the personal help, advice and patience of Jacques Ledoux and the Royal Film Archive of Belgium; Elizabeth Bennett; Sidney Bernard; Raymond Durgnat; Andi Engel; Susan Forrester; Simon Hartog; Leena Komppa; Jonas Mekas; Bobby Ross and Ros Spain. I would also like to give thanks for the direct help obtained from The Museum of Modern Art, New York; the Film-makers' Co-operatives of New York, London, Hamburg, Austria, The Netherlands and Italy; The Svenska Filminstitutet and the Moderna Museet, Stockholm; X-Screen, Cologne; Filmverlag der Autoren, Munich; Film-studio 70, Rome; and The Other Cinema, London. Thanks too to Dan Franklin at Peter Owen.

Stephen Dwoskin

Some films are not dated in the text. For dates of these films please see the Index of Films.

Part One

1 On Location *by Joan Adler*

Really, the way to remember Frankie Francine is not to think of those long, sad stories of his youth and times when he had his own long brown hair and marriageable suitors, but with sharp-pointed features and dark eyes flashing with indignation and fury at Jack's failure to take care of his clothes. His marvellous, worked-over, much-loved clothes. His pink gown with flowers and frills. He wears it at the top of the wedding cake, drowning in a waving sea of tendril arms as he sinks, with many bumps and groans, to the bottom of the cake. And bruises 'That motherfucker doesn't care what happens to me.' Shrill, busy, angry voice. Sharp as his face.

Not like the soft, thickening waist muscles seen years later as he rocks self-consciously onstage in pink stage chorus costume.

Delighted.

And he's right. Jack Smith *doesn't* care. Not like that or for that. Jack's attention is elsewhere. He's getting chimera cameras, film, cars, locations, costumes, people, meeting-places and God knows what other down-bringing affairs to attend to (if they bring him down). And the movie. Getting his creatures to be creatures alone all the time, nurtured, breathed-on, tended, grown. With Frankie it's a matter of giving him the chance; he's set and knows and loves it. Rene isn't Mario yet, he still has another life. Ah, the hell with it. Theories. Frankie loved his jewellery. For hours he and Beverly Grant's room-mate, Zelda, discussed his jewellery, his clothes, houses, furniture, common-character relatives. Long, long before they had finished, other things had started. Jim baiting Zelda because she can say, perfectly sincere, that I think, therefore I am, as the philosopher said. She's got a beautiful American Beauty-in-the-movies face. Not blonde-pretty, dark-pretty. But she disappeared too soon after appearing too late (to Paris and on-the-run boy friend and whoring to keep them both and final return to NY). She was Beverly's room-mate for four months and they had themselves a barely scraping along, girl-about-town's friendship going. But Beverly was really away out of that. Her change was coming and Jack drew her into the Cobra Woman character and miasma skilfully, obliquely. And thus drawn out, she became black, white-faced, mysterious, beautiful and witch-like.

Jack Smith was after a complete feeling-aura. He thought Maria Montez was like that all the time. The altar in the middle of the 14th Street living-room was the giver-out of incense to bemuse the full-time senses of his hosts, his also-creatures but with illusions of freedom. A more practical role for hosts who are car drivers, home-providers. Mamas and poppas maybe. Drivers through New Jersey countryside to find a place to shoot the Yellow Sequence in. And the Marsh Sequence later. But the Yellow Sequence really got out into open country. A field full of golden-rod. Frankie, flowered yellow and black frocked, yellow umbrella'd, flowered hatted, sinking into a field of grass-weeds/golden-rod. Dying broken-hearted because his apartment had been burgled again yesterday and they'd smashed and destroyed a lot of his things for him to find and grieve over. He grieved for the stolen things too. The chandelier he had so painstakingly stolen, carrying it home piece by piece. The armchair he had carried. Carried! On foot for more than twenty blocks at dead never-dead of New York night. Braving policemen all the way. Frankie dying in a field of yellow. Jack lost the film to that sequence, or the laboratory did, and it didn't turn up for ages. He shot another sequence in a yellow-painted wrecked car lot with Tiny Tim holding Vigue and the Mongol in white moving wispily through it. The Mongol was bald and skinny armed and legged. A munshkin of Jack's hospital-grown type.

Tiny Tim was brief, he played a tiny George Formby ukulele and sang Shirley Temple songs. Had long woman's hair and dressed like a dyke. But he was in drag for the Yellow Sequence. Huge face peering into the camera twisting on the screen, eyes all over. Nose all over. Mouth all over. All in one face? Impossible. But true. His whole body was large: well over six feet and big, not skinny. It was Tiny Tim's Yellow Sequence that Jack eventually used, even though the Frankie Yellow Sequence turned up in the end. Both are overlaid by the images in Bob's still pictures. Stills which are utterly vivid and vision-spun. Frankie dying in the yellow golden-rod. Mongol and Frankie dancing finger-tip to finger-tip under the yellow umbrella, white-robed, flower-yellow gowned, heads raised, eyes lowered (Frankie, professional appearer) and squinting (Dave Mongol, apprentice appearer) in the bright sunlight which is, of course, behind the camera because Bob thinks technically, which Jack doesn't. Jack can't remember names of processes or negatives or anything. He's also a marvellous still photographer and was very bitter at his failure to get his pictures on to the cover of *Harper's Bazaar*. Soft, fading, pale-coloured, mysterious-fleshed pictures which *Flaming Creatures* almost got to. But that was only shown in lofts, so that the police couldn't raid it too easily (raids of private showings are much rarer than theatre-licence revoking and the police are very hot that year, what with the Film-makers' Co-operative running a theatre and The Bridge showing the movies too). It got worse as it went on. But they didn't risk *Flaming Creatures* at a public showing at all. They did in Belgium, where, to everyone's surprise, it got into violent controversy. Lots of people seemed very offended by *Flaming Creatures*. The film was shot on the borrowed roof of the old theatre in broiling sunlight with the set falling all over them, high as kites, Jack pouring ceiling plaster all over them (a large chunk bruised Frankie, who got mad telling about those sufferings too) and careening dangerously above them on some swinging, home-made contraption. Frankie mad as hell about the bouncing camera. Even madder at Jerry Joffrin's shaking camera. Which manages to split up all images and thus offends people like me and Frankie who like to see pictures of ourselves.

Rene had been a Spanish dancer in *Flaming Creatures*. Pleased with himself as a Spanish dancer but more taken up now with the Rene version of

Marilyn Monroe as Maria Montez (later known as Mario Montez) in the
'Moon Pool' and the 'Swamp'. The Moon Pool was indoors and gauze-hung
and mirrored. The altar, after months of growth, change and minishment on
the 14th Street living-room floor, had been re-erected on the side of the Moon
Pool. And Rene, her high priestess adorer and reincarnation, lay in her
silver-glistening, blonde-wigged, bejewelled mermaid's costume, worshipping
the stark black and white photograph of Maria Montez around which the altar
was built. Small candles, death's head, jewels, rings, necklaces, plastic flowers,
Art Nouveau vessels, hand mirrors. Out of drag Rene was a small, slim,
tight-bodied, long-faced, brown-skinned Puerto Rican boy with a fairly heavy
accent, full-lipped and heavy-lidded. In drag, a beautiful Hollywood-sex-
appealing woman. Though I've seen him dance with woman's head and
below-waist and man's chest and shoulders and found him bewitchingly
hermaphroditic. At the same Wyn Chamberlain party where Rene danced,
Ron Rice got undressed to shock the mob. Ron loved to shock people. He also
loved to get undressed at gatherings. But at this party he did it across the
middle of Tiny Tim's act. That upset a number of people so Ron was hustled
out again, calling loudly for attention. His physical image was an aggressive
Mexican, Zapata style, black-mustachioed, dark bright eyes, pushed-out chest.
The masculine image from that world, at least according to Hollywood.

The next year he left for Mexico with Amy, whom he married after she
got pregnant and with whom he lived until he died in Mexico. They had no
money and lived in a hut on the beach with very little food. Ron got mad
when Jack, visiting, bought food with his limited available money. Ron wanted
film. Filming was most of what he wanted to do all the time. Amy wanted
Ron and Mexico. She got Ron's child and her father's New Jersey suburban
home for shelter. And a dream of Mexico. Ron died two weeks before the
baby was born, but he stares out at you from the child's eyes and there's still
the same boldness and fear and humour.

Before all that, though, he and Amy lived in a loft just off Canal Street and
towards the end of the summer, when the non-stop effort was over and the
shooting of *Normal Love* had become sporadic, Ron's set was ready for
Chumlum. Jack's creatures set free, Joel, Beverly, Frankie, Rene, Jack
himself. They were three-day sessions which led to despair on the creatures'
part, two days of waiting for Ron to start shooting, left totally to their own
character building and action devices, drained of energy until they slowly
emerged into slow, curving dancers in sequence shot over sequence, inter-
meshing blacks and reds and yellows, curving fabric lines, swaying arms, hair,
bodies. Jack started everyone off into make-up and costumes, then started his
own. It took three days to finish that, too, as everyone explored the heaps
around. Beverly in the hammock. Some of Bob Adler's most commonly
beautiful still shots. But perfect. Jack-as-the-Magician surrounded by Frankie
and Rene as Eastern nun and great splashes of colour. And Guy, Ron's friend,
the painter, slow-spoken Dumb-seeming. Costume-prone but no Jack creature.
Chumlum was the first to get into the mid-town theatre and it was shown at
the Co-op's first press conference which was attended by a large number of

foreign (European and South American) press correspondents and a scattering
of minor United States ones. With Jonas Mekas, Jack Smith, Ron Rice,
Gregory Markopoulos, Stan VanDerBeek, etc., etc., on the platform. *Chumlum* was a part of the statement (at Ron's insistence but they let him win) and
everyone crowded around to watch it, then separated again to fire questions
at the platform. Jonas nominated people to answer. Not a word could be
gotten out of Jack. Gregory made a plain historical statement. VanDerBeek
told what he wanted to do. The press was dissatisfied, they wanted an intellectual statement of purpose, message, structure, categorization of some kind,
and they weren't getting it. One of them was getting very angry in a 'child
of five could do it better' kind of way. And Jerry Joffrin stood up in the
audience and gave them what they wanted. A structural philosophy which by
a miracle of Jerry's intellect was open-ended and life-giving. They didn't
understand it but it shut them up, particularly the angry man, who kind of
subsided. It wasn't any good as a conference with the press, but with each
other it was fine. Everyone was waving arms and talking to each other as
they slowly herded (maybe fifty people) towards the doors.

Barbara Rubin had also got up and made an excited statement in what
later became known as Hippie terms. But she sounded incoherent, so was
easily dismissed by the Gentlemen of the Press (greeted in silence by her
fellows).

The Co-op then was a third-storey crowded loft on Park Avenue South,
opposite the huge neon Belmont Cafeteria which stayed open late and was
the local eating-place for those with money. At the front of the loft, overlook-
ing Park Avenue South and the Belmont, was the office, desk, telephone, type-
writer, drawers, paper, pens, inks, filing cabinets. The sides of all sections
were filled with film racks which were stacked with films and reels. For
screening, the screen would be opened with the office as a dark backdrop
and the audience would drag up chairs, sit on the floor or lie on the sofa to
one side of the cleared space which was the centre of the loft. Maybe 25 feet
deep and 12 feet across. Behind that was the projector and storage space with
more film and cameras and negatives and whatever odd items of equipment
had turned up. There was also table space for sorting mimeographed sheets
and what was once to have been darkroom space but never got used. There
they gave private film showings to prospective backers, sponsors, angels,
distributors, helpers of power and there they got raided by the police a couple
of times and lost a few copies of film (including *Flaming Creatures*) to the
authorities. One lab painstakingly destroyed a copy that they made of a
sequence and threatened to confiscate, virtuously, the negative. Some soft,
fast talking released the negative. But it was a constant question. Nudity in
moving film ain't the same as still life, baby, and the police are angry and
getting angrier the more they are flouted. Open rebellion is not common among
citizens who are not protesting war and not criminals. And even the former
are a passive kind of problem, though disturbing too, in a stranger kind of
way. But this is open, unabiding law-breaking. They hadn't got the Hippies to
occupy them yet.

Barbara Rubin was very militant. She wanted a brave, new, licentious world of film showings with freedom and we all got pretty indignant one time or another. But some went to the court-house to give moral and legal support and some didn't. Barbara did; and she organized what organization there was to the Co-op, and kept Jonas together. She came back from Italy (deported, she claimed, for public protest when goosed by a priest in the Vatican) with her head shaved and wearing a long, heavy, black cloak and looking marvellous. Before that she had been black-hair-tousled and face-hidden, by the hair, by down-bending, finger-plucking. Now her chin was forward and her face out for viewing and she stood straight in her cloak. Still militant and sexy. She it was who brought news of possible or non-existent donors to egg Jack on and keep him out of despair over money doldrums. She was the rumour engineer who kept speculation, intrigue, scheming, alive at the Co-op, and everyone had a good time figuring out what was *really* happening. Jack got his money in dribs and drabs, when the need was most painful, and he got his film processing paid for by the Co-op. If the Co-op had a general policy, it was that. Help the most needy to stay alive while filming; pay for the processing and try to make sure the film gets made. But no fancy things like written contracts and salaries. Beverly would never believe that. She wanted an agent, a manager, a contract, folding money and a regular life. She was really convinced that the world was scabbing her, that everyone secretly had a finger in the pie (lack of evidence notwithstanding) and she was being kept out of the pie. Around her, machinations appeared like spiders' webs, complex, hardly visible possibilities. But they weren't just business, financial-pie webs. They were who-loves-who, who's-making-whom, what-was-meant-by-that, how-much-for-the-cocaine webs too. When we got burned for the C, Beverly got the Mafia. And when the Cobra died and Beverly (she says, of course) threw it into the Hudson at dead of night, with incantations, Jack and Stanley pulled their webs out for viewing and claimed witchcraft. And surely bicycles fell over as she cursed them, men ran screaming from her in the streets, though she wanted to help, and things fell her way at silent bidding. And she believed it, too.

Joel stock-still in the street staring at Beverly and me with wishfully felt fear. Convinced that if he entered the house at our bidding he was lost. And I anxious to get him out of the street and the police danger and Beverly, too, I think. But Joel held her in special awe of her powers and wanted her badly at times. He himself dropped out of the film early on. What he had had for *Flaming Creatures* was not for *Normal Love* and he was too hung up on Jack and Stanley and Beverly (and on being hung up) to be usable. Too paranoid. Jack let him go thankfully.

Uncle Pasty, Arnold, was the film's rapist, his great chance to appear nude and the nearest he had yet managed to get to being in a dirty movie. He was disappointed that it wasn't going to be a real sex scene, but then he said that Diana, whom he was to attack, was one of the few women who didn't turn him on sexually. He felt like a brother, protective towards her, and tried to help later as she became unhappier. With food and money and offers of practical help because he saw she needed them. But by then she had gone to Jerry and his ménage and Arnold savagely despised that scene. Jerry he conceived to be a blown-up fly-speck of a man with unaccountable attractions for women whom he then made mad. By hypnotism, Arnold thought. And he wasn't too far wrong, though it wasn't the settle-down-and-let-me-trance-you hypnotism that Arnold was trying to learn (or talked about learning) out of a book. Jerry was magnetic if you didn't find him despicable. And when he was in full possession of his powers. And if you were prepared to believe and listen. He really believed that he knew and could teach. He jumped his camera until you couldn't see what had been and got a headache. His paintings were for the eye of the viewer only, his loft was always full of people, many of them there sitting gazing silently into the blank air for days at a time. Shooting gallery. But also Frankie, who never shot, could be found there in the same condition. Shelter, sometimes food, presence tolerated, visitors to take one somewhere else always possible. Diana's job became to tidy up Jerry's painting things, trim his canvases, get paints and brushes, etc. Ellen's was to earn money (she was a night-club bar waitress who worked steadily then), and Joyce, I think, kept house, though the function for Joyce and Ellen was never really ritualized. For Diana, in need of a base, it was.

Jack said he had met her in a 42nd Street cafeteria (he had met Frankie in an 8th Street one) and that they turned out to have friends in common in Cuba. Anyway, he took over her life and her apartment for the first period of organizing his film. There costumes were stashed, meetings held, plans made. Until he wanted Stanley and moved into 14th Street and left Diana lonely on the other side of town. And as the affair between Jack and Stanley became clear, she moved towards Jerry and then back, lonely, to her own apartment where she held a dinner of rice and chicken hearts and strawberry shortcake and was a hostess, with Jack and Stanley, and Jerry's ex-mistress Margo there, complaining of how Jerry had ruined her life and showing her 'before' photos to anyone who would look. Then Diana was reported to be sweeping her whole apartment into the street (it had an uncovered little stream running through the living-room) and to be unrecognizing and not eating. Her parents came and drove her to Bellevue and then she went to Hillside out in Queens County for several months of therapy and came back, fat, to Jerry, who by then had lost the loft and a tiny apartment on East 12th Street which may have been Stanley's before then. And grew thin and mad again. She wore a pink goosy and cut pink melon in an early sequence and swung slowly on a swing from a tree branch in a later one. On Fire Island she wrapped herself slowly around a white Grecian plaster pillar and green fabric around herself, it billowing with the wind from the sea and its pattern becoming her face and a mask. She never let go and Jack swore she hated her nose which he thought he could use in spite of it. But she got lost along the way of Stanley and then Beverly.

Uncle Arnold Pasty made a sex film with Barbara Rubin shooting later. Two couples and make-believe fucking. He wanted Barbara he said, for months, but he could never get her alone and if she knew she never let on.

He was annoyed when he went to see the film and found that she had cut it all up into one-inch pieces and spliced them together again at random. Couldn't see anything, he complained. That bitch. He stopped wanting her.

He brought real (made in Mexico) dirty movies to show at 14th Street. Sex between a woman and a dog and then between a woman and a priest. Cunnilingus, for which a married couple got arrested in their kitchen recently, having been copped by cops peering through the fanlight. The surprising judge threw it out as private behaviour and to hell with the written word of the law. Arnold also had stories of almost-sex situations every time we saw him, but after his heart-attack and three hours of lying thus, ignored, in a Brooklyn subway station, and months in hospital after almost dying, and a complete and utter life-shaking-up so, he confessed to erection difficulties and married a plump, laughing Mama doll, whom he met at a relative's birthday party.

Gregory Markopoulos used Beverly for his Greek-costume movie on the shore. He came over dressed in a dark suit and tie and white shirt and sliced-down hair; frozen-faced, polite and odoriferous if approached too closely. Beverly said he was always like that and had a script, organized his expeditions neatly and to plan, and told his actors what he wanted and what to do, and was altogether organized, meticulous and unagonizing. Though he did say at the press conference that three-quarters of all his earnings went on film-making, he paid Beverly when he could, which is more than she's managed to get out of Jack.

The big break-up between her and Jack came, I suppose, during their overwhelming row about her having gotten $100 from Jonas (and/or the Co-op). She needed rent money and food, she said, while working full time for Jack and thus for the Co-op. The Co-op's film-makers, Jack insisted, needed the money for making films and that's what the Co-op was for. Beverly declared the actors to be badly used and in need of a union. Jack declared the film-makers' need of all the tiny available amount of money for film-making. They called each other many names and never really forgave each other.

The search for a swamp had gone on for weeks. Site after site had been put forward, but was non-existent or no good for one vague Jack Smith verbalized reason or another. But one Friday night we packed and got together and chose costumes and got into cars to go to a swamp which the friend of a friend, who had turned up during the night with a car as well as with a site, claimed to exist. And he was to lead-drive us when we got close enough. It was a swamp with his grandparents' house on the verge. But houses on verges are not alone. They tend to have other houses nearby. They certainly have roads. This one was a highway. We parked the cars off on the side of the road. These swamps were in the woods and our tramping company, Cobra Woman, Werewolf, Mermaid (tailless, as yet; we were only partly begun), Mummy, Cutie Pie, Chorus Girl, Yellow Hag, drivers and attendants, skirted gullies and hollows and indentations of swamp, keeping to high ground, twisting, turning, arriving finally at a clearing verged with luxuriant swamp and clearing to a forever mist-blue patch of water. The mud was dark brown and sloshy; walkable but sinky. At one point it rose in a series of rocks and sparse grass before the woods began. And there the company perched like birds, making up, sniffing up, dressing up for hours of sunlight while Jack tramped to and fro, from costume to make-up to scenery, busy and swearing for need of time.

The Mummy and Cobra Woman first ready and usable. But Jack's camera somehow gets stuck on the Mummy and finally settles on his feet churning through the swamp. Camera trouble. Then the Mermaid and Werewolf to the camera. Out into the wetter part of the swamp whence the Werewolf is to carry the Mermaid into dry land. (Heroically? Who knows?) He was in training as an actor and went through many contortions for the camera. A lot of the time it turned out not to be trained on him and then he'd get mad at the loss of his lovely bit of acting. Rene, Marilyn Monroe legless, fish-tailed and set-faced (to sweetness when possible) in the swamp as the Werewolf let slip of her a little and mud got on to her tail, face, wig. The wig finally got lost that day after its final slip-off being ruthlessly filmed by Jack over Rene's screams and head-clutchings and pleadings not to. And comforting himself later with the thought that perhaps the camera wasn't working. So, with to-do, the filming continues.

In the meantime, rockbound, the rest of the company watches, puts on more make-up, smokes a cigarette, another cigarette, chats quietly, wonders when Jack will get to them. Finally, if. The driver-guide was watching and sniffing and talking to Stanley. He was reported by his indignant and scared car-load of creatures to be a reckless driver and they were each bent on getting a seat in the other car going home. He and Stanley depart for a walk from which Stanley returned alone. He had found his companion entertaining, he saw lions and tigers in the trees, figures prowling. Stanley, seeing the possibilities in the vegetation around him, agreed. But Dick was getting spooked and went to his grandmother's house for a rest, he said.

By the time the Werewolf and Mermaid were mud-soaked and the Mummy's costume legs were covered with drying mud, and the blonde wig lost, and the camera bust for the day or out of film, or Jack too tired to go on, Dick's absence had grown alarming. As dusk fell, a bewildered, grumbling, many-lost company was fumbling its way out of the forest (the actor-Werewolf had revealed a sense of direction and led the way, though nobody believed him until we hit the road again) a few hundred yards from the cars. Dick's car was still there, so, scrambling or riding up a hilly private road, we parked near a small, scattered circling of houses, one of which was Dick's grandparents'. Dick was found to be lying in the living-room. When whoever had seen him knocked on the door, waited, then knocked on the window, he called the police. Reported strangers on his roof and under his bed. They had heard it before but they came anyway. And found us all, all except the Mummy who had disappeared and later reported waking up on the floor of Dick's car as he drove into New York. He had a whole conversation with him and couldn't find out what had happened to everyone else.

As searching lights flashed into the car, I saw dark forms quickly fade off the scene, into the trees; just as well, they're only more evidence against. The broad police face followed behind the lights, and his shoulders came through the window a bit too. He didn't say very much for a while, but looked from Werewolf (heavy black facial make-up lines and eyes, pink tights now, fortunately hidden) to Cobra Woman (now a slightly faded green face and tall green neck rearing from hidden green shoulders, arms, legs and blue-green dress), to Chorus Cutie (still heavily pink-lipped, berouged, kohl and cat-eyed), to Mermaid (belipsticked but wigless and tailless, at least). Then the outside of the glove compartment. We held our breath. Then he asked what? And Beverly, green Beverly, answered his questions with all the aplomb and friendly dignity of a well-set-up Jersey matron who does this kind of thing all the time, and doesn't everyone? She included the policeman in that everyone, so that by the time he got to asking about the film he was a little softened. Bob and Stanley had gone into the house for questioning with Dick and the other policemen.

Fourteen in the Volvo in two loads to the bus stop and relatively mild paranoia of public transport into the city.

Tall, quiet, smiling Angus was the Mummy for that sequence. Holding what was probably the Cobra Jewel, he advanced mysteriously through the swamp, moving ever towards the Cobra Woman whom he eventually strangles and spreadeagles in the dark water-filled cave in the cliffs. Not that you can see the water. The hole in the roof admits only enough light to catch the two faces, jewel-like in the deep black velvet. With a suggestion of moving, dim limbs in slow aquatic subterranean movements of death. Further glimpses of the Mummy walking through the swamp overlaid by Beverly, witch-like incantatory Cobra Woman, peering into her crystal jewel. The blue-green scintillating fabric of her dress among the lichened, glistening rocks.

Slam away to the pink and white of the birthday cake sequence shot on a Claus Oldenburg on-site constructed birthday cake loaded with cavorting, simpering, preening chorus cuties, layer over layer. Lot of extras for this sequence, which is a weekend away in the country at Wyn Chamberlain's summer house, lent for the occasion. Cake is in a hot glade in the woods a scrambly walk away from the dressing-barn, which is also a bedroom and across a large clearing from the house. On top of this cake Frankie is to sink, Andy Warhol is to be the only person to keep his sun-glasses on while the camera is turning, Diane di Prima is to be the Most Pregnant Woman (had her baby twelve hours after getting back to New York, a day later), the Mummy is to attack a chorus cutie and be finally machine-gunned down by a then-new Mongol, whose climax came as his foot went through the cake. His machine-gunned water and the cries and groans of dying cuties were real enough as the cold water hit their sun-warmed skins, almost all of which were showing. But they were nothing to the curses of purely naked Arnold, hit by a cold stream of water just as he got into his attack-on-Diana scene. Agonized contortions and twists over the ground with unsunburned strip prominent. Diana, stripped of dress, rescued naked by Stanley in long, yellow-flowered gown. He can't get her off the ground. Drops her, groans, tries again, up and off again. Reach the end of the run by the end of the fourth stagger length.

Bruised Diana in fits of giggles. Dying screams of laughter from watching
birthday cake cuties. Bob collapsing into laughter after his final (still) shot.
Jack mad at the incompetence. And at his difficult, borrowed, strange camera
of whose pitfalls he was just learning.

Pasty, he called it. And decided on a pasty film. But the later sequences with
Beverly and the Mummy were something else, and those at the Moonpool
with the White Bat and the Priestess-Mermaid and the Black Spider were
something else again. They were both richer and more pleasing visually than
the Melon and Birthday and Fire Island sequences. They were solo or couplet
sequences; the pasty ones were larger group sequences. So he was left, perhaps,
with many films. They have never come together into the commercial success
he had declared himself to be intent on. He's made later movies, too. But, like
those before *Flaming Creatures,* they are shorts.

The Co-op, as was then their habit, showed rushes in the theatre after their
scheduled programme. The Gramercy Arts was their theatre then, on a cross-
town street. We saw Frankie waiting outside the theatre at the top of the
steps, in baby-blue embroidered shorts which ended just above his knees; in
self-patterned white, short-sleeved shirt, brylcreemed hair, hairy legs, short
socks, heavy dark-brown shoes. I didn't recognize him until he smiled and
waved his hand. It was our first public meeting. At the birthday party for
Jack on the stage of the theatre after the show, the Co-op presented him with
a wedding gown at which, to their dismay, he took offence. Wouldn't even try
it on. He and Ron cavort on the stage, a few others wander up there for
short, uneasy periods. Jonas stands on his head when asked for a speech.

Kenneth Anger's *Water.* Gentle, flowing, night-timed, full of quiet hallu-
cination. His *Scorpio Rising,* violent, clashing, angry, sharp-edged with Jesus
sequences slotted in from some TV standard. Later to be raided at the Bridge.
His view of Hell's Angels.

Night after night the 14th Street apartment is crowded, sometimes quite
literally to the doors. Stanley's room, 6 feet by 8 feet box, is occupied by a
littered bed and chest of drawers, made-up bedside table, hangings, mirrors
and at least four people, usually more, in deep conversation or silence. The
living-room, grey walls and floor, Maria Montez altar in a state of change,
creatures working on their costumes, waiting for attendance from Jack, eating,
sheltering from outside. Incense burning, candles lit and electric lights turned
off, dinner cooking or coffee keeping hot.

Jack is grooming Rene at the moment. They have chosen a name, Mario
Montez, and Jack is arguing, explaining, demonstrating about the character.
Obliquely, with many facets of obliquity. Never so directly that Rene won't
have to work it out for himself, but with enough felt direction to keep him
headed there. Rene is surprisingly set in his ideas, he *must* look glamorous at
all costs, and all Jack's requirements are measured against that one of Rene's.
If he can't look glamorous he won't do it, and his idea of glamorous is well
defined. It necessitates almost complete stillness for Rene and nobody's plead-
ing, not White Bat's, not Black Spider's, not Jack's, can get him moving from
the spot he's chosen. He'll wriggle on it but not from it. Jack moves the camera.

The White Bat is John Vaccaro, and he's deathly beautiful for the part with skeletal face and acrinous skin. He's acted before and he feels the need to move, but the Moon Pool is small and he shares it with Mario, a black cat, Johnny Foster, Diane and her suckling infant, and billowing Naomi inches above where they lie, a hovering Black Widow of a fat spider. Her rope breaks and she crashes on to everyone except, fortunately, the still-suckling baby. Jack is shakily perched above it all on the framework which holds up the white gauze in which the Moon Pool is enshrouded. He looks as dangerous as Naomi.

Ron and Gerry lived together at Gerry's loft for a while, during which Jack and Tony were constant visitors. There's a sequence shot by Ron under Gerry's direction with Jack costumed in black suit and hat and white gloves by Gerry. It's a beautiful, strange piece, but they couldn't work so together for long enough. Each was his own film-maker, though together they did well. A world of constantly shifting realities, illusions, hallucinations, mysteries, possibilities. Where madness waits for those who falter, beauty for those who are involved without selfconsciousness. Plots appear, shimmer, threaten, evaporate or die. Roles change, shift, take on new meanings, mean them all at once, and shift back to which one you decide to live with for now. They are just as convincing in all the good ones; those in which they're not convincing die. Being is required, not questions about being; the questioners are a different role and only one, the be-ers as many roles as they choose or have chosen for them. All are painful and probably necessary, though I have doubts about the questioner's role. It doesn't seem to help anything, not even the questioner.

Steve Dwoskin is uptown, making films. Quietly, quite efficiently, overcoming great difficulties without shouting too loudly. Or loudly enough, sometimes. He needs people, but the ones he needs have to be shouted to and he doesn't shout. He knows more about what can be done to film, he knows the results of certain deliberate action. He and Bob get along well, they know of the same things. Steve is a black and white man of sharp, decisive images and starker imagination than the others. He wouldn't throw Jack's scenes, but then he might kill someone if he did. Jack's biggest physical violence was to smash a mirror over Stanley's head and that was at the end of their affair. Steve would break your head with one angry swing of his crutches; he's a strong man.

His apartment, he shoots his films there, is a calm refuge compared to the other locations. He's also pleasant and has a skeleton action plot in mind. This one is a game of Chinese checkers with two participants, both women. The shooting action is broodingly calm and slow, caught so in the film but crescendoed there with music and editing cuts. It's a good film if still a little afraid. Beverly responds to this camera too, comes alive into it, gives a thousand hints of possibilities into it. Steve doesn't make up for his camera's relative stationariness by moving the characters but by building on the static scene.

And what's the truth about Jonas? Innocent? Dedicated film purveyor? Money-maker? Fame hunter? Scheming cunning Latvian refugee who's out to make a place for himself in money-rich USA where even the deserving can

make it? Or poetic, quiet, soul-hungry film-maker and merchant, out to spread
the good word for and about his protégés, the film-makers? He's the root
and heart and trunk of the Co-op; he's the moving force behind it, the sooth-
ing glue which holds its multi-diversities together. He says little, leaves most
of the front work to his helpers. And everyone has a completely different picture of him, each of which is firmly believed to be the all-embracing truth. He's
really a mystery, with his low-intelligence *Village Voice* column which so belies
his achievements as a Co-op operator.

And, watching all this happen, except for the few times when I was happening too, with it. But also for a long time in another kind of exploration
which could only watch the rest occasionally. But I learned to look with
wider eyes and how to look with narrower ones. I had good teachers and they
were eager to help, even when it was painful because they couldn't live any
other way, actually. And I think they're right, in all realities. But a slow
start quickened its pace considerably during that year and I began to learn that
I wasn't so sure at all, in any terms that I could accept.

So film followed film; scene followed scene; act followed act; and the people
are people, not the frightening monsters that society sets up for her children
in the hopes that it will frighten them out of growing up, and out into the sun.
But it's all very painful and that year was an increase in pain as well as in
the sources of pleasure. Because there is a keen, sharp delight in seeing with a
many-faceted or all-open eye. It's agonizing and it's beautiful. I don't really
see why it should be agonizing at all, I think that that's a lack of acceptance.
Whenever you have a pain, think about that, which leads to a lot of pain-
dwelling. Perhaps if one dwelt more on the pleasure it would be less painful.
Rising puritan hackles. 'Pain is a part of life', intone even those Far East
Churches of my admiration. The West says embrace it with joy; the East says
accept it; and I say, is it necessary? Is it? Because to the real West, back at
root and heart, away from sword-bearing limbs, the story of the Hero also
belongs. And the Hero makes it, like the Buddha who stands at the doorway
to heaven, waiting for his last fellow, all of life, to get through first. He pipes
the way, sort of. And we do indeed have our messengers and ferrymen and
witch-guides, for the time needed. And sometimes it seems hard without
them, even after years. But that's looking back, you can't have the same
guide twice, except, of course, the ferryman if one comes back. But does
one come back the same way ever? Only Hollywood ever thought so. It's
such an absurd image to be wrestling against. But it's stealthier than it looks,
and creeps into many aspects of life. It's how you see things, say things,
think things. It is nurtured by society at large, all of the aspiring and middle
classes pump it into their children, and it is ramified by the equally extraordinary teachings of the other classes of society, and publicized as desirable.
Upholders.

2 Early History

The film-makers search. The names and places change. The talk goes on. Definitions are attempted; books are written; the press has more chat. The police move; the professionals watch; the critics play. The hustler exploits; the parasites linger; the groups form. Within all this there is the artist who tries to develop his ideas, dreams and fantasies out of the mainstream of contemporary society. There are individuals and there are feelings still somewhere in all this, yet somehow much gets forgotten amid the hustle and bustle of controversy and sensationalism. It becomes a movement, a new activity, another fixed point to aim at and somehow, from somewhere, a label is stuck to it. This time it is 'underground'. Last time it was Dadaism; or Surrealism; or Expressionism; or Cubism; or the pre-Raphaelite Brotherhood. The labels unravel as from a tape. Though in any such movement there are many people, many ideas and many feelings, all beyond the limits of any one definition, the outward impression given is often one of narrowness, even superficiality.

It can glibly be assumed that there might be some link with underground war activities in the use of the term 'underground' for films. The films and the film showings took place in this underground way to avoid disdain, and persecution from overground authorities. It seemed, at some points, that whenever a public showing was attempted the police were there to take away and destroy the films. The standard commercial outlet would not look at them and the censors would not pass them. On the other hand, independent film-makers do not believe in censorship in any form and would never consider presenting the films for review. So they went 'underground'; they wanted a free cinema. The term became, at least by 1960, a much-used label, at first with films but later spreading to a number of other creative and experimental activities, such as small theatre, 'happenings', light-shows; the concept even evolved into an underground press syndicate, including *International Times* (IT) and *Oz* (both in Britain), *East Village Other* (EVO), *Other Scenes* and *RAT* (New York), *Chicago Seed*, *The Argus* (Atlanta), *LA Free Press* (Los Angeles), *Berkeley Barb* (California), *Win*, *Liberation*, *The Rag* (Detroit) and the *San Francisco Express*.

As far as films go, those that are loosely grouped together under the heading 'Underground' are, for the most part, made by individuals. They have not been initiated by a commercial or business enterprise. These films have no fixed scope, no fixed budget, no fixed audience, no fixed style and often no fixed script. They are personal works, individually motivated, like any other creative activity. The painters and poets have become film-makers.

The film-makers themselves do not like the term 'underground' and are constantly trying to get rid of it. American film-makers employed the term 'New American Cinema' instead. At the Fourth Experimental Film Festival held in Belgium in 1967-8, a conference between representatives of the various European and American film co-operatives stressed that the word 'underground' should be avoided, since the term is vague and largely meaningless, blinding outsiders to the scope and value of the films themselves. To some it meant dirty movies, to others amateur films; some people even thought 'underground' films were made by London Transport! Nonetheless, the word remained and the press plugged it; it became a flag to rally round and a group to be in or to criticize. It is not and never will be descriptive; it is poetic; it is horrible; it is good and it is bad. It is many things, but it is mainly films.

Film itself has been confined by a vast range of philosophies, applications and standards. Film is art; film is entertainment; film is industry; film is recording; film is creativity; film is. . . . The search for a definition for film goes on and on. We try so hard to pin things down, making definition possession. Any medium, material or idea is only as good as its user, and each individual can pick his own philosophy from whichever end of the scale he chooses and make it come out well. As long as it is real and true to him, this still seems to work. If we work very hard at stripping away our preconceptions then we may stand a chance of responding to the thing in itself, as opposed to our preconception of what it should have been. By giving ourselves a chance we can respond instinctively and emotionally and make judgements. If both creation and response are true and uninhibited, then we can know by feeling without a definition. In time, we can view a thing without the bias and association of the period in which it was made. To view something after some time is, of course, possible only if it is still in existence. Out of all that is being done, how much dare show itself now, much less in the future – film or otherwise?

Within the physical limitations of ciné there exists freedom, limited only by the individual. Yet ciné, more than most other media, has evolved not only with a mosaic of definitions, but with an intellectualization that inhibits application. The great majority of filmgoers see and consider films in a purely literary way, with perhaps a soupçon of knowledge of simple technique thrown in (camera work, soundtrack and so on). In fact, ciné is a far broader medium than this outlook admits. It is perhaps necessary for film to develop a language and a set of references of its own, drawn where appropriate from the other visual art forms, before it can develop the seeing powers of its audience; and even in some cases of its makers.

Because film can capture the sense of movement in naturalistic terms, there has been a tendency to document actions occurring in front of the camera. Beyond this is the use of the movie camera to create sensations and display ideas that cannot be expressed in other forms, the only limitations being imposed by the film-makers themselves and by audiences.

Much of the difference developed out of the economic situation in which film found itself. Because of its technicalities, its science and its machinery, film requires a larger amount of money than the other media. Then, too, ciné film, like still photography, got caught in the wonder of recording things, in the magic of capturing lifelike realism, with lifelike movement added. The economics, of course, tended to demand that a film be seen by as many people as possible to recoup the financial investment. In order to ensure that a lot of people would pay to see a film, it was assumed that it should be presented in a form that was already familiar to the audience and in an already proven format. It became the stories the audience knew – a 'poor man's theatre'.

This is where the split occurs: either film remains a recording device for a theatrical reference, or it establishes its own identity. Naturally these categories can be split again, overlapped and intermixed; it is all still film and everywhere there is a splendid and complete array of theories and attitudes, each perfectly valid.

It was in France in the 'twenties that cinematographic philosophies came to the fore, and with them came attempts at defining and justifying film as an art form of its own. Film became an art in its own right, Malraux said, only when the camera discovered mobility. Attempts were even made to define 'experimental', just as more recently there have been attempts to define 'underground'. No one came up with any clear definition, and most provided even greater confusion. Even the term 'experimental' seems inadequate, since it implies incompleteness; and yet many of the films, then as now, were complete entities. One of the clearest definitions of these films is: 'All that is out of the everyday rut of film production at any given time can be considered experimental.' Even this fails.

Before the 'twenties the motion picture evolved through a rather sensational and picturesque history of experimenters, industrialists, opportunists and showmen. There were Edweard Muybridge, Marey and Anshütz who, with scientific interest, explored movement in sequence. The investigations of J. A. F. Plateau and of Simon Ritter von Stampfer led to further development of the 'persistence of vision' theory, which is the concept underlying the number of frames per second needed to create a sense of continuous movement. There were

Horner's Zoetrope, Reynaud's Praxinoscope and Uchatius's experiments with
projection. There were also, of course, the great industrialist inventors like
Edison and Lumière, who made film work physically. Edison put the sprocket
holes in film and Louis Lumière started the cinema theatres, as well as inventing a vast array of vital gadgets, including cameras and projectors, and,
naturally enough, he made films to go in them. So it went on, with the show-
man George's Méliès and his magical films in France, and in Britain the wild
'Brighton School' of C. A. Smith and James Williamson as well as the frustrating activities of William Friese-Greene. There was Émile Cohl, with his
so-called 'magic cartoons', making trick effects of multiple transmutation,
and the obscure 'Futurist School' of films by Guilio Bragaglia and Marinetti.

But it was in France, which in the 'twenties was still far from the influence
of Hollywood, and preceding the Hollywood dream factories, that film developed depth. The film-makers came from the other arts and the influences
came from Surrealism, Dadaism, Futurism: from Rimbaud, Valéry, Mallarmé
Gide, Jarry, Apollinaire, Picasso and Canudo. The influences themselves were
not strictly concerned with film. It took film artists such as Louis Delluc,
Germaine Dulac, Abel Gance, Jean Epstein, Marcel L'Herbier, Hans Richter,
Fernand Léger, Viking Eggeling, Walter Ruttmann, Oskar Fischinger and Luis
Buñuel to free the cinema from being only 'poor man's theatre' or a sideshow
toy, and give it its aesthetic. 'Cinema is painting in movement,' said Delluc.
'Cinema is the music of light,' said Gance. The French philosopher Gilbert
Cohen-Séat thought the film equalled the importance of printing as a major
influence on knowledge. The thoughts and the philosophies continued:
'We do not, or should not condemn music because it is primarily concerned
with emotions so why should we do so in films?'

It was not until the end of the First World War that the poetics of film
took root. Louis Delluc was one of the first of these film poets, and he also
wrote on the aesthetics of cinema. In 1919 his first piece was published,
Cinéma et Cie, and later came *Photogénie Charlot, Drames de Cinéma* (not
to be confused with the film *Photogénie* [1925] by Jean Epstein). He saw the
rhythmic potential of film and related cinematographic rhythm to the rhythm
within music. He declared: 'I have seen an admirable technical phenomenon –
I have seen cadence.' Herein began the great and constant parallel, both in
practice and in theory, between music and film. Both can fulfil themselves only
in the element of time. Delluc, though essentially a writer, began directing his
own films mainly because he believed that film was the only modern art. He
made *Fièvre* (1921), a relatively simple film in which all the action occurs in
one room and which is still conceived within the dramatic framework of the
theatre situation. To create the sense of memories and the past he juxtaposed
images as flashbacks. This juxtaposing he called 'montage'. Delluc also wrote
the script for *La Fête Espagnole* (1920), a film made by Germaine Dulac.
Mme Dulac went a bit further in her attitude towards the film. She felt that
the film 'carries in itself the very essence of the universal movement'. For
her the ideal film would be one that brought into force rhythmic movement
without any dramatic characters, and emotional response from the move-

ment of lines and shapes. It should not necessarily be dependent on a realized idea. In other words she wanted a symphony of vision and the poetry of seeing.

From the Dadaist artists came the first attempts at a more abstract visual 'symphony'. *Le Ballet Mécanique* (1924), made by Fernand Léger with Dudley Murphy, broke into the new art freedom provoked by the Dadaists. The film takes what often seem to be chance elements of objective images and juxtaposes them in rhythmic movements. The editing is the essence, involving as it does an infatuation and exploration of the time/movement possibilities of the film. Here is an early example of physical potential being used, the structure being built up from the image content. The repetition of a woman climbing stairs, or the spinning of wheels as a close-up, gives a sense of freedom to the visual motion inherent in the subjects.

Man Ray's *Le Retour à la Raison* (1923) was one of the earliest films of this period that were made for their own sake, without any commercial intent or outside financial aid. From here possibly emanated the spirit, if nothing else, that brought films made for small private viewings and friends, films of individual statement and experiment. It may have been the first Dada film and was shown at the 'Evening of the Bearded Heart'. It was in this spirit and in this way that Léger and Marcel Duchamp worked. Man Ray went on to make *Emak Bakia* (1926) and in 1928 *L'Étoile de Mer*, a visual translation of Robert Desnos's poem of the same name. Before making these two films he worked closely with Duchamp on the latter's *Anemic Cinema* (1927).

Duchamp's obvious interest in movement in his painting ('Nude Descending a Staircase') and his general attitude to the scope of art led him to film and the *Anemic Cinema*. Duchamp, whose involvement in time and movement extended beyond that of most other artists of his time, also had an interest in creating the abstract illusion of a three-dimensional effect. The *Anemic Cinema* is an attempt to do this. It is a 7-minute film made up of off-centred concentric circles filmed while spinning. The effect created was one of spatial depth in the form of spirals and cones. Duchamp inserted a 'pun' or statement between sets of optical revolutions in which he intended to offset the spatial effects of the patterns. 'Anemic' is an anagram of the word 'cinema', tending to symbolize the forward/backward movements of the film. At earlier stages Duchamp worked with Man Ray on various kinetic and optical devices to create three-dimensional illusions and eventually published a dozen printed optical discs derived from this film work, which he called *Rotoreliefs*. As early as 1921 he was working on three-dimensional film experiments using red and green lenses. These created a reasonable effect of three dimensions, though the film has since been lost.

René Clair continued to concentrate upon building up from existing realities to create poetic movements and visual rhythms. He worked more closely within the commercial framework of the cinema and was mostly concerned with what he called 'pure cinema'. He believed that no amount of previous writing of a script could anticipate the form that the film would take: '. . . a film exists only on the screen' and 'does not appear on paper'. This is of course true in film analysis, where it becomes difficult to describe anything that is as visually based as, for example, Clair's films. This is also true of many of the films made at this time (or later) that are visually based and without previous literary references. The films made by Léger, Duchamp, Ray, Richter, Buñuel and others present this difficulty. One may indulge in a repeat of the story-line if there is one or try to describe certain actions, but for most of these individual films the whole point is seeing.

Entr'acte, made by René Clair in 1924, is so highly visual that it can exist only on the screen, as Clair intended. The thematic line involves a funeral procession, but this acts only as a means of continuity and plays less than a secondary position to the action of poetry, rhythm and visual humour. *Entr'acte* has a wide range of imaginary camera angles, cuts, split-frame and high-speed movement, but retains great balance and unity. Clair shows here a degree of influence from Sennett and other American comedies in some of the action and in the chase (after the runaway horse). This influence is also apparent in his pantomime film *Le Voyage Imaginaire* (1925). *Entr'acte* itself is probably Clair's most influential film, especially among the younger non-commercial film-makers. One interesting point is that it was the first film produced wholly with financial support from outside the film industry. It was made to be put on with the Swedish ballet *Relâche* from a script by Francis Picabia. Before *Entr'acte* Clair made *Paris Qui Dort* (1923), from his own scenario. After *Entr'acte* he made *Le Fantôme du Moulin Rouge* (1924), using much superimposition, and *Le Voyage Imaginaire*, which Brunius describes as 'a succession of gags skilfully linked by a sort of pantomime justified by a dream'. Clair moved more into the commercial arena with *La Proie du Vent* (1926), followed by *An Italian Straw Hat* (1928) and *Les Deux Timides* (1928), and then came his great success *Sous Les Toits de Paris* (1929). Throughout these films Clair was the first to use a basic troupe of actors in film in the fashion of the repertory theatre, a characteristic adopted by Bergman in the late 'fifties.

The poetic dream of highly personal atmosphere where the exploration of inner emotions dominates is to be found in Germaine Dulac's *The Seashell and the Clergyman* (1926); (various sources put the date alternatively at 1926, 1927 or 1928). This was from a script by Antonin Artaud, the surrealist writer, and the film was laden with symbols revealing the sexual repression of a clergyman. The frustration is laid bare in the breaking of phials from a seashell, the pursuit of a woman, and in fairly obvious masturbation by the clergyman beneath his robes. Through the symbols and actions the film becomes real but far from literal. The clergyman crawling through the streets on his stomach, the endless doors and his pursuit drive home the emotions of a man trapped and tormented by his self and his instincts, an effect achieved without words.

Though not highly thought of by Jacques Brunius, Abel Gance's role in film history should not be neglected. If nothing else, the methods he employed and the images he achieved expanded the physical vocabulary of film. Originally a playwright, he made his first film in 1911. From him came the phrase

'Cinema is the music of light'. In 1915 he made *La Folie du Docteur Tube*, and in 1918 *La Dixième Symphonie*, plus the war film *J'Accuse*. Yet not until 1921 with *La Roue* did he really begin to develop the physical aspects of film in order to enhance and dramatize his subject. In effect, he began to unfold ideas that would not have been possible in any other medium, using concentrated shots of relevant objects to stress the drama of the situation and making effective use of mattes to break the frame shape into more emphatic images.

Gance went beyond the technical conventions of his day (though not as far as D. W. Griffith) with what were to be the beginnings of an applied use of the 'expanded cinema'. He produced his major work *Napoléon* (1925/7) as a three-screen film, which expanded not only his subject, but film as a whole. He employed virtually every ciné effect imaginable to emphasize his subject as strongly as possible. He became the first film-maker to shoot with a hand-held camera (a difficult task considering the primitive equipment of the day), a technique virtually forbidden in the commercial film world for at least thirty years afterwards. He employed a camera on a pendulum (soaring back and forth above a crowd scene), cameras mounted on horses, or two or three cameras running together to give different views of the same action. He even used a camera that did a full circular pan by itself. From him came the quick cutting method known as 'montage'. This direct cut from scene to scene (as opposed to fading in and out from scene to scene) proved to be a particularly effective method for creating sharp tensions and rapid time changes and was probably the most influential of all the methods Gance introduced, affecting Eisenstein and the other Russians and Akira Kurosawa in Japan.

However, his greatest influence came with his rediscovery, which formed the backbone of the French *Nouvelle Vague* in the late 'fifties, when directors such as Godard found the scattered bits of his films luckily preserved by the French Cinémathèque. Even the idea of Cinerama and the use of stereo sound are attributed to Gance, while on acting he commented that actors must *be*, not act.

During this period, too, numerous small, esoteric films were being made along personal and poetic lines, many now forgotten, a few hardly seen. Henri Chomette played with abstract images from landscape, cities and crystals to make such films as *Jeux des Reflets et de la Vitesse* in 1924 and *Cinq Minutes de Cinéma Pur* in 1926. Eugene Deslaw, fascinated by the beauty of machines in motion, made *La Marche des Machines* (1928), and with the patterns from flashing electric signs made *La Nuit Électrique*. For Claude Autant-Lara close-ups were enough to tell a story in *Fait-Divers* (1924). One of the most poetic attempts was achieved by Joris Ivens in Holland in his film *Rain* (1929). Here the patterns, and, most important, the moods created by rain falling on a city were enchantingly and effectively expressed. Film animation suggested other possibilities, an example of which was *Une Nuit sur le Mont Chauve*, made in 1934 by Alexandre Alexeieff, based on Mussorgsky's piece of the same title and done with austere, charcoal-like drawings in motion. Gradually, but continually, every possibility presented by film started to be explored.

In 1929 the film *Un Chien Andalou* (made in 1928) hit, and hit so hard that its impact still causes vibrations. The film was made by Luis Buñuel with Salvador Dali, both of whom were virtually unknown at the time. The film was a deliberate attempt to destroy rationality and avoided using any over-worked film tricks. It is without any intellectualization, and in fact its nature prohibits such an approach. It contains images, situations and movements that shock, confuse and obscure, and it confronts the viewer with himself. The film is banned in many places even today because of its shock effects (cutting the eye), or simply because it cannot be classified into any category. *Un Chien Andalou* has survived the period during which so many thousands of films were lost and has become one of the main inspirations of the New Cinema.

Buñuel's second film, *L'Âge d'Or* (1930/1), caused riots and a police ban and with them the eventual decline of the avant-garde film of this period. Richter describes the film show at which, after an hour when there was 'something anti-Church or anti-Royalist on the screen', someone screamed and a bomb was thrown at it. Battles broke out all over the place and objectors even tried unsuccessfully to storm the projection-room.

In Germany, *The Cabinet of Dr Caligari* (1919), made by Robert Wiene, became one of the first great leaps into the art of the film. Its influence gave film its own language. This film, with others such as *Nosferatu* (*Dracula*, 1922) by Friedrich Murnau, introduced painterly sensitivity and expressionist moods to the medium. They increased the magic of film and showed its potential.

As in other countries, other artists in Germany began to explore the film medium as an expansion of their own personal language. Here the correlation of film with music appears again. Hans Richter, probably the most notable of these experimentalists, spent a couple of years (1916-18) searching for sources with a view to creating rhythms in his paintings. He began studying the works of Bach and in 1918 started to discover 'negative–positive' relationships. Richter then met Viking Eggeling, a Swedish painter, who was struggling with similar problems. Eggeling had developed a complete theory and system that inspired Richter. Richter explains this system as 'using contrasting elements (counterpoint) to dramatize two (or more) complexes of forms and used analogies (of opposites) in these same complexes to relate them again. In varying proportions, number, intensity, position, etc., new contrasts and new analogies were born in perfect order until these grew into a kind of "functionary" between the different form units, which made you feel movement, rhythm, continuity. . . .' Eggeling called this system of an all-encompassing relationship of forms *'Generalbase der Malerei'*. In 1919 Richter and Eggeling published *Universale Sprache*, establishing a vocabulary of abstract visual forms.

Richter and Eggeling began working together on this principle, first with drawings, in which they made transformations of individual form elements (themes) and thought of them as 'instruments'. The process led to attempts at continuity by means of a form of 'orchestration' (different stages of the theme). The idea of continuity began to demand a definite situation, since it was no longer a single fact being explored but a process. They began to work with scrolls, with which they built transforming phases. Richter states that 'it became evident to us that these scrolls, as a whole, implied movement . . . and movement implied film'.

After his second set of scrolls Eggeling finished the first version of his film *Diagonal Symphony* (1921), while Richter completed *Rhythmus 21*. Richter explains that 'it was not only the orchestration of form but also of time relationship that we were facing in film. The single image disappeared in a flow of images, which made sense only if it helped to articulate a new element . . . time.' They found the technicalities of the new film medium a big hindrance to their early efforts. The shapes and forms called for animation and the method was, even on a professional level, very crude. Richter translated his drawings into cut-out paper squares and shapes, which were easier to handle in front of the camera than the more refined drawing. Eggeling pressed on with trying to use drawings and had a considerable struggle with his *Diagonal Symphony*. He remade the film three times and was never completely satisfied with it. In 1922 it was shown publicly in Berlin, but it earned no money. Eggeling died in 1925 without making another film.

In *Rhythmus 21* Richter created rhythm by trial and error with animation methods, and found that the technique allowed him to make the squares jump, disappear, slide and so on. In some cases he used film methods in ways that film-makers cannot employ today. Film-printing machines were not yet fully automatic and he could use them flexibly to obtain stop action, and backward and forward motion, by running the machine that way. *Rhythmus 21* lasted only a minute and a half. It was not shown publicly in Berlin until 1925, after parts of it had been mixed with his second film *Rhythmus 23*, which contained lines as well as squares.

At the same time, in Germany, Walter Ruttmann was making abstract films. Technically, his films were better than those made by Eggeling and Richter, but they lacked much of their sensitivity. Ruttmann worked with small plasticine shapes mounted on a revolving structure, and in a few of his earlier films made attempts at hand colouring. His films were shown before those of Eggeling and Richter, his *Opera* being screened in Berlin at the end of 1921. He was originally a painter, as were Eggeling and Richter, and he became more formally committed to film when he worked with Fritz Lang on *Nibelungen*. His big breakthrough was with *Berlin, die Symphonie der Gross-Stadt*, (Berlin, the Symphony of a Great City, 1927) which was supported by Karl Freud of Fox Films, Berlin. With Berlin as its theme, it was made with a poetic rhythm and sensitivity that brought new life to film in the documentary style. It was accompanied by the first musical score for a film, written by Edmund Meisel.

Richter, in the meantime, had produced *Rhythmus 25*, in which he continued to use lines and squares with hand-painted colour. He then acquired better animation equipment and in 1926 made *Film Study*. He stood by his ideals and continued to work on the sense of relationships through rhythm in film time. He began to get a few commissions, one of which was an introduction to a UFA film, the piece he did being called *Inflation*. This was again built up on visual rhythms, but this time he used more literal images, based on the cause of inflation itself, money. This was the beginning of a series of so-called essay-films that Richter was to make. He began to earn enough money from this enterprise to continue making his own films, trying to retain in his commercial ventures the essence of his earlier personal films; in this he succeeded.

Richter was directly involved with the Dada movement and therefore knew the set-up quite intimately. The whole Dadaist/Surrealist feeling is successfully emulated in his *Vormittagsspuk* (Ghosts before Breakfast, 1927/8). This film, Richter's most widely seen work, was built out of natural objects, in contrast to the abstract geometry dominant in his earlier films. Four hats travelling their independent way and four hat-owners travelling in independent and irrational time as well – all manage to be mingled with pistols, beards, lamp-posts and the eternally timeless clock. To a lesser degree Richter managed to keep this Surrealist feeling and use of juxtaposition in his later films, even the commissioned ones.

Then sound came. Ruttmann made the first attempt at it, composing a sound piece without any picture called *Wochenende* (Weekend). He composed this sound as if he were composing it for a film; that is, the sounds to him had image connotations. This was in 1928, which was also the year when he made *Toenende Welle* (Sounding Wave), a film about sound. Then in 1930 he made *Die Melodie der Welt* (Melody of the World). Meanwhile Richter made *Alles dreht sich, Alles bewegt sich* (Everything Revolves, Everything Moves), a documentary about a funfair. According to Richter this brought him into a fight with two Nazis, which got his name into the newspapers. Thanks to this, two years later Prometheus-Film in Berlin commissioned him to direct an anti-Nazi film called *Metall*, about a metalworkers' strike in Henningsdorf. It was a confused affair that was plugged, changed and altered with the quick tide of Fascist political movements. It began as a documentary, but with the quick change of events and with at least seven rewrites became a standard fiction film.

At about this time, in 1929, a younger generation of more experimental film-makers began to emerge. Wilfrid Basse, Carl Junghans and Ernoe Metzner explored the documentary possibilities of film. Oskar Fischinger, one of Ruttmann's students, continued to develop the abstracted animation methods of film by organizing images more tightly round the sound. Fischinger worked painstakingly on numerous colourfully abstract films, all of which had a remarkable purity and brilliance. The movements were based on the sound, as with *Hungarian Dance* (1931) from Brahms's composition of the same name, while in *An American March* (1939) they were linked to Sousa's 'Stars and Stripes Forever'. Fischinger also made a series of animated geometries called *Film Studies*, numbered 1 to 12 and continuing until 1930. He also made *Optical Poems* (1937) in America and other films such as *Allegretto* (1936), based on jazz, also made in America, *Motion Painting No. 1* (1949), *Composition in Blue* and *Circle*. Fischinger seemed to have brought the abstract film movement to an end in Germany and, like so many others, showed where the next phase would be by leaving Germany and going to America.

The Nazi oppression began. For the Fascists the avant-garde became 'degenerate art' and had to be forced out. The movement was rapid. In 1929, at La Sanaz, an International Congress of avant-garde film-makers was formed, but only a year later, at the second meeting in Brussels, the Congress revealed an ideological split and was finally dissolved. The split was between those members who wanted to use film as a political weapon against the Fascist movement and those who wished to concern themselves as before solely with poetics. Richter, Fischinger, Junghans and Metzner eventually made their way to the United States. Ruttmann stayed in Germany and made the film *Stahl* (Steel) for Mussolini, also working with Leni Riefenstahl on her film *Olympiade* (1936) for Hitler. He was killed on the German-Russian front in 1941. After doing some work in Holland and Switzerland, Richter became director of the Institute of Film Techniques at the College of the City of New York (CCNY). At this point he made *Dreams That Money Can Buy* (1944/45), a film composed of various dream sequences, each constructed by such friends as Marcel Duchamp, Max Ernst, Fernand Léger, Man Ray and Alexander Calder. Richter wove the sequences into a structure based on a man who sells dreams, but this catalyst was weak and further weakened by the commentary which, a narrative rhyme, was not Richter's forte. None the less, the individual dream sequences remain quite strong. In 1957 Richter made *8 x 8*, a film that also developed round his notable friends. Fischinger went to Hollywood, where he worked on *Second Hungarian Rhapsody* (from Liszt) for MGM, and made the Bach 'Toccata and Fugue' sequence for Walt Disney's *Fantasia* (1941) besides continuing his own work.

In the early days the development of avante-garde film in America had been very scattered. Hollywood did of course start and grow and it could be said that this, in itself, was an experiment with film as a medium. However, the more subjective and personal films took a long time to show themselves. As is the case in Britain today, the earlier experimental film-makers in America were called amateurs and brushed off as a group involved in a casual, part-time activity. America was a late developer and it was not until the arrival

C

of European artists, workers and philosophies that avant-garde film-making began to take firm root; it gradually established itself a few years before the Depression. In the late 'twenties and early 'thirties American artists went to Europe to experience the art explosion. This was originally stimulated by such earlier influences as the 1913 Armory Show in New York. By the 1930s Paris was overrun with American artists. At the beginning of the Second World War the Americans returned to the United States, and with them came many European artists and the new arts. During the Depression the US Government had given about $75 per week to almost 70,000 artists, the only condition being that they should continue their work. The government never stipulated *what* they should paint or write. Unfortunately, this state of affairs lasted only a short time, but it did coincide with the influx of European art movements to America. America's entry into the war postponed this creative flowering until hostilities had ended. From then on American art grew at a fantastic rate, through painting, dancing, literature, design, music and poetry up until the 'sixties, and through films.

During the 'twenties and 'thirties Hollywood had built up its empire of candy-coated film and fed everyone, everywhere, every day with it. As the war ended Hollywood began to decay. During the more fragmented days of the 'twenties only a few films on an independent and personal level were attempted in America. Even fewer have been preserved. In 1921 the painter Charles Sheeler and the photographer Paul Strand made a one-reel film called *Manhatta*, which was partly inspired by a Walt Whitman poem, plus the unusual beauty of Manhattan. The film was a simple, poetic documentary, showing patterns and movements of the skyscraper city and with clear and selective shots of buildings, ships, crowds, smoke and canyons, all edited into a delicate visual rhythm. *Manhatta* hardly made any impact at all – it never had a chance to be shown. In 1925, along the same lines as *Manhatta*, came *24 Dollar Island*, made by Robert Flaherty, already a well-known film-maker. This was also based on the abstract patterns made by the skyscrapers of New York. Flaherty, whose great influence came later with strong and individual documentary films such as *Louisiana Story*, was at this point inspired by a telescopic lens and the strange sense of vision that can be obtained from the top of one New York building. The film, when finished, got its major showing only as a backdrop at the Roxy Theatre for dance routine entitled 'The Sidewalks of New York'. (To make it more heart-breaking, the managers of the theatre took the liberty of cutting *24 Dollar Island* from two reels to one.)

Others at the time who might have wanted to make films were stifled by lack of money and equipment and by an environment concerned with economic and industrial expansion. Whatever equipment there was could be found only in Hollywood, and it was here that the first independent film was made. In 1928 Robert Florey, a French journalist working as an assistant director in Hollywood, wrote and directed a film called *The Life and Death of 9413 – a Hollywood Extra*. This film was edited, designed and photographed (with the exception of the close-ups) by Slavko Vorkapich, a painter, and is about a Hollywood extra who leads a frustrating life to reach stardom. He wears his number, 9413, on his forehead and is constantly rejected, whereas a Mr Blank becomes Number 15 and reaches stardom with a star on his forehead instead of a number; 9413 dies of starvation and goes to heaven, where his number is removed. The whole film was done in miniature, with cut-out cardboard figures and sets, tin-cans, paper and other bits and pieces, all handled in a very stylized and impressionistic manner. It consisted of one reel, cost only $100 to make and was reasonably well circulated.

After *Hollywood Extra*, Florey made two other films, *Johann the Coffin Maker* and *The Loves of Zero*, both economic productions and similarly stylized. Also at about this time came a larger film, *The Last Moment*, directed by Paul Fejos and with strong impressionist overtones. It was composed of rapid sequences of images expressing a man's life as he sees it on the point of death. *The Last Moment* probably had a stronger impact on the American film at this time than almost any other production. It attempted a subjective and personal theme with many film experiments and strong camera work, all successfully linked together with exceptional editing. It was also made outside the commercial studios.

German expressionism, notably that of *The Cabinet of Doctor Caligari*, now began to reveal its influence on American films, though this became crossed with the imaginative force in the stories of Edgar Allan Poe. In 1929 Charles Klein made *Tell-Tale Heart*, with painted sets akin to those in *Doctor Caligari* through which he attempted to create the surreal and haunting atmosphere found in Poe. Another film based on Poe was *The Fall of the House of Usher*, directed and filmed by James Sibley Watson, with sets by Melville Webber. This version was a personal interpretation rather than a literal translation and achieved its individuality through exterior illusory features, an aspect that can be so well displayed in film. The highly distinctive use of film – its optical distortions, multiple exposures and extensive use of lighting – created the mood and background and at the same time helped project the story-line, though the acting was rather poor.

In 1929 Ralph Steiner, a photographer, made H_2O. This was simply a cinematographic study of water reflections and was one of the first attempts at a strictly visual, non-narrative piece. It used no camera or optical tricks but rested on one subject, presenting it with a good photographic and editing sense. At about the same time, Joris Ivens in Holland was working on similar non-dramatic films such as *Rain* (1929), *Branding* (1929) and *The Bridge* (1928). The essence of this kind of film was the use of the camera to project the basic visual nature of the subject-matter. In the case of H_2O, water with its reflected light and movement gave way to an endless array of abstract patterns sought, selected and recomposed by Steiner. He adopted the same attitude in his other two films, *Surf and Seaweed* (1930), based on the motions and rhythms of the surf and tide, and *Mechanical Principles* (1930), based on close-up movements of machine parts.

An orchestrated structure was the physical basis of *The Story of a Nobody* (1930), made by Jo Gercon and Hershell Louis. The theme was a boy/girl love story. The film's structure came from the sonata tempo (moderately quick, slow, very quick), and a variety of optical effects such as reverse motion, split screen, superimposition and so on were employed. *The Story of a Nobody* originated with an earlier film called *Mobile Composition*, made by Gercon and Louis with Lewis Jacobs. These two films attempted to be subjective in that the camera's eye became the eye of the characters witnessing other movements.

By 1931 philosophical attitudes to film-making came strongly under the influence of the super-realism of the Russians, notably the work and writings of Eisenstein, Pudovkin and Dziga Vertov. Vertov and Eisenstein developed the technique of montage to such an extent that it tended to dominate all levels of film-making for a long time to come.

Dziga Vertov (whose real name was Dennis Arkadyevich Kaufman), with his more dynamic verbalization, had the most immediate influence. His 'kino-eye' (he called himself and his followers and their films 'kino-eyes') and his *Kinoks-Revolution* manifesto (first published in 1919) stressed a highly revolutionary attitude, for its time, to film-making. The 'kino-eye' films laid the foundations for the documentary and *cinéma vérité* style of film-making that eventually spread beyond Russia to Europe and by 1930 to America. The attitude here ranged from breaking the currently standard sixteen frames per second to regarding the camera's eye as better than the human eye. As for the camera's ability to copy exactly, Vertov said: 'As of today we will unshackle the camera and will make it work in the opposite direction, further from copying.' He said that 'kino-eye' films should observe what the human eye does not see and avail themselves of all the possibilities of the film medium, such as high-speed action, microphotography, multiple exposure and so on. He also insisted that films should be shot in natural locations without a narrative and without actors; they should unmask 'and find the correct and necessary line among the millions of phenomena which relate to the theme'. 'Kino-eye' was to make full use of montage to link and draw together this phenomenon of time into a 'ciné-thing'. In other words, montage organizes pieces of film (which includes 'found' pieces of film) and relates them to each other. As Vertov states in his 'Lecture II': 'Kino-eye is a victory against time. It is a visual link between phenomena separated from one another in time. Kino-eye gives a condensation of time and also its decomposition.'

This attitude became the major basis for film-making among young, inexperienced, independent film-makers, giving many of them sufficient confidence to feel that large production companies were not necessary. It was at this point that avant-garde film-making began its slow but strong growth. With the elimination of sets, actors and crews a great deal of footage began to be shot of places, of people and of activities, all very much in a documentary newsreel mood to which selective composition was applied by careful editing. The main consideration was the visual aspect of the surrounding natural environment. The footage was cut mainly to achieve strong visual rhythms and thematic orders resulting in ciné poems and symphonies similar to Ruttmann's *Berlin*. This style was adopted by the early experimental (and later influential) film-makers in America, many of whom worked closely together.

Among them were the painter Emlen Etting, who made *Oramunde* (1931), *Poem* (1932) and *Laureate* (1939); Jay Leyda, who made *Bronx Morning*, and Lewis Jacobs, who made *Footnote to Fact*.

Just before Vertov's influence took hold, a film that transformed the phenomenon of the time sense was made by Charles Vidor in 1931. It was entitled *The Spy* and another version of it, by Robert Enrico, appeared in 1958, this time called *Incident at Owl Creek*. Both were derived from Ambrose Bierce's story, *An Occurrence at Owl Creek Bridge*. The film, like the story, rests on the moments before a man's death by hanging up to the moment of death and uses these moments to create a forward projection in time, coinciding with the dying man's hallucinatory mental flashes. The impact is created by an unusual approach to time since in the film, as in the story, all actions appear to follow a normal narrative time sequence. This sequence, which relates to his thoughts, is cut in between the moment before death and after death. The effect is that you do not realize that he has died until the end, but think he has escaped; the escape is simply the victim's fantasy.

In the early 'thirties, in the wake of the Depression, came films based upon social situations, often worked out in a satirical mood. One example is *Mr Motorboat's Last Stand*, by John Flory (with Theodore Huff), about a Negro who lives in a car-dump and sells apples; he dreams of riches but then loses everything, including his apple stand. Another film, *Pie in the Sky* (1934), which also takes place in a city dump, was an attempt at film improvisation. This was made by Elia Kazan with Ralph Steiner, Molly Day Thatcher and Irving Lerner. At about this time Lewis Jacobs made what might be called a pre-Pop Art film entitled *Commercial Medley*, which was a take-off of film trailers. Another film made in this 'take-off' spirit was *Even as You and I* (1937), by Roger Barlow, with Le Roy Robbins, Harry Hay and Hy Hirsch. Hirsch was later to make some important abstract colour films in Europe.

With the beginnings of war in Europe attempts at experimental film-making became more difficult and more obscure. While production innovations such as sound increased the commercial possibilities of film, they made experimentation more difficult, for to use sound naturally made production far more costly and more complicated technically, which put it out of the reach of most independent film-makers. But a few experimental sound films were made, one of the more notable being *Lot in Sodom* (1933/4) by Watson and Webber. Taken from the biblical story, it attempted to use film as allegory. Much emphasis was placed on optical camera effects, in rather the same vein as in *The Fall of the House of Usher*, but with a greater degree of control. Experimental film-makers were constantly attempting to exploit the physical potential of the ciné medium, so that it became more than a mere story-recording device. In *Lot in Sodom*, for instance, optical effects were used to create dream-like situations and to enhance and 'magically' develop the film's content. In contrast to this, Joseph Berne made a sound film called *Dawn to Dawn* (1934) – from a story by Seymour Stern – in an attempt to create a completely natural story of a boy/girl relationship without the pretensions of Hollywood drama. Yet another approach was adopted by Lewis Jacobs and Thomas Bouchard in their satirical sound film, *Underground Printer*, in which the effect was created by dramatic and stylized solo dance movements.

During the last few years before America's entry into the Second World War few esoteric films were made. Most seem to have been the work of Mary Ellen Bute, a designer, with her husband, Ted Nemeth. Mary Ellen Bute's introduction to film had come with drawings she did for *Synchronization*, made by Joseph Schillinger and Lewis Jacobs. Her own films followed the thematic lines of music, to which she applied abstract movements and patterns. She made in black and white *Anitra's Dance* (1936), *Evening Star* (1937) and *Parabola* (1938), and in colour, *Toccata and Fugue* (1940), *Tarantella* (1941) and *Sport Spools* (1941). These films evolved systematically and rhythmically from the music that accompanied them through Mary Ellen Bute's use of three-dimensional objects. This type of abstracted animated visual with related sound seems to have received most of its inspiration from the work of Oskar Fischinger. (There is, of course, a natural affinity between film as vision in motion and music as sound in motion.)

In Britain, meanwhile, the independent and avant-garde film movement was rather meagre. After the earlier 'Brighton School' much of film exploration centred round the documentary, more particularly the social documentary (Vertov again), though there was also some activity in animation. More often than not the films were sponsored by some official group such as the Ministry of Labour. If there is any hero in the early British film movement, it is John Grierson. Working with Sir Stephen Tallents, Grierson laid the foundations for the General Post Office Film Unit (Crown Film Unit and the Ministry of Information Films Division) in the 1930s. It was Grierson and the GPO Film Unit that gave the first real opportunity for film expansion in Britain, as for instance when Grierson invited Robert Flaherty to join the unit and later introduced Alberto Cavalcanti, a Brazilian film-maker working in France. Both had great influence. Also in the group were Humphrey Jennings, Harry Watt and Basil Wright. Wright (who was later director of the Crown Film Unit from 1939 to 1945) made what is considered to be the most outstanding documentary of its time, *Song of Ceylon* (1934/5), while Watt made *North Sea* (1938), one of his best films, and worked with Wright on *Night Mail* (1936).

One of the most important members who worked for the GPO Film Unit was Len Lye. Born in New Zealand, he had his first real break when he discovered that he could evolve his own philosophy about art instead of adopting someone else's. He therefore began to develop his own theories of motion and light, and was particularly inspired by the idea of motion when he learnt that Constable had made numerous oil sketches in order to understand the movement of clouds. After seeing a film called *Pearls and Savages* made by the Australian Captain Frank Hurley, he decided that film was for him and went to Australia to study animation. After producing bits of animation he arrived in London. His first complete film, finished in 1927 and done as straight animation, disappointed him. It was not until a few years later that he finally began to develop, in cinematic terms, a greater sense of tempo and motion. For him this meant breaking motion down and then building it up again. On the basis of his first film he was able to persuade the London Film Society (the first in the world) to sponsor the photography for his next film. He spent two years making it and ended up with a ten-minute piece called *Tusalava* (Samoan for 'Things go full cycle'). He showed it to Grierson, who gave him the go-ahead to make films for the GPO.

Lye now made one film roughly every six months for the GPO, in each case animated abstractions with the occasional GPO slogan and based on the rhythmic motion of shapes and lines. The imagery was created by painting and scratching directly on the film, examples being *Colour Box* (1934), *Rainbow Dance* (1936), *Trade Tattoo, The Lambeth Walk* (1941), and later *Free Radicals*. Lye related his films closely to sound in their tempo and rhythm, finding accents of the particular sound and synchronizing them to a related visual accent. In *Trade Tattoo* he used three rhythms at once, while in *Lambeth Walk* special sounds were used to relate to the image – a guitar twang, for instance, was linked to an image resembling a guitar string.

In *Colour Box* the method of direct painting on to film was used for the first time, and Lye is considered to have originated the technique. (In fact the American film-maker, Harry Smith, unknown to anyone else, also began to develop the technique of painting on films in the late 'thirties.) Lye later went to New York, where he received no encouragement or commercial support for his films, though *Free Radicals* was to win the second prize at the Second International Experimental Film Festival in Belgium in 1958.

In the United States Lye continued to explore his ideas in kinetic sculpture and environmental situations, but only one other person (apart from Harry Smith) managed to pick up and develop these ideas. Norman McLaren came from Scotland and became a member of Grierson's Film Unit. When Grierson left for Canada at the outbreak of the Second World War to establish the National Film Board of Canada, McLaren went with him. He decided to stay and eventually, continuing the painting-on-film method, plus the relationship to sound, made dozens of such films, some with the GPO in England and the rest in Canada. In 1943 he formed an animation film unit in Canada which produced some of the best animators and animated films in the world. In 1952, with his film *Neighbors*, he developed what became known as the art of 'pixillation'. This technique involves animating live people, or creating animated effects by using actual objects instead of drawings or painting. In 1956 he developed a method of animating cut-out shapes, which he used in films such as *Rhythmetic* and *Le Merle*, writing at one point: 'Animation is not the art of *drawings-that-move* but the art of *movements-that-are-drawn*. What happens *between* each frame is much more important than what exists *on* each frame. Animation is therefore the art of manipulating the invisible interstices that lie between frames.'

In 1943 the seeds of the New American Cinema were sown. Maya Deren, a dancer living in California, started to work on films and to talk about the new film freedom. She inspired many independent American film-makers, her influence reaching its full force by the mid-1960s. Her highly individual films were guided by her own personal visions, symbols and involvements and strove for a subjective rendering. Coupled with her almost mystical sense was the fact that she was a dancer, which enabled her to do her own choreography. Her films are therefore dominated by a sense of flow and movement and she often danced in them herself or used other dancers as expressive vehicles. Working first in California, she subsequently moved to New York, where she became one of the main spokesmen for the New American Cinema. Her first film, *Meshes of the Afternoon* (1943), made with her then husband, Alexander Hammid, and starring the two of them alone, is a dreamy, surrealist attempt to express frustration and isolation. It drifts from a woman's dreams to reality and back to her dreams, becoming a ciné-exploration of the unconscious and conscious side by side and intertwined. The editing intercuts between dream and reality, and uses film to displace a normal sense of time and space.

Maya Deren also played the main character in her second film, *At Land* (1944). In this an Alice in Wonderland figure travels through a banquet after being washed ashore, then follows the Queen from a chess game back into the sea. In her third film, *A Study in Choreography for Camera* (1945) she juxtaposed time and space relationships with a dancer (Talley Beatty), whose movements start in one location and finish in another. This effect is achieved by cutting into the movement before it is complete, with the continuation from a similar movement shot elsewhere. Deren's constant attempts to break up the formal dance with highly personal intentions, as in *Choreography for Camera,* allowed her to overstep the formal limitations of film as well. Another film involving the flowing and the freezing of choreographed movement was *Ritual in Transfigured Time* (1946), which develops the theme of a woman's spirit as 'the changing of a widow into a bride'. This is Deren's most conceptual film and reveals her interest in primitive mysticism, in the concept of mortality becoming immortality. As with *Meshes of the Afternoon,* it also mirrors her own anxieties as a woman. Her next film was *Meditation on Violence* (1948), made with a solo dancer. It is weaker than her others, probably because of its more objective approach and because it contains less personal introspection. Of her last completed film, called *The Very Eye of Night* (1959), she said: 'I have made this film because the techniques of this medium make possible the most accurate metaphor for this particular complex of ideas and emotions and also because, for intricate personal reasons, I have a greater creative facility in this medium than in most others.' Again it involved the immortalized dancer transfixed in motion.

Maya Deren soon became the heart of the new personal film movement. She stressed the poetic qualities of film, led the debates and brought the few independent film-makers together under the wing of her Creative Film Foundation, which attempted to give grants. In 1946 she had herself been the first film-maker to receive a grant from the Guggenheim Memorial Foundation.

Her idea of hiring the Provincetown Playhouse in New York to show her own films inspired Amos Vogel to follow her example and establish his 'Cinema 16', which showed experimental films for sixteen years. Her idea of mutual collaboration among the film-makers for distribution purposes later became the reality of film-makers' co-operatives. So, here in the 'forties, the germination took place and the film-makers began to appear.

Among the small pioneering band were Willard Maas, Marie Menken (Maas's wife), Charles Boultenhouse, James Broughton, Sidney Peterson, Ben Moore, Ian Hugo, Stan Brakhage, Gregory Markopoulos, Curtis Harrington and Kenneth Anger. They formed the link between two generations and walks of life and were instrumental in bringing American films down from their ivory tower. They found themselves together through the existence of the Guggenheim Foundation, the Museum of Modern Art in New York and the San Francisco Museum of Art. The Guggenheim Foundation (one of the major achievements of broad-minded capitalism) gave money to support the arts, to support abstract and experimental art, to support American art. Marie Menken was assistant curator when the Foundation bought prints of films by Richter, Eggeling, Fischinger and McLaren, but there were hardly any organized attempts to do this in America in 1940, and even as late as 1967 there was no government support for the collection and preservation of film.

At the time when Marie Menken was at the Guggenheim Foundation McLaren arrived from England, showed his hand-painted films and asked for money. The Foundation bought some prints and he soon became friendly with Marie and with Maas, who describes McLaren at work in Flushing, New York:

It was something to see Norman at his home-made contraption, a magnifying-glass attached to a board through which the film was placed (old thirty-five millimetre that he had washed down – the method lent itself to poverty), drawing infinitesimal sequences of drawings. He has invented hundreds of other techniques, some of them pretty exciting, including hand-drawn sound, some sounding quite lovely, others sounding like farts. . . .

Maas and Menken made their *Geography of the Body* (1943), at the same time as Maya Deren was making *Meshes of the Afternoon. Geography* is a travelogue of the body made with cheap magnifying-lenses in front of the camera. Why the body? 'Because our bodies were nearest at hand when we wanted to try out the lenses, (being a ten-cent magnifying-lens), we looked at our hands, our lips and even our tongues,' says Maas. George Maker wrote and read the poetic commentary on the soundtrack. Maas also made films such as *Images in the Snow*, finished in 1948, in which he sought to express a homosexual's inner conflicts. Then he made *The Mechanics of Love* (1955) with Ben Moore, followed by *Narcissus*, also starring Ben Moore, while Marie Menken made animated and pixillated films using such things as jewellery and sculpture. With *Visual Variations on Noguchi* she explores Noguchi's sculpture; in *Dwightiana* she uses objects; in *Hurry Hurry*, sperm; in *Mood Mondrian*,

Mondrian's painting 'Broadway Boogie-Woogie', filmed to a boogie-woogie rhythm. She filmed simple, everyday things in the early days and continued to do so throughout the whole film explosion, making *Andy Warhol*, a day in the life of Andy Warhol seen in ten minutes, and *Wrestling*, a speeded-up wrestling-match filmed from television. Later on, in 1965, she starred in Andy Warhol's film *The Life of Juanita Castro* and a year later appeared in *Chelsea Girls*.

Also, in these early days, came the animated films of John and James Whitney, who later called them 'motion graphics'. In their first animated film, *Variation* (1941/3), they followed Fischinger's example by developing movements from sounds. Though working separately later on, they continued to develop more complex machinery for their 'motion graphics' and in a truly experimental fashion evolved animated imagery that had infinitesimal variations in movement and involved fluid subtleties of change.

Then there were Sidney Peterson and James Broughton, who made *The Potted Psalm* (1946) together but worked separately afterwards. Peterson made such films as *The Cage* (1947), with its runaway eyeball, and *The Petrified Dog* (1948), as well as the stretched and squeezed anamorphized film *The Lead Shoes* (1949), while Broughton progressed from *Mother's Day* (1948), a strange satire of adults acting like children, to *The Pleasure Garden* (1953) and *The Bed* (1967), which involves many people and various activities in a bed placed in a field. Curtis Harrington began in 1946 with *Fragment of Seeking*, which was concerned with adolescent narcissism. Meanwhile in 1939 Harry Smith was painting on film and by 1947 had completed the work now called *Early Abstractions*; the painter Jordon Belson began abstract films with *Transmutation* in 1947, while the long-neglected Hy Hirsch, an American working in Europe, produced films of solid rhythm and strong photographic qualities. From his *Autumn Spectrum*, built round reflections in the water in the canals of Amsterdam, to *La Couleur de la Forme*, a free-wheeling collage with superimpositions of orange skies, Hirsch produced films of pure imagery, while in *Come Closer*, *Gyromorphosis* and *Défense d'Afficher* the images are based on sound rhythms, sculpted forms and patterns. Hirsch died in 1960 and his films have seldom been seen; as with many of the individual film-makers, his first aim was to make films of his own choice in the way he wanted, and then hope that someone would want to see them.

Finally, a Wall Street businessman, with no training and at the age of forty-two, began to work on engraving and etching at the Atélier 17 in Paris. By the time he was fifty (in 1948) he was making films and finding that 'he was using images as if they were notes in a symphonic composition'. His name was Ian Hugo (Hugo Guyler).

Hugo would refilm already projected film and use it for superimpositions, as in his *Ai-Ye* (1950), a lyrical film poem of man as rower. This work was followed by *Bells of Atlantis* (1952), based on Anaïs Nin's book *The House of Incest* and including the author reading her work to the accompaniment of Hugo's images. Two years later came *Jazz of Lights*, featuring the glittering lights round Times Square; then at the age of sixty-five – with his youthful idealism still intact in spite of the pressure of the business world – Hugo made *The Gondola Eye,* a chamber piece on the canals of Venice and incorporating his earlier film *Venice Etude No. 1.*

The generation gap now started to close and the catalyst formed. In the late 'forties and early 'fifties the younger film-makers began to emerge. Kenneth Anger, Gregory Markopoulos and Stan Brakhage all started work during the time of Deren, Maas, Menken and the others. Anger, born into a world of gloss, chrome, magic and Hollywood, made his first film in 1941, at the age of nine. This was *Who Has been Rocking My Dream Boat?*, a question that seems to have become Anger's lifelong preoccupation. Made completely by Anger himself, it is described as 'a montage of American children at play, drifting and dreaming, in the last summer before Pearl Harbor. Flash cuts of newsreel holocaust dart across their reverie. Fog invades the playground; the children dropping in mock death to make a misty landscape of dreamers.' Also in 1941 he made *Tinsel Tree,* concerned with the build-up and destruction of a Christmas tree (the film was hand-tinted), and *Prisoner of Mars,* structured as a serial chapter with the ten-year-old Anger playing the 'Boy-Elect from Earth'. By 1962/63 Anger had made his powerful and famous superchrome hell film *Scorpio Rising.* As with all Anger's films, this reflects the growing influence of the 'American way of life' which, like the theme of dreams experienced and yet broken, became an important element in the raw material of the growing New American Cinema.

Gregory Markopoulos began making 8mm films in 1940 at the age of twelve, but it was not until 1947 that he began his long film venture into his own self. Part one of his homosexual trilogy was entitled *Psyche* (1947) and this was followed by *Lysis* (1948) and *Charmides* (1948). Using himself as his central theme, Markopoulos went on making film after film throughout the 'sixties, including his long work *The Illiac Passion.*

Then in 1955 Stan Brakhage appeared on the scene. When he first met Deren, Maas and Menken in New York he had made only a few rather awkward films, the first of which was *Desistfilm* (1954). This was followed by *The Extraordinary Child* (1954), *In Between* (1955) and *The Way to the Shadow Garden* (1955), in each of which he attempted to express adolescent claustrophobia. His involvement with the other three film-makers proved fruitful, and in 1955 he made *Reflections in Black* and *The Wonder Ring,* after which came *Flesh of Morning* (1956/7) and a number of others, including the majestic and intensely personal *The Art of Vision* (1961/5), which lasted four hours.

With all these an era came to an end. It had included many other film-makers – who knows exactly how many? – and is best summed up by Maya Deren, who described it as one of 'agony and experience'.

The first striking revival of the new avant-garde film started in the 'fifties. By 1958 the New American Cinema had begun its real growth from the foundations laid by Deren and her followers and great impetus also came with the arrival of the Neo-Realists in Italy, the *Nouvelle Vague* in France, Ingmar Bergman in Sweden and the 'Free Cinema' documentary forms in Britain. The

air was finally cleared of the stifling oppression of the million-dollar Hollywood film blanket that caused a dreamy, sleepy gulf between film and reality.
As the 'fifties rolled on, television had begun to grind out the Hollywood
magic, taking audiences away from the movie theatres. The bubble of the
Hollywood film industry began to burst. The industry itself scrambled and
turned to television to find a new outlet and new material. Paddy Chayefsky's
Marty is an example. Though this is still in traditional form, it presents a
situation that has a wider application; it came closer to people, bringing the
film into the living-room. It also became clear that a feature film could be
produced for far less money than the vast sums that Hollywood normally
consumed.

An even greater impact came from the *Nouvelle Vague* in France. Jean-Luc
Godard's *À Bout de Souffle* (1960), Francois Truffaut's *Les Quatre Cents
Coups* (1959), Alain Resnais's *Hiroshima mon Amour* (1959) and Louis
Malle's *Les Amants* (1958), were among a whole group of films that suddenly
appeared at Cannes one year. Their makers – along with Claude Chabrol –
were heard of everywhere, especially in America. They demanded that each
individual film should be, fundamentally, the work of an individual film-
maker (or director), and should bear the stamp of his own personality. Their
work showed that this approach could be highly successful. These new French
directors explored the archives at the Cinémathèque Français, thus getting
away from the boredom of Hollywood and rediscovering the great wealth and
power of the early cinema. Some of the films that inspired them had been
buried for almost twenty years, while others had been saved (if only in bits)
by the Cinémathèque, the least inhibited of all film archives.

The *Nouvelle Vague* had a shattering impact on the lethargic American
film scene – and its audiences. The shock came from the directors' individual
styles, statements and techniques, which were as alive as everyday life. The
cameras shook with the movements of people, intertwining with their subjective characters. The camera thus became a greater part of the film. Cinema
became more direct; the atmosphere became freer. The *Nouvelle Vague* films
paved the way for the new generation, giving the feeling that you too could
make a film without the Hollywood hullabaloo, the costumes and the whole
Mexican army. Their makers also stirred up the past, uncovering Buñuel,
Vigo, Gance and Delluc, Eisenstein and the rest. The older voices began to
reach newer ears and the obscure words and works of these individual directors, whose belief in film was so sorely crushed and isolated by the Hollywood
giants, soon became apparent.

Even the so-called 'Free Cinema' in Britain had its effect. This group was
formed in the mid-'fifties, producing at first short films, then later features in
a direct documentary style that pushed a sort of plotless realism into a mood
of contemporary life. With their films and a small magazine called *Sequence*
the group challenged the very dull and rather trite British cinema, as well as
a stilted society that still conceived of the cinema and its entertainment in
terms of its Victorian past. As the Beatles did in the 'sixties, so the 'Free
Cinema' group tried to open up the tightly knit class structure that was ever-

present in Britain. They tried to show in their films a frustrated and restrictive society that was causing social strangulation and inhibition. If they did not achieve their aim in this, at least they opened up television and cut into the innately dull feature film, creating works such as Lindsay Anderson's *O Dreamland* (1953) and *Every Day Except Christmas* (1957); Karel Reisz's *We are the Lambeth Boys* (1958) and *Momma Don't Allow* (with Tony Richardson, 1955) and later his feature *Saturday Night and Sunday Morning* (1960); Tony Richardson's *The Loneliness of the Long-Distance Runner* (1963); Lorenza Mezzetti's *Together*; Jack Clayton's *Room at the Top* (1958); John Schlesinger's *A Kind of Loving* (1962) and Bryan Forbes's *The L-Shaped Room* (1962). Oddly enough, this spell of activity had little hold in Britain. Once out of the hothouse of a cohesive movement, the leading members of the 'Free Cinema' lost their intensity and adventurousness in the commercial structure. But in America the Free Cinema, along with the Neo-Realists and the *Nouvelle Vague*, created the film climate from which the New Cinema was to emanate.

This climate was part of a larger eruption in the United States. After the Second World War the country found itself in Art; its own art; its own avant-garde – finally! The new avant-garde unfolded in New York thirty years after Paris. The environment was electric with excitement and was stirred into high-pitched activity and ideas. Painting, poetry, writing, dance, theatre, music, design and eventually film broke into life. There were the 'Beats' and the Abstract Expressionists such as Pollock and Klein, who translated subjectively caused moments into painterly forms and dynamics. Pollock went out into space and left behind a survey of the pieces on earth, of things around. With the survey came another label, machined out by the press as 'Pop' art. This represented the break from pristine attitudes towards art and the artist, from the usual habits of seeing. This was the era of the immediacy of time, of the 'now' and of the 'thing'. Historians tried to tie Pop to Dada. The two did have some visual similarities and for cinema they represented the points when film began to see. The difference was that the Dadaists withdrew and established a particular dogma within their social structure, while Pop artists delved into and adored all the things their society involved. They had no dogma of withdrawal and no political attachment. Instead they created a structure that was available to anyone and appealed directly to the senses, not to the intellect.

This climate was the confirmation of everyday life: the car we drive; the soup we eat; the noise of traffic; the ads stuffed into our faces; the comic books we read as kids and the pin-ups hidden from Mom. It was the flag we flew; coughing in the theatre; the half-tone dots of the printed picture; the false eyelashes and the dolly wigs; or just our toilet. It was everything that our environment directly felt and directly expressed, even to the point of actually using the things. The results were felt so strongly because everyone had been so exposed to them that no one could see them any more, so when they were pointed out it really meant something. We knew it. As the Surrealists' images are our subjective reality, so Pop images are our objective reality.

Much of this attitude was fostered by John Cage, whose philosophical and physical impact was undeniably one of the greatest influences on the post-war generation. His attitude was to allow art to 'be the affirmation of life – not an attempt to bring order out of chaos or to suggest improvements in creation, but simply a way of waking up to the very life we are living'. He considered that any form of self-expression, conscious or unconscious, becomes a way of adopting a false picture; it simply perpetuates the myth of the 'artist'. He wanted to go beyond the limitations of his own taste, his own consciousness, as well as going beyond thoughts of tradition or future. After studying oriental philosophy (Indian and Zen) and then studying with Suzuki he arrived at the philosophy of 'waking up the very life we are living'. Thanks to this he relinquished almost all traditional ideas on musical procedure, pointing out that no sound is musical in itself, but that any sound becomes musical by being heard in the context of a piece of music. From 1957 to 1958, when he composed 'Concert for Piano and Orchestra', he became increasingly interested in audio-visual possibilities, which took him more into the area of theatre (although his 'Water Music' of 1952 already reveals earlier stirrings of this interest). He evolved his theatre concept in such pieces as 'Music Walk' (1958), 'Sounds of Venice' (1959), 'Water Walk' (1959), 'Theatre Piece' (1960) and '0.00' (1960), in which the performer carried out an activity that he would have carried out anyway. In other words, other parameters than audio ones (such as visual elements and physical movements) are used. Cage once said: 'Music is an over-simplification of the situation we actually are in. Hearing is not being; music is one part of theatre.' This notion of music-as-theatre is part of his belief in pieces that are indeterminate as to their performance.

His 'Music of Changes' (1951), for piano, involved a very complex system of chance operations devised from the 'I Ching', which was used to determine what a pianist should play. Although the establishment of the elements and their sequence was initially based on chance, it was later fixed by notation. This process restricts the performer to whatever is eventually determined. In a piece like 'Variations IV' Cage provides a number of plastic transparencies with various ink-marks on them, and these are placed in any position over a plan of the performance area. The intersection of the ink-marks indicates where the sound will come from, but nothing else, leaving the performer free to choose the nature of the sounds. Cage is sure that his methods of working – whether by chance, indeterminacy or theatre – are those that most accurately reflect modern life, or rather *are* life. 'Everything we do is music' – there are no sacred cows, nothing is considered reverent or insignificant. This is not quite the same thing as saying 'anything goes'. As Cage has said many times: anything does go, *but* 'only when nothing is taken as the basis'.

One of the things that disturbed Cage most was the way orthodox musicians became irresponsible when playing pieces that gave them freedom in performance (*vide* the 1964 performance of 'Concert for Piano and Orchestra' in New York and Cologne in 1958; in the New York and Illinois performances of 'Theatre Piece' some performers were either showing off or were embar-

rassed at their new responsibilities, though of course others performed well).
Cage said: 'I must find a way to let people be free without becoming foolish
so that their freedom will make them noble.'

Not many of Cage's disciples, even in this climate, were prepared to take
nothing as a basis; so much of their permissiveness seemed foolish and ill-
considered, or else they used chance merely because they found it made
composition easier. Almost nothing is harder than accepting responsibility for
an indeterminate situation that you have to set up (Cage's position), or assum-
ing responsibility *in* an indeterminate situation set up in part by someone
else (the performers' position). Cage's attitude to the hexagram (a combination
of two elements in threes) on art in the 'I Ching' is significant:

> . . . it discusses the effect of a work of art as though it were a light shining
> on top of a mountain, penetrating to a certain extent the surrounding dark-
> ness. That is to say, art is described as being illuminating, and the rest of
> life as being dark – naturally I disagree. If there were a part of life dark
> enough to keep out of it a light from art, I would want to be in that dark-
> ness, rumbling around if necessary, but alive; and I rather think that con-
> temporary music would be there in the dark too, bumping into things,
> knocking others over, and in general adding to the disorder that character-
> izes life (if it is opposed to art) rather than adding to the order and stabilized
> truth, beauty and power that characterizes a masterpiece (if it is opposed
> to life). . . . All that you can do is suddenly listen in the same way that
> when you catch cold all you do is suddenly sneeze. Unfortunately European
> thinking has brought it about that natural things that happen such as
> suddenly listening or suddenly sneezing are not considered profound
> [*Composition as Process 111 Communication*, 1958].

This attitude of Cage's filtered into the environment and into the whole art
community. It was not just listening and music that was affected; the theatre
and the performing arts were too; and so were seeing and the visual (plastic)
arts; so was film. Morton Feldman said of Cage: 'Just to change one little
thing in music was a life's work. But John changed everything. We got out
of that strait-jacket, and it made everything much more simple in one way and
a lot harder in other ways. What we learned was that THERE ARE NO CATAS-
TROPHES.' It was not that everyone swung over to follow Cage, but he helped
to open many doors. The effect was there and many other artists, such as
Jasper Johns and Bob Rauschenberg (Cage worked with Rauschenberg and
Merce Cunningham, the dancer, in 1952) knew Cage personally or studied
under him, or else had experienced his performances.

The environmental period of the 'sixties not only brought artists into the
theatre, but the theatre provoked a rich extension within itself as exemplified
by such groups as The Living Theater, the La Mama or the Theatre of the
Ridiculous, each of which had its feedback to and from the new growth in
film. In this period too, came the development of so-called 'Minimal' art
(dealing directly with the nature of the experience and the perception through

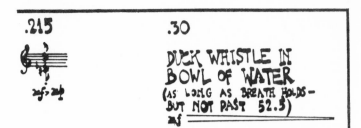

reaction) which fed its concept into every area, particularly into film and dance (where Yvonne Rainer produced some of the most brilliant examples of the minimal in movement). This period also produced a neo-dada group like the Fluxus at the same time as it produced a social/political consciousness that was realized all over the world – the two ends meeting in the vital re-birth of the film. By the 1970s, the controlling Establishment showed clearly how extensively alive and open the environment was becoming by its frighteningly strong return to oppressive and totalitarian measures. Obviously this generation had so strong a sense of change that the Establishment feared its own overthrow.

It was at this time that some painters broke away from the enforced shape and flatness of the painted area, moving instead towards the theatre concept – not the traditionally narrative one, but the visually sculptural one. In 1957 Alan Kaprow created the first 'happening'. The 'happening' was time and space, an environment in itself. The room or the area was filled with objects; with materials; with sounds and smells; with lights; and most important, with people. What happened depended on the people present, who were no longer viewers but were part of the piece. The action was all round; they were surrounded, involved (or forced by the situation to be involved) and they occupied space. The objects were everyday ones; the materials were materials; bodies were bodies and materials became bodies and movements, materials and lights transforming it all. The whole 'happening' happened and, like a Tinguely sculpture, went through itself and developed itself until it had exhausted itself. The artist created a situation, as it were, for people, which lived only as it happened. Here too came minimal art, which had become a force by the late 'sixties and which deals directly with the nature of experience and with perception through visual reactions.

If you are in a crowded shop you are surrounded by an environment made up of people and objects. You are involved. You notice things – a box, the counter, the salesgirl – and you can react to the things about you. You move in its space, you touch the objects or bump into the people. You are not fixed but can project yourself on to the environment or the environment can project itself on to you. It is real; it is life; it is happening. It initiates emotional, subjective response by the affirmation and association of the thing itself.

Kaprow was the first to start 'happenings', but other artists such as Red Grooms, Robert Whitman, Jim Dine, Claes Oldenburg and Carolee Schneemann soon joined him. The scene is described by the Underground reporter,

Sidney Bernard:

> One of the first practitioners of Happenings was Claes Oldenburg who, along
> with other young artists, would open their walkup flats – some located on
> Third and Fourth Avenues, below Fourteenth Street – to a public audience
> and would proceed to involve that audience, in a most off-the-cuff manner
> in a casual building of the atmosphere of play, discovery, group singing or
> recitation, games and what-have-you, often with the use of made-up on-the-
> spot props, or costumes, to lend the verisimilitude of a group experience,
> with an emphasis on performing, on theatricality, all of which added to an
> evening of what might be called 'found experience': hence Happenings.

The idea and practice of the 'happening' spread quickly and soon newspapers
like the *Village Voice* were giving space, both in short write-ups and in their
weekly 'What's On' columns, to this new development in New York 'avant'
art circles.

From the start there was a big difference, at least in degree, between the
limited public impact of 'avant' film-making, and the more immediate and
open impact of the 'happening'. Indeed with the possible exception of *Daisy
(Pull My Daisy)*, which did catch a wider audience via the campus film clubs,
and such 'avant' film-houses as Dan Talbot's New Yorker, few avant-garde
films could hope to make their way into the mainstream. In one sense, then,
the 'happening' was predictably the medium of a social art form, much more
easily accessible, much more 'tuned' to a current style than the medium of the
'avant' film-maker, who more often than not dwelled, and worked, in his
own private world, with little or no thought for the impact of his footage on
anyone but himself, first, and perhaps on very close friends and other movie-
makers in his set, second. Since their beginnings in the early 'sixties 'happenings' have spread widely, and are even used by – to take one example of wide
public application – the New York Park Department for a huge paint-in in
Central Park, behind the Metropolitan Museum, with as many as ten thous-
and people, children barely out of prams included, making use of as much
paint and canvas and as many brushes as they needed. The result of one such
event was a mammoth, 200-foot-long collective canvas that had everything
from kids' musings and scrawls to art students' *ad hoc* creations, activists'
political graffiti and slogans, and hundreds of other examples of instantaneous
art.

The adaptability of the 'happening', its easy use of space in virtually any
circumstance that the artist may visualize, is what gives it impact at a time of
great social and political change. It is a vehicle not only for the artist, but
for a broader spectrum embracing rock groups and even politically oriented
groups such as the SDS campus rebels, the Yippies and the East Side anar-
chists like the Motherfuckers. That the impact falls into political areas as well
simply means that the 'happening' is pre-eminently an event of artists, activists
and masses of people moving in an atmosphere and in a space and time that
are most conducive to great change.

By 1958 the influence of the 'happening' on the feature film became appar-

D

ent with the appearance of the low-budget *cinéma vérité* film *Shadows*, made by John Cassavetes at a cost of only about $15,000 – a tiny amount compared to the Hollywood productions, which often ranged near the million-dollar mark. It was shot on 16mm, then blown up to 35mm, and was essentially plotless and improvised. It was based on moods and attitudes within a Negro family in New York and on the wandering life engendered by the frustrated atmosphere existing between black and white people. The most important aspect of this film was its use of improvised, unscripted action, with the director setting up a situation and following it through with the camera, later creating relationships by editing. In many ways this improvisation technique is closely related to the feeling in much of American jazz. (A point to mention here is that there are two versions of *Shadows*. The original version was freer and more daring, but it shocked the distributors so much that they persuaded Cassavetes to remake the film to suit commercial theatrical standards. The second version was the one most widely seen.) The roughness and comparative naïveté of *Shadows* tended to emphasize the reality and naturalness of the characters and their situation. It achieved its breakthrough by reaching more into the 'soul' of people and the life round them.

At this time artists were once again reaching towards film, since the current attitude to materials, technology, happenings, time and contact with 'now' related to film. For the artist even more than for 'professional' film-makers, film meant fluidity, movement, space juxtaposed, illusion, parody, reality, fantasy, twenty-four paintings a second, subtlety, exaggeration, boredom and repetition; it was drawing, photographic scrutiny, scratching, colour, tone, mathematical relationships and patterns. It was all, part or one of these things for each of the individual artists who stepped into film. Even in the 'beat' and 'pop' generation, film artists grew up with the same sense of response as painters and sculptors. What the comic book and the soup-tin were for painters, Hollywood and home-movies were for some film-makers; the film was the machine of dreams, gloss and stylized exaggeration, and the obsessive, every-day object, made to be played with. It was part of mass materialism and the environment of exaggeration. For others it was the freedom and 'camp' attitude reflected in Dad's home-movies; the commonplace sense of the living-room; friends and family and an uninhibited mood of 'why not?'. For many it represented an extension and exploration related to the basic concepts of form, space and time; and an emotional transference to the development of their imagery in the tradition of Duchamp.

Pull My Daisy might be called the first 'underground' to appear in this atmosphere. Made within a fictional concept and filmed as documented reality, it was directed by Robert Frank (a photographer) and Alfred Leslie (a painter) in 1958/9. It retains the feeling of a freely improvised film in the style of 'Beat' poetic ramblings, using local, contemporary colloquialisms. It was silent and was based on a scene from an unproduced play by Jack Kerouac, who speaks for all the characters on the soundtrack, adding comments of his own. He recorded the track in a free-form manner on his first viewing of the film. *Pull My Daisy* represents in essence the 'Beats'' anti-middle class attitude, starring as it does the most notable of the 'Beat' poets – Allen Ginsberg, Gregory Corso and Peter Orlovsky. It takes place one evening in the Greenwich Village flat of a young 'railway worker' (ex-drug addict) called Milo, who is visited by some poet friends and a 'bishop' (of no church). The 'bishop' has been invited by Milo's wife in the hope of converting him to middle-class ways. The camera wanders through the place, picking on the slightest details and scanning the people. Nothing much happens and that is the beauty of it, its deliberate point of contact with life. Frank's photography, as in his still work, manages to scrutinize obliquely the details and characteristics of everyman's life. (In 1961 Frank was to make the short film *The Sins of Jesus,* a religious parody on a run-down farm.) In his work as painter Alfred Leslie maintained an awareness of paint and spontaneity. It was this spontaneity, combined with the ramblings, colloquialisms and improvisation of the poets, that produced *Pull My Daisy.* The film marked the coalescence of the movement towards the New American Cinema, which spread rapidly as the so-called 'underground' film, and into a fuller independent cinema.

3 Contemporary Background

Like most artists, the serious personal film-maker commits his time, his energies, his emotions and his money to producing a film. But films need to be projected, even to friends; this is one of their distinctive properties. A FINISHED FILM IS A PROJECTED FILM: that is its function. To make a film that is personal, experimental, avant-garde – call it what you will – in other words, to make a film that is not produced primarily for commercial gain, and to get it projected for others to see, can put the film-maker into a world foreign to his own, the world of bureaucracy, politics, organization, economics.

Traditionally, the commercial film functions in a sphere unlike that of the personal film. In general it has been tied by the investment in it, an investment intended to reap a financial return. This meant that a type of film was developed and fostered that was based either on a previously successful style or on the lowest common denominator of public values (the acceptable, the untroubled). Then, of course, films of any genre must be seen. That means distribution and exhibition. As the basic function of the commercial film is profit, to control its distribution and exhibition is to increase the backer's insurance against loss. In most places distribution and exhibition has become the monopoly of the few – those who have money – and they inevitably select films to maintain their profit levels.

Film has also fallen at least partly under the control of governments, as have all the mass communication media. If governments have not completely inhibited the production of films, they have certainly inhibited their exhibition. Film works in the ambiguous sphere of art and art makes use of the values that exist within a culture. A society's culture is more pervasive than its politics, which means that any alteration, or even questioning, of existing values is an alteration of society. The established cultural hierarchy maintains itself by protecting and enforcing the ideas that keep it in power, so that anything that attacks, questions or provides new values is a threat. The hierarchy allows only material that will not challenge its assumptions; everything else must be forced out – or forced underground.

However it is made, the personal and independent film seeks its own path rather than following an established commercial pattern. The style and themes

52

of this New Cinema differ from country to country (sometimes even within one country) because each grows out of a different cultural, economic and political situation. In the economically more highly developed countries films have a cultural emphasis; while in under-developed countries they tend to aim at precise socio-political objectives. Because of this, and because such films are often highly personal, the subjects dealt with are the taboos of the society in which they are made. These taboos range from the sexual, to the religious, to the political. If and when such films are shown they attract condemnation and persecution from those conditioned by the hierarchy to accept certain values and, in many cases in which cinematographic technique itself is challenged, from the film industry and critics.

The harassment and oppression meted out by the authorities have taken various forms, but they have occurred (in varying degrees) in most countries where an independent cinema has sprung up. The primary method is censorship, which uses certificates, licences and so on to control the public exhibition of films. The decision to pass a film is not generally based on definable laws, but rather on laws that leave the decision to the judgement of the censor (or committee of censors) and his interpretation of what 'might be damaging to the public health, welfare and morality' or 'tend to deprave and corrupt'. Often the film industry itself creates a censorship designed to protect it from public or political criticism. The term 'obscenity', for example, has never been clearly defined, so that its interpretation is totally dependent on the values held by those who apply it to films. Yet it is used all over the world to stop films. In Britain the Obscene Publications Act of 1959 and 1964 states that it 'shall apply in relation to anything which is intended to be used, either alone or as one of a set, for the reproduction or manufacture therefrom of articles containing or embodying matter to be read, looked at, or listened to . . .' and extends to that which 'shall be deemed to be had or kept for publication. . . .' Interpretation of the Act is left to the authorities and their agents, who can enforce it when they have 'reason to believe' that an infringement has taken place. Such action can be taken not only when the films are shown publicly, but also when they are merely in the possession of a private individual. Fears of potential oppression from the authorities spread, naturally enough, to the film laboratories, causing the technicians to behave even more cautiously than the authorities in interpreting material as obscene and to refuse to process or print anything that they consider may bring police action against them. These fears, encouraged by the hierarchy in each particular society in order to maintain its values, of course extend to film exhibitors as well. Thus it is the values, not the laws, that become the real oppressors.

In this situation, when the independent film-maker has made his film, whatever the subject, and intends to show it, he will often find himself going underground, rather than battle with the obstacles put forward by the film industry and by the values of his society. One of the earliest possibilities for showing such film has in many countries been offered by film clubs, which exhibited films 'privately' and therefore bypassed the laws regarding 'public' exhibition (though in some countries, including Britain, the obscenity laws still apply). These clubs were the first places where many independent and experimental films could be seen – often the only places. In the mid-1920s the first showing of some French avant-garde films was in a few clubs such as the Ciné-Club de France, Club des Amis du Septième and the Tribune Libre du Cinema. There were also one or two sympathetic theatres, such as Cinema 28 in Montmartre, which witnessed the first violent reaction against a film when Buñuel's *L'Âge d'Or* was shown in 1930. By showing these new films the clubs helped to spread some of the ideas that were being developed at the time and thus contributed to the avant-garde movement as a whole. As their popularity grew, besides attracting genuinely interested people they also drew into their orbit pseudo-intellectuals and pseudo-artists, who did not really come to see the films, but merely to be associated with the movement. Soon more clubs and cinemas sprang from the success of the earlier ones and began to exploit the growing interest in the new cinema and its money-making potential. The actual films and the film-makers gradually became submerged.

Film clubs and societies, many within the universities, still provide the major viewing facilities for the independent cinema. By now most countries have established film archives that have attempted to preserve many of the older independent films and often screen them, though some of them still ignore most of their contemporary counterparts. Yet even though the clubs and archives have been able to show films, they have seldom been in a position to distribute them, and some have been completely unable to do so. In 1933 the British Film Institute established one of the first film archives (and now distributes a few of the films), but it was not until 1937 that the Museum of Modern Art in New York began to distribute avant-garde films to other non-profit-making organizations. There was no commercial distribution and only a few other organizations, such as the San Francisco Museum of Art, the Guggenheim Foundation and the Cinémathèque Française, made any attempt to preserve early independent films.

The United States

After the war American film-makers continued their efforts to promote and achieve a greater degree of public exposure and at the same time to gain some financial return for their films. Maya Deren, for instance, began to lecture and write about the personal film. She hired a small wooden theatre, the Provincetown Playhouse off 3rd Street in New York City, to show her own films and with the money she received from her screenings and from the attendant publicity set up the Creative Film Foundation, which was intended to help other independent film-makers. Deren's attempts, plus those of Frank Stauffacher of the San Francisco Museum of Art, encouraged Amos Vogel to open his Cinema 16 and to help build up the Creative Film Foundation. Cinema 16, functioning as a club, assembled the first exclusive library of contemporary avant-garde films for distribution and exhibition. Vogel initially, like Deren, used the Provincetown Playhouse, but eventually he would hire larger commercial cinemas (costing five times more than the Provincetown) a few times a month to give the films a wider audience. Cinema 16 gave the first showings in the United States of many of the new films by men such as Kenneth Anger and Stan Brakhage. Economic problems eventually caused the disappearance of Cinema 16 in the early 'sixties, the whole library being bought by Grove Press in New York.

In 1957 Robert Pike, a film-maker in California, after fruitlessly attempting to get his first three films distributed, decided to distribute them himself by founding the Creative Film Society. He also distributed the films of other West-Coast film-makers who were in the same position as he was, among them John and James Whitney (noted for their 'motion graphics'), Jordan Belson, Jane Belson, Leroy Robbins and Hy Hirsch, plus Curtis Harrington, Kenneth Anger, Bruce Conner and Robert Nelson. Pike also released such well-made but neglected films as *Even As You and I* by Leroy Robbins, Roger Barlow, Hy Hirsch and Harry Hay, which had been lying around unseen since 1937. Pike's own three films: *A Thin Dime, Desire in a Public Dump* (beauty and rubbish contrasted in an allegorical use of colour intercut with black and white) and *The Tragicomedy of Marriage* (spoofing adolescent American experimental films of the 'forties and 'fifties and marital shortcomings in America). Pike's statement about his first film exemplified, in part, the influence of the earlier experimental film-makers plus that of the newer independent film-makers: 'The original intent of the film was to be a lyrical editing exercise in symbolic passion, inspired by a sequence in *Psyche* by Gregory Markopoulos and in *Lot in Sodom* by Watson and Webber.'

the village VOICE,

movie
JOURNAL

by Jonas Mekas

Probably the most important initiative for the presentation and distribution of independently made films came with the foundation of the film-makers' co-operatives. The co-operatives are, in principle, groups of film-makers who bring their films together into one central library and proceed to show and distribute them jointly. The first of the co-operatives was begun in New York at the beginning of the 'sixties and was led by Jonas Mekas. Mekas was one of the most influential people to give life to the personal film, becoming spokesman, critic and organizer for the whole of the New American Cinema, while facing arrests, court cases and mockery. As a film-maker, poet and dedicated voice, he became the patriarch who held the respect of other film-makers and kept them united. Because of this the co-operatives grew and the films they showed rose more and more to the surface.

Jonas Mekas was born in 1922 in Semeniskiai in Lithuania. During the Second World War, when first the Russians and then the Germans occupied the country, he worked against both enemies as the editor of an underground newspaper. Eventually both he and his brother, Adolfas, ended up in a labour camp. The end of the war brought them to a displaced persons' camp and finally to the University of Mainz. Here Mekas discovered a book called *Dramaturgy of Films* and he later said: 'When I read the book, I realized that, no matter where we went, Cinema was the tongue in which we could reach anybody.' In 1949 the International Refugee Organization brought him and his brother to New York.

In 1955 Jonas and Adolfas started a magazine called *Film Culture*, having spent the previous six years working as loaders, maintenance men, dishwashers, messengers, photographers and darkroom technicians. *Film Culture* became the only regular journal devoted almost entirely to the new independent films, to avant-garde films and to the new people and ideas in the cinema, though without neglecting important people and activities within the commercial cinema. The magazine gave the first tangible voice to the whole personal and independent cinema, both contemporary and historical, while in his widely read, weekly column in New York's *Village Voice* newspaper, Mekas kept alive the sense and the spirit of the new films throughout the year. His reviews and descriptions of film, his news about activities among film-makers and organizations (including reports on police harassment) informed people and gave the film movement unity.

In 1961 Mekas, aided by his brother, made *Guns of the Trees*, which he described as an 'anti-police, anti-government and anti-film' film. Then in 1963 he directed *Hallelujah the Hills*, a parody of the styles used in the commercial films, but composed in a delightfully wild, free style. In 1964 he directed *The Brig* (which was produced by Barbara and David Stone, who also produced such important independent films as Robert Kramer's *Ice*, and their own film *Companeras and Companeros* with Adolfas Mekas), shot round a special performance of Kenneth Brown's play by Julian Beck's and Judith Malina's Living Theater group. This film turned out to be a strong and very raw rendering of cruelty based on a US Marine prison. The Living Theater is an astounding group in itself and in conjunction with film made *The Brig* a formidable production. In 1966/7 Mekas made *The Circus Notebook*, which he described as 'the Ringling Brothers – but really, it's the circus of my childhood, with all the fantastic things going on, and colors, and mystery, and exotic, and dreams, and amazement'. *Hare Krishna* followed in 1967 and by 1969 he was finishing off an autobiographical film called *Diaries*, part of a collection of films made by using the camera as a personal notebook. In 1971, Jonas Mekas, with his brother Adolfas made a return trip to Lithuania. Adolfas made the film *Going Home* on this visit, while Jonas made his film *Reminiscences of a Journey to Lithuania.*

Mekas's greatest efforts, however, have always been towards giving free and personal films a chance to live the life they deserve. Obvious examples are his development of the first film-makers' co-operative and later his estab-

lishment of places where the films could be shown, such as the Film-makers'
Cinémathèque in New York (which was eventually forced to close). His
writings, criticism and actions always give the others new heart, though his
fight for a liberated cinema often placed him in direct conflict with the
authorities – he has been in prison and appeared in court more than once.
For example, when he was one of the judges at the Third International
Experimental Film Festival, held at Knokke-le-Zoute in Belgium, Jack
Smith's *Flaming Creatures* was refused a screening; Mekas resigned and then
proceeded to take over the projection room. When the Belgian Minister of
Justice protested, Mekas projected the film on to his face. As a critic Mekas
insults, attacks and praises both commercial and non-commercial films. He
uses such point-blank statements as 'Stinks! ', or simply lists films he does not
like under the heading: 'Walked out of'. He has said, 'Children and wise
men never argue about movies. Everything is clear to them. Only we –
those in between – are all shook up, confused and lost in the pastures of
art.'

The New York Film-makers' Co-operative became the first open distribution structure. In its ideal and original framework, it was intended for the
film-makers and used by them alone, as a collective force, a basic economic
and social structure held together by a unity of effort. Before it began in
1961 hardly any personal and independent film had any chance whatever of
being distributed. The Co-operative was a sound and practical solution. The
system is that any film-maker can place his film or films into the co-operative library. He pays for the film and the prints and thereby owns all the
rights in them. The depositing of a film entitles him to any rights and privi-
leges that the co-operative can offer. He can also withdraw, restrict or determine the hire fees for his own films. There is no preselection or censorship,
and no aesthetic judgement is made on any of the films. The idea is that
everything should be done to encourage film-making and nothing to inhibit
the development of film and of individual film-makers. This undoubtedly
means that the quality of the films will vary considerably. On the other
hand, it ensures the survival of many good films and the discovery of a few
great films, some of which would otherwise never have been seen at all.

As a collective body of people who deposit their films in one central
agency, the co-operative can easily handle the complex business of film
distribution, exhibition and promotion. The financial system is based on a
percentage of the hire fees going to the film-maker and the remainder going
to the co-operative to cover its overheads. The percentage that goes to the
film-makers varies from co-operative to co-operative, ranging from 60 per
cent to 75 per cent of the total fee. (In New York the rate is 75 per cent.)
This system works because no single film-maker could handle his film alone,
since the necessary financial investment and paperwork would severely restrict the time and money he has available for making films. Whereas an
individual film-maker has a limited output and cannot offer selection possibilities in order to expand outlets for distribution and showings, the co-
operative unit can provide a reasonably steady circulation of films, with a

wider range, plus the publicity, secretarial duties and cataloguing necessary
if the films are to be seen by as many people as possible. (In the early days,
when the system was often struggling, the film-makers had to do most of
the secretarial work themselves.) There are no contracts or binding agreements and the structure is held together by common interest, friendship and
exchange.

   In this climate there is an opportunity for the individual film-maker to
turn up with his or her film and show it on the spot. This system, one of the
main advantages of the co-operatives, is known as 'open screening', since it
involves no prejudgment. Each film and each film-maker must find its own
audience, the only limitation on the maker being his own imagination. In
the independent cinema there tends to be no division of labour, as in the
commercial cinema: the film-maker conceives, shoots, edits (and sometimes
even processes) his own film. Often this total commitment and financial investment on the part of the film-maker arouse his fears about how others
will handle what amounts to his only print. This kind of protective fear has
often resulted in conflicts within co-operatives. They are run as a kind of
democracy – which often verges on anarchy – and there are many ambiguities and vague situations. This often results in paranoia becoming rampant,
in personal vendettas emerging and in subgroups dividing themselves off
politically and socially from the others. The open structure of the co-operative also allows many people to enter it solely for their own personal gain.
Yet the co-operative structure can function only as long as it remains open
and free from personal tastes or political ambitions.

FILM-MAKERS' COOPERATIVE

So-called 'underground' film screenings began to be run by the New York
Co-operative in 1962. At first they were conducted anywhere that was available. At the original office at 414 Park Avenue South there was a projector,
so that rushes could be viewed and friends could watch films, and some editing equipment for film-makers to use. Spontaneous screenings would occur
in lofts and other places in and around Lower Manhattan as audiences began
to grow and the screening of rushes to more open audiences also became
a commonplace activity. This both gave the film-makers a chance to see what
they had shot, since many of them could not afford their own projector, and
also brought in money to enable them to finish their films. These various
film shows were sometimes announced by Mekas in the *Village Voice*, but
more often news got round by word of mouth or cryptic notices pinned to
lamp-posts round Greenwich Village. For example, the first screening of
Jack Smith's frequently confiscated film *Flaming Creatures* took place in
a storage loft just off Washington Square Village. Various members of the

press managed to get in and it was rumoured that Fellini and a few other 'known' film people were there as well. The seats were planks of wood stretched across boxes, with a few old lavatories that had been stored there also turned into seats.

Screenings also began to take place once a week at Dan Talbot's Charles Theater on Lower East Side. (Talbot also ran the New Yorker cinema on West Broadway, the first public cinema in New York to revive the early classics and later to show the independents.) But it was in the Gramercy Arts Theater that the main activity and regular (almost daily) film shows took place. It was always full, attracting long queues of festive people. The films were projected from the small balcony on to what amounted to a home-movie screen. Most of them had sound on tape, or else records would be played, since most of the film-makers could not yet afford sound transfers. It was during these shows that police harassment became evident. They first tried to stop the screenings by stating that as tickets were sold at the door they constituted a public exhibition. As New York did not have the freedom of the British 'club' structure, a New York State licence was needed for each film, which involved presenting the film before the censors' board. (This was never done, firstly on principle, since it meant limiting freedom. and secondly because many films would clearly never have been passed.) To counter this, film shows were conducted free and contributions asked. The arrests and the confiscation of films began soon after. Mekas and three others were arrested at the Bridge Theater on East 8th Street when they were showing Jean Genet's film *Un Chant d'Amour* in early 1964. (I myself had a three-minute film showing with it called *A newsreel of two underground film stars having breakfast in bed.*) Mekas wrote of his arrest:

> The detectives who seized the Genet film . . . did not know who Genet was. When I told them that Genet was an internationally known artist, I was told it was my fantasy . . . while I was walking toward my cell I was pushed on my back by the cop. I told him not to push me since I was not resisting. For this remark, the cop kicked me full force in the back. When I reminded him again not to use force, I was pushed again. . . .

When the New York Co-operative finally opened the Film-makers' Cinémathèque, located on 41st Street, regular film shows began. Distribution increased rapidly, especially on the university circuit, as well as to a growing number of small theatres round the country. By 1968 there were approximately 150 cinemas regularly showing the work of the New American Cinema. Various 'experimental' film societies also began to spring up and the teaching of film and the use of film in teaching rapidly increased. A few entrepreneurs now became active, such as Mike Getz, who developed the Underground 12 circuit in California. This supplied programmes to a regular group of cinemas, films often being sought outside the co-operatives. Some entrepreneurs hunted out films not yet generally seen, or went abroad to find material. Unlike Getz, a few of these entrepreneurs tried to buy up all the rights in such films, hoping to corner part of what seemed to be a growing market.

Meanwhile, in California, the second American co-operative and distribution structure was formed, calling itself the Canyon Cinema Co-operative. It functioned in the same way as its New York brother and was made up of West Coast film-makers working in close affiliation with New York. Soon the New York Co-operative opened a second cinema on Wooster Street and for a while managed to run it along with the Cinémathèque on 41st Street. But then both had to close, the Cinémathèque for financial reasons, the Wooster Street Cinema because of pressure from the authorities, who constantly found fault with the building that housed the cinema, applying building codes and fire regulations. (These faults could also be found in about half the buildings in New York City.) The Co-operative's screenings went into 'exile', as Mekas called it, giving shows at the Jewish Museum and the cinema of the Gallery of Modern Art (not to be confused with the Museum of Modern Art, which showed independent films and films from its own archives on a highly selective basis). The screenings in exile, however, attracted only very tiny audiences – often only ten to twenty people, and many of these were 'friends' of the film-makers. Places like the Millennium film workshop still gave regular film shows, and the Gate Theater, run by the film-maker Aldo Tambellini, struggled along by plugging a sex-sensational line. The members of the Co-operative, still with Mekas to the fore, then began work on a project to establish a repertory cinema in New York called Anthology Cinema. It was to show pieces regularly from its own collection of 'classics', whether they were so-called 'underground' films or not. It would be rather like an archive with film shows and the films would be selected initially by a committee. It would not be open to all films as under the co-operative system, and thus marked the end of an important phase in independent film-making in the United States.

This phase also marked the beginning of a commercialization process based on many of the 'underground' techniques and styles. Hollywood's expensive operations and their neglect of the new and younger audiences, many of whom had come to accept the new cinematographic language fostered by the New American Cinema, had led it into partial bankruptcy. The dinosaur story began to come true once again: the giant studios were sold or auctioned off, along with their theatrical authenticity; mergers began to take place; companies found themselves becoming subsidiaries of larger industrial combines and the remaining companies had to cut back drastically on productions and budgets. Old styles of film-making no longer worked and small-budget, more loosely structured films started to become the norm. The 'underground' feeling started to become an overground method.

In the years following 1962 interest in the personal film had grown at an astonishing rate in America. Hundreds of young people began to make films and film-making and the study of films spread to many universities, though it is true that film audiences often came out of curiosity rather than through a genuine interest. By the end of the 'sixties audiences in a place like New York had declined rather rapidly, though university and film-society distribution continued on a regular basis. The rapid influx of half-committed, 'imitation underground' films tended to wear heavily on an often none-too-sure and sensation-seeking audience.

But by now the spirit of the independent film had already begun to spread to Europe once again, as well as to Japan, Canada, Australia and parts of South America. There were two main stimuli for this. One came from the four International Experimental Film Festivals (1949, 1958, 1963, 1967) held in Belgium. The most influential were the last three (the 1958 festival was held during the World's Fair in Belgium), which were organized by Jacques Ledoux (one of the few individuals to have had any true feeling and understanding of the independent, experimental and personal cinema) and the Royal Film Archive of Belgium. These festivals not only took the New American Cinema into Europe but also brought together for the first time a major portion of the world's experimental and avant-garde film-makers. The second impetus came from the films of the New American Cinema brought to Europe by Jonas Mekas in 1964/5. He was followed in 1967/8 by a year's tour of a sixty-hour programme organized by P. Adams Sitney from the New York Co-operative. This tour coincided with the Fourth International Experimental Film Festival, held at Knokke-Le-Zoute in 1967. In almost all the countries that Sitney visited a film co-operative or some form of consolidated independent film activity soon appeared. By the beginning of 1970 there were co-operatives in Britain, Italy, Germany, Switzerland, Austria, Holland, Sweden, Australia, Canada and Japan, with rumours and stirrings and other levels of film activity in Argentina, Brazil, Belgium, Cuba, France, Portugal, Spain, Israel and India.

A CERTAIN GREAT
AND POWERFUL KING ONCE
ASKED A POET
"WHAT CAN I GIVE YOU
OF ALL THAT I HAVE ?"

HE WISELY REPLIED
"ANYTHING SIR...
EXCEPT YOUR SECRET"

Britain

Of the many film-makers' co-operatives that began to spring up in Europe the London one was the first. It began in October 1966 before the New American Exposition toured Europe, in a room at the back of the Better Books bookshop in Charing Cross Road. It grew out of a very different situation from that surrounding the New York or Canyon Cinema Co-operatives, for there were hardly any indigenous films or film-makers about at the time. It began rather from an interest in film, with the support of only a handful of film-makers, many of them Americans, and apparently with the optimistic hope that film-makers would suddenly emerge from secret hiding-places. Very few in fact appeared. The London Co-operative was clearly a premature venture, but it none the less continued, with many ups and downs, showing the few films that were available plus more from abroad.

It is important to realize that the British environment has never been conducive to the practice of the visual arts, including film. It is one of a prevailing literalness, of classification, of systematizing, a maze of labels, endless compartments and rigid class structures. To have any sense of achievement or recognition in Britain one must always reach some intellectually definable position. The undefinable and the unclassifiable must remain introspective secrets. This is important, because artistic self-expression has nothing to do with definable positions but works in a world of ambiguities and abstractions. If we look at Britain's visual history, we find few highly personal, individual and non literal painters (the outstanding exception is Turner); similarly Britain has produced very few memorable exponents of that most abstract of the arts, musical composition, whereas in literature and science she has excelled.

The visual arts have chiefly developed in two directions: towards the so-called decorative arts, involving surface embellishment and patterns (which are now giving way to mechanical solutions and computer ideology); and towards story-telling, satire, documentation and allegory, in the tradition of Hogarth. In terms of film, the second of these *genres* is the backbone of the British documentary – the predominant form of film-making in the country and the basis of the Free Cinema group in the 'fifties. It is noticeable that attempts at other forms of visual expression, especially more personal ones, tend to be copied from elsewhere. A good example is Pop Art, which originated in the United States as a dynamic personal response to a way of life; in Britain it tended to become narrative and highly picturesque.

The London Film-makers' Co-operative began as one of the many liberating influences that hit Britain in the mid-'sixties, along with the Beatles, the miniskirt and 'swinging London'. It was a time when the Vietnam War brought in many young Americans; when first Pop Art then Op Art came to the Whitechapel, the Royal College, then everywhere. Plastic. The Albert Hall poetry Wholly Communion. The Beats, the hippies, the Provos. Marijuana. Underground press and the Anti-University. The new generation that came of age no longer knew or cared about the Battle of Britain. It opened up and each little group soared like roman candles. The light burnt and died because there was nowhere to go; the old rules still held sway and Swinging London merely rocked the boat a bit. But the ground had been prepared for new values.

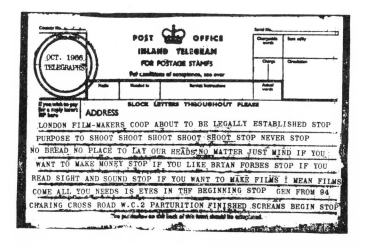

POST OFFICE
INLAND TELEGRAM
FOR POSTAGE STAMPS

OCT. 1966
TELEGRAPHS

BLOCK LETTERS THROUGHOUT PLEASE

ADDRESS

LONDON FILM-MAKERS COOP ABOUT TO BE LEGALLY ESTABLISHED STOP
PURPOSE TO SHOOT SHOOT SHOOT SHOOT SHOOT STOP NEVER STOP
NO BREAD NO PLACE TO LAY OUR HEADS NO MATTER JUST MIND IF YOU
WANT TO MAKE MONEY STOP IF YOU LIKE BRYAN FORBES STOP IF YOU
READ SIGHT AND SOUND STOP IF YOU WANT TO MAKE FILMS I MEAN FILMS
COME ALL YOU NEEDS IS EYES IN THE BEGINNING STOP GEN FROM 94
CHARING CROSS ROAD W.C.2 PARTURITION FINISHED SCREAMS BEGIN STOP

In 1966 attempts were being made to make London an all-night city like New York. Among the first of these was the UFO Club, which opened in a mirror-lined Irish dance-hall in Tottenham Court Road (later to be used for the Open Space Theatre) and stayed open all night. Pop groups played, such as the Pink Floyd; there were light-shows and films; people dressed in anything and everything you could imagine. Much of the idea for the UFO Club developed from earlier events in Notting Hill Gate, in and round the London Free School and the week-long First Notting Hill Festival (1966), during which one night was given over to underground films. The patriarch of such events was John ('Hoppy') Hopkins. This was also the time when London's first underground newspaper, *International Times* (IT) began. (Like other underground publications it was the victim of constant police harassment.)

The UFO Club continued to thrive and its example was followed by the Middle Earth Club. Under UFO influence three vast and memorable twenty-four-hour film/light/pop/sound events came into being, one at the Round-house, to celebrate the first issue of *IT*, the second, called the *Technicolour Dream,* at Alexandra Palace, the third, called *Christmas on Earth Revisited,* at Olympia. These events also attracted a large number of film companies, mostly Italian, who wanted to use the 'with-it' London scene as their back-drop. (Examples are Antonioni with *Blow Up* and Godard with *One Plus One* – later called *Sympathy for the Devil.*) The Roundhouse (a converted railway roundhouse) became a film-set for many other productions and later housed happenings and festivals plus more orthodox shows (such as Tony Richardson's *Hamlet*) and the Living Theater. When the UFO Club was chased out of its dance-hall it went straight over to the Roundhouse.

Both the UFO Club and Middle Earth eventually sank into oblivion, but this period also saw the opening of the first Arts Laboratory (Arts Lab), in

Drury Lane in 1967. The Arts Lab concept, fostered by Jim Haynes, involved a place where new ideas and attitudes in art could flourish. The Arts Lab contained a theatre (for live drama and musical performances), an art gallery, a bookshop, a cinema and a television room and also tried running a restaurant, though without success. Meanwhile the back room of Better Books was still a centre for poetry readings, 'happenings' and small-scale performances, including the much-talked-of International Destruction in Art Symposium. It was also a central meeting-place, as was another bookshop called Indica Books.

The London Film-makers' Co-operative, still based at Better Books, ran weekly film shows to increasingly large audiences. At this early stage it also managed to put on a week-long Spontaneous Film Festival at the Jeannetta Cochrane Theatre, building up its programme from the few new independent films available in London, plus some seldom-seen films by earlier independent film-makers, which were dug out from layers of dust in the libraries of private distributors and the British Film Institute. But the days of the Co-op's life at Better Books were numbered. The shop's manager, concrete poet Bob Cobbing, who was also secretary of the Co-operative, was told by the owners to remove the Co-operative and its films, along with any books, prose or poetry dealing with controversial subjects such as drugs. The Co-operative had to go into temporary exile, though it managed to continue its distribution and was held together by the few remaining committee members.

The Arts Lab in Drury Lane now formed its own group of film-makers, which fragmented the Co-operative effort. Eventually a difference of approach caused a split within the Arts Lab itself, forcing one group out. This latter group formed a New Arts Lab (known as the Institute for Research in Art and Technology), where the Co-operative finally had an office, plus film-processing and editing facilities. The original Arts Lab closed soon after that. By the end of 1969 the Co-operative's film library had grown to about two hundred films, though the bulk of them were from the New American Cinema. In the early stages, only a few British-based film-makers supported the Co-operative. Apart from myself, among the first were Jeff Keen, John Latham, and Simon Hartog, who were later joined by David Larcher, Peter Gidal, Malcolm Le Grice, Fred Drummond and Mike Dunford.

Younger people were gradually becoming more aware of this type of film and a whole new attitude towards the cinema was emerging. By the beginning of the 'seventies the Co-operative had also begun to build and operate its own processing laboratory, which was essential for experimental and economic reasons. As we have seen, it also built up editing facilities to complement the processing. The existence of this equipment brought in many 'interested' film-makers. The Co-operative had by this point already brought out three issues of its magazine *Cinim*, originally under the editorship of Philip Crick and later under Simon Hartog.

Many of the Co-operative's American films came with Carla Liss, who took on the job of its full-time paid secretary. The presence of a full-time person increased distribution, improved co-ordination of films and activities, and provided a sort of core for the organization. The lack of a core had been the main weakness of the Co-operative, and has remained one of its main weaknesses. Not only had it been formed without a strong body of film-makers or a central figurehead – as Jonas Mekas was for the American Co-operative – it also failed to cement a strong social bond between members. At least half the people involved were after all not film-makers themselves, but were merely interested or involved with films in another capacity, perhaps as writers or poets. Personality differences were often extreme, even among the film-makers, so social communication and exchange was slim, and functioned, if at all, in small cliques. Emotionally the Co-operative never formed a whole, though its members had the same intellectual approach. Co-ordination and co-operation were often difficult, and unfortunately remained so. This is perhaps endemic to all such activities and groups, but it certainly has a retarding effect. It is also within this social and co-operative gap that the hustlers and spoilers begin to move. Yet distribution did continue and film shows did occur, at least in universities, film clubs and societies and in the increasing number of Arts Labs throughout the country. Thus the ideas, interest and possibilities inherent in the new cinema became an effective reality in a country that had previously been starved of such stimuli.

In Britain anyone who wants to make a film independently runs into even more frustration than in other countries. Any Briton who has managed to get away from the oppressive classification (professional, amateur and so on) and from the social conditioning that regards success as greatness and failure as an incurable disease is also confronted with an economic problem; aliens living in Britain are of course exempt from all but the latter consideration – they have other hang-ups. Personal economics are the primary concern. Film is expensive anywhere, and when the general cost of living becomes greater than one's earning power it is even more expensive; but in Britain the government imposes an additional 50 per cent tax on such material. Exemption from this tax can be acquired only by a 'professional business', not by the independent artist/film-maker. Film-processing laboratories, being expensive and geared to professional, bulk users, have little sympathy for the small user and experimenter. They also act in Britain as censors, because the authorities invoke fear of reprisals against them if they do not (and any censorship, especially based on fear, is confused and dangerous). Lab censorship does not take into account the context in which the images are used, or even consider whether the images will be used at all in the finished film, but is based on the appearance of the isolated image (a single frame of the film).

One of the greatest restrictions on film-making in Britain (for after all economic and censorship problems exist in most countries) is the cataloguing of attitudes and actions that is due in large part to educational conditioning. The Establishment's attitude towards film-making is well expressed in

E

this statement from a proposal to establish a National Film School: '. . . in our view great emphasis will have to be placed on practice training and acquiring a high level of knowledge of all the numerous technical aspects of film-making so as to equip the successful candidates ultimately to take their place as practical film-makers within the industry.' The report further considers that: 'Although film-making may derive some sustenance from its association with visual arts and design, it seems to us self-evident that the visual arts are in themselves quite different from film-making, both as an art and as a craft. . . . The drama undoubtedly has close links, in some ways closer links than that of the visual arts, with the art of film-making.'[1] This attitude is the product of the accustomed commercial tradition in the film industry, but it is peripheral to the art of film as a whole. To teach this as the major and, in a sense, the only aspect of film is to control the general public's view of what film is and should be.

In an environment that establishes singular and narrow definitions, such definitions become the direction towards which the interested turn, and the sole criterion of success. For many people this might seem a satisfactory arrangement, but if any creative form is to develop its potential it must be allowed the broadest possible arena for discovery. This means the widest definition, not the narrowest, and it applies to all the arts, not just to film. Yet emphasis is constantly placed on definition, on the need to have a place within society (such as a job).

It is in this basic situation that young people must grow up. Those who want to become film-makers are taught that these definitions exist, and find it difficult later on to consider any other possibility. Luckily, a few people in Britain have managed to break free of such bonds. Social difficulties in Britain, especially since the Industrial Revolution, have produced not only a survival problem but a strong environmental influence. Most people experience other people, their struggles, living conditions and attitudes within a technical environment, rather than trees, mountains and landscape. Thus when independent films are made they tend to express and reflect this environment. This has given Britain its predisposition towards the documentary style of film-making.

If we consider the physical landscape of England (as opposed to Scotland or Wales) the visible impression is one of moderation: of subtle rather than dramatic change; of repetition and of closeness. This landscape is lit generally by a diffused, mellow and almost shadowless light (though there is some sunshine!). The roads are small and winding; the views offer little sense of scale. This induces a feeling for pattern (decorative design), which basically involves surface treatment and textures without any strong central points or dynamics. Hence the British supremacy, for example, in textile and typographic design, with such visual movements as the one originated by William Morris. Combined with the ordered landscape, the reduced sense of scale and the technical facility, a concern with details and pieces emerges that shies away from direct self-contained gestures.

The mock paternity of 'socialized' governments, combined with social and economic classifications, is another constricting force. Legislation to provide for the arts involves a number of narrow and inflexible definitions, yet since support is provided, it creates a feeling of dependency on the government. In their mock-paternal attitudes the various governments have given people the feeling that the arts will always be granted provision and support, as will education in the arts. Almost every county in Britain supports at least one art school at the higher-education level, and in London alone there are almost as many specialized art colleges (as opposed to those that are part of universities) as in the whole of the United States. But this abundance of art and design education has tended to make most of these schools function on the level of middle-class 'finishing' schools, or else as purely functional training establishments. Most of them are state-supported, with fees paid by county councils, which encourages many people to expect continuous and regular financial support for their activities in the arts. The government also maintains its sense of patronage through such a body as the Arts Council, which deploys sums of money for art exhibitions, theatre groups, literary journals and the like. But the deployment of money is dependent on strict definitions of art activities. In regard to film, the Arts Council will provide money only for films made about an artist (such as Richard Hamilton) or by a qualified artist (a graduate practising painting or sculpture) as an extension of his work. Film as an art form is not considered as art in this context, and all other applications concerning films are referred to the British Film Institute.

The British Film Institute (BFI), which also embraces the National Film Archive and the National Film Theatre, was one of the first of its kind in the world. It represents a well-ordered, nationalized way of administering, preserving, showing and making films and providing the public with information about films (library, stills collection, publications, lectures). It also works in conjunction with the Federation of Film Societies. But the Institute's definition of film has primarily been determined by the commercial concept, as reflected in the proposals for a National Film School. It has managed to foster and support the narrow traditional concept of the cinema, not only through its activities but through its widely read, subsidized journal *Sight and Sound*, and it neglects newer forms of independent and personal cinema. The way in which the BFI runs its London Film Festival is another example of this attitude. It has been so closed to the new cinema that even staunch traditionalists have become bored. The National Film Theatre has certainly managed to show a great range of classical and traditional cinema, much of which would not otherwise have been seen, but this has been at the expense of the newer cinema and the film archive has shown virtually no interest at all in acquiring new avant-garde films. It is worth mentioning here that though there are also two film schools in the London area – the Royal College of Art's Film and Television School and the London School of Film Technique – both of these institutions have upheld the concept of film as a commercial activity.

The BFI has also maintained the British Film Institute Production Board, which was formed to aid the production of new films by young people. Ironically, the Production Board was originally called 'The Experimental Film Fund', yet one of its criteria for providing funds to young film-makers was that they must present a script, though more recently this requirement has been diminished. One submitted a script but was refused help because she had had no previous experience in directing (though she had made 8mm films); she was told however that her application would be considered if she could find an acceptably experienced director to make the film for her. On the other hand, the Production Board (with the BBC) sunk good money in producing such an embarrassingly poor film as *Herostratus* (poor even by commercial standards) and followed this up with a bleak propaganda campaign to promote it as one of Britain's major achievements in experimental film. The Board also produced a film called *The Park* and sent it to the Fourth International Experimental Film Festival as a representative example of a British short film. A rather dry and unsympathetic story of an old man seeing his favourite park change, it was booed more than any other film at the festival. (To be fair, the Board has produced the occasional good film, such as Anthony Stern's *San Francisco* and *My Childhood* by Bill Douglas.)

Within this narrow establishment interest in the new cinema began to be apparent by 1970. A surprisingly large number of small magazines and independent film groups, clubs and distributors began to appear. Not many felt any sympathy for the Co-operative, or for the co-operative ideal; many, in fact, thought of it as a specialized film-distribution organization, dealing solely in a fixed style of film-making. But this sudden growth did show that the traditional view of the cinema in Britain was changing.

Three groups, The Tattooist, Cinema Action and The Other Cinema were among the most important. The Other Cinema stated that 'its aim is to provide a system of film distribution and exhibition which will function as an alternative to the existing methods of distribution which repeatedly prove themselves unable to handle the numerous independently made films for which there is clearly an audience'. It grew out of an invited meeting held at the Institute of Contemporary Arts (ICA) to establish a 'parallel' cinema and an alternative distribution circuit. This had become necessary because much major cinema distribution is run by monopolies that own cinemas, control the types of film made and make their own films for their own circuit. For example, the drab *Look at Life* series is made by Rank for themselves. A weak anti-monopoly action was taken by the government against Rank, and this did make the company agree to give up thirteen weeks each year to other short films. So Rank's own films run for only thirty-nine weeks a year instead of fifty-two. No other change took place.

The idea voiced at the original 'parallel' cinema meeting was, in principle, similar to that of the co-operatives: to establish a distribution circuit by which any money received could be fed into making new films. The difference was that the group would gather the money collectively and would thereby be able to act as a production company. In other words, the group would support the production of films, whereas in the co-operatives a percentage of the money earned by each film goes to the individual film-maker. One view expressed at this parallel cinema meeting was that if a film was to earn enough money to support the production fund it must have considerable public appeal. Films were therefore to be generally feature-film length (around the 90-minute mark).

Other groups beside The Other Cinema now began to distribute films, with names such as PolitKino, Newsreel and Cineindependent, while various individuals acquired a few films and the smaller commercial film distributors also began to buy many independent films. (An important point to mention here is that in these early stages only a small number of the films acquired were by British film-makers. For example, the first films handled by Andi Engel's PolitKino were by the German film-maker Jean-Marie Straub and included his *Chronik der Anna Magdalena Bach* (Chronicle of Anna Magdalena Bach, 1967) though he did also acquire *Events*, by the British film-maker John Llewellyn.) The increased interest in the New Cinema is also exemplified by such successes as the New Cinema Club and the Electric Cinema Club. The New Cinema Club, formed by Derek Hill, grew out of his Short Film Service, which functioned as an agency to place films with distributors and other buyers. Hill began to show feature films as well as short films under the club banner in order to create an interest in such material. He showed them in hired cinemas and as interest increased expanded his repertoire. The Electric Cinema Club became a great success after acquiring the old Imperial Cinema in Notting Hill. It ran late-night shows and showed a large variety of films, from classics to 'underground'. It had fuller houses than many commercial cinemas, though we must not forget that it was in Notting Hill, which has a younger and more cosmopolitan population than many other areas.

Interest did not emerge solely in London, but was awakened in many centres throughout the country. The Film Co-operative's distribution to universities and film societies was constant and widespread. Requests for lecturers with the films were also regularly received. A New Cinema Club and an 8mm Film Co-operative opened in Oxford, another in Southend, while film shows began to take place in Liverpool, Brighton, Birmingham, Cambridge, Portsmouth and Edinburgh, among other places. In London, places like the ICA, the Arts Lab and The Place increased audience awareness by allowing much of the new, independent cinema to be shown. But probably one of the most striking signs of interest in film was the rapid increase in film publications. Books on all aspects of the film poured out from numerous publishers and one, Lorrimer Books, was virtually founded on scripts of well-known films, which it continues to publish today. The number of big and small magazines being issued seemed by 1970 to be greater than in any other country. They ranged from the glossy, commercial film magazines like *Sight and Sound, Films and Filming, Continental Film Review* and *Film* to semi-glossy independent journals like *Cinim, Movie,*

Cinema, Cinemantics, Independent Cinema, Fiba, After Image and *Cinema Rising,* plus numerous university magazines, while commercial art and 'underground' journals also gave a good deal of space to the newer cinema.

Yet however much *interest* in film had increased at this point, a corresponding increase in new indigenous films and film-makers was not so apparent. One recurring feature of all these various interested groups and publications has been the activity of non-film-makers. In the early Film-makers' Co-operative half the active members were not film-makers but critics, journalists, writers and the like, and so it was with many of the newer activities. As their interest tended to be verbal and intellectual, this meant, to some extent, that concern for film depended more on theory, politics, documentation and technique. The innate (or latent) recording and propaganda attributes of the film medium make it an available and tempting means of communication for people who think in journalistic terms. Whereas painting, poetry, music, sculpture and so on rely on conveying more abstract and subjective matter, film can also act as a recording system for literal and objective imagery strung together like sentences. In this way it is related to the journalist's method of describing within a literal and verbal structure. Thus those with verbally descriptive ideas would turn first to film (or television) as the most immediate way of visualizing them. Similarly, since film's whole physical existence is dependent on machinery, optics, light and chemistry, people whose interests are with such technicalities also find themselves at home with it. It is in these two general areas that many of the newer, independent film-makers were working by 1970, not only in Britain but in most other countries. These directions explain in part the early absence of film-makers from the London Film-makers' Co-operative. Some potential and existing film-makers assumed that it was concerned only with films that they considered to be 'poetic' or 'art' films. They did not understand or want to understand that the co-operative idea merely involved co-operation between film-makers making any kind of film outside the established commercial system. The journalistic film-makers were not in sympathy with the so-called 'art' film-makers, while for others 'art' had nothing to do with films – all these definitions are of course a *'grande illusion'.* Some came but went away again because, in the early stages, the co-operative could not provide them with equipment. When it announced that it now had processing and editing equipment many interested 'film-makers' did turn up. (Of course, a large number of film-makers do genuinely prefer to be part of the established film industry.)

One wonders if all this lack of co-operation and the formation of different groups (even within the Co-operative), plus the existence of so many different independent film journals, are not symptoms of megalomania. To quote from the Tattooist group:

> The terrible problem in England is that there are large numbers of talented people who have lived for years in total isolation, and vicious competition with each other. They believe that nobody understands them, that everybody

is warping against them. And by now they've built up an almost classic tradition in British films – so that their isolation speaks more loudly than their borrowed politics.

The journalistic attitude we have been discussing fitted the growing involvement in politics, the use of film as a direct political weapon. Much of the political direction, particularly in Britain and on the Continent of Europe, involved an increasing swing to the left, with a strong Marxist line against existing capitalist/imperialistic systems in Europe and America, with special emphasis on American domination and the Vietnam War. Other activities were aimed against the capitalist, 'bourgeois' film industry itself, which was alleged to put forward a false reality in order to uphold its own consumer ideologies, and to work as a closed capitalist system for making money. The more extreme political attitudes of the Left have seen the cinema as the art of the masses, and in these terms transform films into an active means of revolution rather than mere entertainment. The camera then becomes a gun, and the cinema must be a guerilla cinema.[2]

The Hour of the Furnaces

The extreme cinema of the Left was already in action in Latin America (particularly in Cuba), but it gradually became a primary approach in most European countries, in Japan and in America. Examples are the 'Zenga-kuren' documentaries in Japan, the *Cinegiornali Liberi* films in Italy, the *Cinétracts* in France and the active political film-making of Jean-Luc Godard and Chris Marker in France or the 'Newsreel' group in the United States. In Latin America there was a whole wave of films from Cuba by film-makers such as Santiago Alvarez; the first 'Cinema Nôvo' films from Brazil, with Glauber Rocha; strong political film-making in Argentina, with Octavio Getino and Fernando Solanas (*Le Hora de los Hornos* – The Hour of the Furnaces); and so-called 'Third World' cinema activities in Bolivia, Uruguay and Mexico.

A dominant attitude behind many of these new political films was that the films, as a weapon, come with the revolution. Before this (in political terms) the change in the cinema (or 'liberation', in leftist terms) had had to wait until the revolution had occurred; films changed only after the particular culture had changed (as is exemplified by the USSR). But now the prevalent attitude was that cinema can be instrumental in bringing about change. The previous attitude had been based on the mystique of the commercial cinema, a cinema that set a standard for heavy equipment and complicated technical skills, as well as standardizing film size (at 35mm), running times and even camera and editing qualifications. This standardization was a legacy from the established commercial (Hollywood-style) cinema and until recently it had been considered to be the only form the cinema could take. Godard once said that up to this point film-makers had been 'trapped inside the fortress of the industry'. The political cinema (often called 'guerrilla cinema'), like the 'underground' or personal cinema, now began to reject the methods and attitudes of the Establishment cinema (for instance by using 16mm and 8mm film).

In Britain, though the more revolutionary ideas of political film-making were causing increased interest, active political film-making followed the journalistic approach. Some followed the American 'newsreel' style, with political footage of protest marches and police beatings, as in *The Hornsey Film* by Pat Holland. Some of the politically oriented film-makers directly challenged the audience, as with the 'tattooist' films, their idea being to 'try to involve the audience as a potential participant in the medium'. Tattooist films often use words as images, projected on to the screen in the form of questions; or else they attack both with a voice on the soundtrack and with projected words. They sometimes even use the image of a microphone for the audience to answer into. Film-makers can also alter the projection according to the situation to further harass or annoy the audience or otherwise stimulate them to react. Another form of political film-making, which again breaks with traditional forms, involves a *cinéma vérité* style of improvisation in which political and social questions are discussed by those in the film. Such films depend, of course, on synchronized sound. Two good examples of this style are John Llewellyn's *Events* and Bill Brodie's *Terry Whitmore, for example*. Both are low-budget feature films. *Events* cost only £5,000 to make. (The Tattooists manage to make films for £50, while the standard commercial feature film starts at £50,000 and can run into the millions.)

Yet political films made in Britain tend to be more passive than those in other countries. This is largely because Britain is not directly confronted with or involved in issues that loom large elsewhere. Political films such as *Point of Order* (about the McCarthy hearings) or *The Year of the Pig* (about American involvement in Vietnam), both made by Emile de Antonio, or Peter Gessner's *The Time of the Locust* (also about Vietnam) or Lenny Lipton's *We Shall March Again* (about protest marches and police action in Berkeley, California) are among many films dealing directly with problems confronting the United States. Similarly, the French *'Cinétracts'*, made jointly by several film-makers, dealt with the student uprising in May 1968 that had an emotional effect in their lives. Latin American films also have have strong emotional content in their action against their own countries' reactionary and military governments, while Cuban films are direct propaganda weapons against the Capitalist system. On the other hand, British political films of recent vintage do not deal with domestic political issues directly (with the exception of the Marxist-oriented Cinema-Action group), though many influential social documentaries have been made in a reformist rather than a political tradition. The only direct effects achieved by British films have been related to altering acceptable methods of film-making. Most films showing an involvement with specific political problems have been concerned with other countries, such as Vietnam and America. It took someone from outside Britain (Godard) to make a politically meaningful film about Britain (*British Sounds*).

The interested film-makers and the non-film-makers offered a stronger confrontation by *verbalizing* ideologies. Some went further in exploring traditional forms, others adopted more extreme left-wing vocabulary. The political Left began to challenge the terminology and the values of the Establishment, such as 'aesthetics', 'art' and 'beauty', which, to them, were being exploited for profit, while people's minds were being nullified. This approach, it was hoped, would establish a new non-commercial cinema. Maybe it will, but all these theories and suppositions are being bandied about in Britain before any strong, new and active film-making or any unified movement has emerged. This intellectual theorizing runs the risk of avoiding the process that causes change and causes things to occur. To deny an established order means first to experiment, search and explore the possibilities of other things which will create something original. Values and language will then be altered. In these areas the artist and the scientist are alike in that they both discover new methods, new values and a new language. Theory comes later. Too much theory too soon can create its own mystique, limiting the search and inhibiting the free development of a meaningful language.

It is in the technological area that Britain, along with America and Germany, and to some extent Holland and Sweden, has shown particular interest and activity. Technological progress, along with materials, has created another mainstream activity in the arts, with a major growth in the audio/visual areas. The availability of technological information and equipment has not only brought about new audio/visual techniques, it has affected many political and theoretical attitudes. The existence of simpler and more accessible technical tools has given greater opportunity for more people to use film (or even printing) for political purposes. Theoretically, new techniques have given a new perspective to evaluations and ideas. From this new perspective, older definitions can be scrutinized afresh. Some argued about whether the illusions caused by films are 'unreal', or whether the subjective experience that one gets from the illusion is 'real'. Some even considered that only the physical presence of the film material could be considered 'real', though for others even a dream is 'real'. Regardless of the philosophical attitude, the technological bias began to create a new, or additional, aesthetic, whereby the physical properties and possibilities of the material took on their own meaning. This technocratic age has also placed new emphasis on technical aptitude and technically derived form, and it made the relationship between artist, scientist and technician more complex.

Sometimes the three were rolled into one, sometimes they interacted and worked together. On other occasions mere technical aptitude ignored, or even replaced, creative insight and feeling. More and more film-makers gravitated to this technical camp, using multi-media (films, slides, live action, sound, lights) and environmental activities. Television, video-tape and computer began to predominate.

One aspect of this technical orientation is a constant search for an individual film language. Besides the exploration of film through camera techniques and subject-matter, through optics and projection possibilities, film began to be explored through the laboratory process. This process, which includes the chemical process (developing the latent image) and the printing process (negative into positive, positive to positive, blowing up, reducing, copying), became the next step. Much of it has been confined to large commercial laboratories, mainly because of the expense, size and technical complexity of the processing equipment. Basically the process is the same as for still photography, except that the length and the continuously appearing image complicate matters. Yet some film-makers began to build their own equipment and many smaller and simpler pieces of basic processing equipment were put on to the market. On occasions film-makers have even found a commercial lab willing to do a few experiments, though others have made do with a bath. (These activities are not peculiar to Britain; much of the simpler processing equipment was first available in the United States, for example.) This exploration of the laboratory process has revealed the visual potential of altering the 'normal' process. Scratches, sprocket-holes and frame separations have become part of the basic language of film. Similarly, the solarized image, the repeated image, the frozen image, the negative image or the altered colour image have become a vital part of film vocabulary. Once they had been used merely to enhance a drama; now they became voices of their own.

The new technical orientation also led many film-makers to experiment with the computer and its relationship to film, just as many artists began to explore the relationship of the computer to imagery. 'Cybernetics', as this new art-form is known, involves programming computers to produce imagery ranging from animated literal images to abstract rhythmic patterns, which are then recorded on film. So some film-makers have become programmers and film-making has turned into making punch cards. Some film-makers even began to abandon film and explore the video tape and television. Conceptually, video-tape has much in common with ciné in that both involve a camera and a lens. They differ in that video-tape records electronically and makes instant playback possible. No laboratory processing is involved and the whole editing process is different. Film is a light-projected image while video-tape is electronically received. Video-tape can be used over and over again and this alone makes it ultimately cheaper than film. It can be played back on an ordinary television set, whereas film needs more cumbersome and more expensive equipment, that is not so easy to obtain. Though at the moment video playback lacks the scale of film, it is becoming a vital area for visual exploration and will provide a whole new range of visual experiences and expressive possibilities.

The continental European countries also gave film an official seal of approval at an earlier stage and more thoroughly than in the United States. This took the form of film institutes and archives, which were designed to collect, preserve and exhibit the art of film; to provide libraries and educational facilities devoted to film; and in some cases to support and develop experimental films and to foster exchanges with other countries. These institutions were generally government sponsored, though in some countries the commercial cinema was heavily involved. The development of independent film-making tended to be dependent on the relationship to the state or commercial systems. For example, in countries where 'official' support existed there was very little or no action to create something like a film co-operative. In countries where there was less 'official' support or where the industry held itself aloof, co-operative and 'underground' film activity of this kind did evolve. This is particularly true of Italy, and to some extent of Germany. It is also interesting to note that in those countries where there was little or no official support for film independent film-makers generally came from the other arts, whereas in countries where there was greater support they came from some branch of film or theatre.

So far as Eastern Europe is concerned this reply from Russia to an inquiry about the individually made film is illuminating: 'The matter is that *Gosfilmofond* [the Russian Film Archive] of the USSR does not collect and reserve individually made experimental films. But such kind of films are extensively made in our country and some of them have been awarded in domestic and international festivals. Film amateurs section of the Cinematography Union of the USSR deals with this question.' From Hungary came this reply: '. . . in Hungary – as the film production is state-run – there are no films shot individually. For the experimentation of the ideas of young directors in order that they receive the necessary practice there are two forums which can give the necessary financial help: the Academy for Dramatic and Film Arts during the years of study, and afterwards the Studio Béla Balázs.'

Attitudes to film in Western Europe were very different from those in the United States. In many European countries awareness of film came from a 'nationalized' acceptance of it whereby it was treated as an activity open to anyone. In other words, it was basically treated like any other profession, and the official bodies concerned, sometimes even the cinema industry itself, made attempts to encourage new film-makers. Thanks to the existence of schools with official backing and socially conscious film institutes, those who found themselves interested in film had somewhere to go. To the American film-maker, the idea of film as a profession seemed rather remote and he therefore thought of it in more fanciful terms. Many Europeans thought of it in more practical terms. Then too, European culture, compared to America, has been predominantly coloured by a stronger political conscious-ness and a greater social concern. In a way, the New American Cinema started with film from scratch, while the Europeans expanded or reacted against what they already had.

Holland

Holland is an example of a country enjoying official support for film-making. The Netherlands Film Academy has been in existence since 1958 and there is also a Netherlands Film Museum. The Dutch government has officially supported two categories of independently made short films: those that seem commercially viable, and experimental films. Yet a reaction has still occurred in the form of an energetic, independent film-making movement. Many of the film-makers who fostered the new Dutch cinema were, at one time or another, students of the film academy and many of them therefore knew each other. (They also produced the revolutionary film magazine *Skoop.*) By the early 'sixties the young revolutionary PROVO movement was coming more and more to the fore in Holland. This political/social reaction · against the established older generation is reflected in the new films. But the whole feeling was like that of someone trying to break away from dominating parents, yet not really wanting to leave home. One important point to note here is that Dutch film-makers make films in the hope of earn-ing money from them. This is a slightly different attitude from that of other independent 'underground' film-makers, who rarely set out specifically to make money.

One of the complaints voiced by Dutch film-makers concerns the distri-bution of their films, which is carried out by the Government Information Service (RVO). Since most of the money to make the film comes from the government, technically most of them are government-owned. Yet the makers complain that RVO is the worst possible distributor; that when a circuit wants to show a film RVO asks too high a fee; if television wants the film RVO says that it cannot have it since a cinema circuit is interested. The result is that no one gets it. The other complaint is that RVO does not attempt to distribute films outside Holland. But still, Dutch film-makers are better off than many of their contemporaries in other countries.

In 1965 two Dutch film-makers, Pim de la Parra and Wim Verstappen, both ex-students from the Netherlands Film Academy, formed their own company (which they called Scorpio Films), in order to gain some independence from government sponsorship and to maintain continuity of production. Pim and Wim alternate the roles of director and producer, and many other Dutch film-makers become involved in their productions as well. Their early shorts, *Aah . . . Tamara* and *Heart Beat Fresco*, began to attract international notice before they made their first feature film (shot on 16mm), *Joszef Katús' Not Too Fortunate Return to The Land of Rembrandt* (1967) about a man who tries to find out what the PROVOS are after by joining them. The description of *Joszef Katús* put out by Scorpio Films conveys the general attitude that prevails among the new Dutch film-makers:

As 'Joszef Katús' was made for only DM 10,000 it must be clear that we are by far the most efficient film producers in the world. We shot the film within two weeks on a 1:1.5 rate, which of course ruled out retakes. We worked without the usual crew of light-technicians, dolly-pushers, make-up specialists, focus pullers and other assistants that were highly necessary some years ago, but who now feel superfluous when working with Eclair Coutand (a French-made 16mm camera, for those who don't know). This camera can be easily hand-held. We shot entirely on 16mm without any tripod, not even during some 4 minute takes. Our crew consisted of a director, a producer, a camera-man and sometimes a sound-operator; often however the director or the producer or even the camera-man himself, or a friend who happened to pass by did the sound. So before we started we knew our technique would not be impeccable. We realized that occasionally a microphone boom would show in our frame. Of course some passers-by would look into the camera during our shooting. Our soundtrack would prove mediocre at best.

Remember we did not make retakes. So, at crucial moments, we made our actors look into the camera. We did this, not only to get a kind of 'Entfremdung', but also because we knew that this and the other 'technical faults' mentioned above, would help us catch *the spirit of anarchism in Amsterdam*.

PROVOs deliberately print their magazine (20,000 copies sold of each issue; a copy of the forbidden first issue can be seen in the film) in a dirty and clumsy way. They even look dirty with their long hair but are not, as there is enough hot water and soap nowadays to wash and bath; so you don't have to cut your hair short for sanitary reasons as your father had to do.

PROVOs often seem to spoil their best plans by explaining them in a deliberate stupid-silly way. This attitude makes PROVO the only important movement in Western civilization which captures the spirit of Mao Tsetung's guerilla philosophy.

The spirit of 'Joszef Katús' is PROVO. If you get the point, you will like the film; if it passes you by, you will hate it.

A look at the cast shows that support came from other Dutch film-makers. For example, Mattijn Seip (who made *Schermerhoon* and *IJDIJK*) and Nouchka Van Brakel (who made *Bobby and Bako* and *Sabotage*) both appear in the film and Wim Van Der Linden was on the camera.

Van Der Linden is one of the most prominent of independent Dutch film-makers. He made a string of revolutionary and satirical films labelled 'Sad Movies', all of which are produced by a unit calling themselves the Dodgers' Syndicate (which suggests a play upon the American capitalist/gangster scene and the popular American baseball team the Dodgers). Van Der Linden's films often have a looser narrative structure than those of Pim and Wim. In his best-known film *Tulips*, he merely films the Dutch national flower straight. All that happens during the 10-minute stare is that a petal falls. In his *Hawaiian Lullaby* the projected image is an old Vaudeville-type backdrop, a still, hand-painted scene complete with moving spotlight. On to the stage with the spotlight comes a real live girl, half naked in a grass skirt, who does a hula dance in front of the film. Some of Van Der Linden's films do have a stronger narrative structure but they are all heavily satirical – (his screenplays are attributed to other members of the Dodgers' Syndicate) – as in *Rape*, where a wandering nun is surprised in the woods. Satire and anarchism ride high among many new Dutch film-makers.

Among the many new film-makers who have received notice are Nikolai Van Der Heyde, Adriaan Ditvoorst, René Daalder, Kees Meyering, René Van Nie, George Sluizer and Erik Van Zuyler. Besides this, a film-makers' co-operative exists in Holland (to which incidentally none of these film-makers belongs). It is probably the smallest co-operative in the world and is based in Eindhoven, not in Amsterdam. Its initiator is Piet Verdonk, but the most striking films it has produced are those of Frans Zwartjes. The group's attitude is akin to that of other co-operatives in that the films are concerned with pure film experimentation and abstraction. Zwartjes's films – good examples are his *Faces* or *Birds One* – are strong, high-contrast black and white films built up from strangely irregular staccato movements with equally strangely transformed subjects. Zwartjes processes his own films, using black and white reversal stock. By doing so he achieves a special 'soft-edge' contrast, which gives his films an extraordinary depth of tone. Verdonk has also experimented with phosphorescent material for cinema screens, which retain the projected image while subsequent images build up on top of those retained on the screen.

Sweden

Sweden does have a film co-operative, Filmcentrum, but it is hampered by paternal socialism. Its original office was housed within the Swedish Film Institute and membership is open to known commercial directors as well as to unknown, independent film-makers. This means, of course, that bookings tend to favour known and well-publicized films. In such towns as Uppsala, just north of Stockholm, groups of independent film-makers were working away on their own, often on 8mm equipment. Twenty-five to thirty film-makers were involved (rather a large number compared to some of the largest cities in Europe) but, on the whole, only a small number of films are produced. Sweden is a film country and though its population is small it produces a large proportion of the world's films. This has been helped by a system whereby the government and industry have made a conscious effort to support and develop film. As with many nationalized systems, there is a bias towards the commercial film, but compared to similar systems, the Swedish one is exceptionally liberal and open to experiment.

One of the major supports for avant-garde and experimental film in Sweden is the State Museum of Modern Art (Moderna Muséet) in Stockholm, which was established in 1958. The director, K. G. (Pontus) Holtén, is himself a film-maker, having made *En Dag I Staden* (*A Day in Town*, 1955/6), a funny dadaistic film. He was therefore quite willing to give film a place alongside the other modern arts. The museum had its own film society and a small 16mm film library where films could be rented for non-commercial screening. It ran six to seven major film programmes each year and it was there that the New American Cinema had its first screenings in Europe. In 1963, by an act of the Swedish Parliament, the Swedish Film Institute was formed, its main purpose being to promote the production of Swedish feature films for theatrical presentation. It does claim to support 'experimental' film-making (this being rather a vague term that by no means infers personal, independent or avant-garde work) and is directly engaged in producing films whose scenarios have been considered too 'difficult' by Swedish film companies. It also establishes co-production agreements with other countries and gives awards (and often annual cash prizes) to the best independent films. The Swedish film archive, Filmhistoriska Samlingarna, which was established as a private foundation in 1949, but had actually operated on a minor scale since 1933 with the help of the Swedish Film Academy, was incorporated into the Film Institute in 1964. Sweden also has two film schools.

Whatever the official structure for film in Sweden, there remains, as in so many other places, the problem of distribution and exhibition especially of short independent films. There are no specialized cinemas to present such films and the so-called 'art' cinemas, which are maintained by the big companies, have mainly commercial interests at heart. So the only places where these films can be shown are the Institute, film societies (usually in universities) or the one or two experimental stage theatres with multiprojection facilities, such as the Pistol-Teatern in Stockholm. Only one other commercial theatre in Sweden has facilities for showing 16mm film. Films from the archive are screened within the framework of a film club belonging to the Film Institute. The club runs a specially hired theatre and functions in

a similar way to the National Film Theatre in London, but with an important difference in attitude: it is prepared to present experimental and independent films at short notice, for instance if a film-maker arrives unexpectedly in Stockholm with his films. The only other outlet in Sweden, as
is beginning to be true in other countries, is television. Sveriges Radio-TV
not only screens a certain amount of independent, avant-garde material
each year, it also supports the production of various experimental films.
For example, the company may provide a film-maker with raw film stock
and pay laboratory costs for projects in which it becomes interested. If it
likes the results it will, of course, show the film, and in some cases will
retain the maker under contract. Of the four Swedish films in competition
at the 4th International Experimental Film Festival (1967/8), three were supported and entered by Swedish television. One of these, Ake Arenhill's
Besöket, won one of the five major prizes. One of the others, Altisonans,
by the contemporary Swedish composer Karl-Birger Blomdahl, is based on
sounds from space – recordings of sound signals from satellites and birds
coupled with abstract images and visualizations from radar screens. The
fourth film, Anima Mundi, was entered privately by the painter Erling
Johansson and conveys the 'in-the-dark-woods' fantasies of Swedish children's stories.

Before all the television interest, and before the Swedish Co-operative was
formed, a free cinema group did exist in Stockholm. Bringing together many
important figures in the arts, it was originally known as Svensk Experiment-
filmstudio, or the Swedish Experimental Film Society, and was started in
1949. In 1954 it changed its name to Arbetsgruppen för Film (AFF), or
Film Workshop, and concentrated on making and supporting independently
made, personal and experimental films. It was in fact a co-operative unit,
its main efforts being directed at creating joint production facilities and finding sponsors and distribution channels. It did not distribute films itself but
thrived on close contact between members and a good deal of commitment.
By 1960 its activities seemed to be on the decline, though it continued to
function in a rather looser way. In 1967 it became a foundation without
any individual members.

The group's first president was Mihail Livada who, like the first secretary, Arne Lindgren, is still an active film-maker. During its ten active years
more than fifty films were made by members of the AFF, one of whose
members was K. G. (Pontus) Holtén, who later became director of the
Moderna Muséet and made A Day in Town, X and Ett Mirakel (A Miracle,
1954), a crazy collage film about the Pope. But the most prolific film-maker
of the group was Peter Weiss who later went on to be a successful playwright. Weiss made many films, such as Hallucinationer/Studie II (1952),
which consists of twelve surrealist tableaux about the hypnotic phenomena
that arise between waking and sleeping; Växelspel/Studie V (Interplay Study
V, 1955), also a surrealist film in tableau style; Ateljéinterior (The Studio of
Dr Faust, 1956), an abstract colour film about Dr Faust's fantastic workshop; Enligt Lag (According to Law, 1957), a strong and moving 19-minute

documentary about a youth prison; and *Hägringen* (The Mirage, 1959) based on his book *Dokument I*, which tells of a young man's difficulties in adapting to life in a big city. Weiss became an enthusiastic spokesman for the independent film and wrote a book called *Avantgardefilm*. In an article called 'To Go Underground' he wrote:

> If one wants to work with film as an artistic, expressive form there is only one choice: one has to go underground. . . . Even the State shows an enemy attitude towards film. It does everything to choke independent artistic production. . . . One has to go and borrow a camera. . . . One learns to beg. Beg together money, beg film material. It is a process that is no more demanding and time consuming than writing a book, a composition. . . . Instead of worrying about the lack of interest of the State and industry one can look for a handful of interested friends. . . . Film is the all concerning art, the dreamt *Gesamtkunstwerk*. Film attracts me because in this art most of it is still unexplored. The whole of the visual, auditory and emotional world is waiting to be expressed. In my no-man's-land I have the freedom to speak as I like, there is only myself clamouring for truth. Why turn to that which only smooths, banalizes and perfumes. . . ? But this is an isolated fight. It should not prevent one from uncompromised film work.

Norway, Finland, Denmark

Scarcely any strong independent film-making activity exists among Sweden's Scandinavian neighbours. Norway, for instance, has shown virtually no films of her own, though screenings of foreign, independently made films, especially from the New American Cinema, have been given in Oslo. The New American Cinema programme was also shown in Finland, but the country has developed more along the lines of an architectural and crafts centre, with no notable film activity of its own (with the exception of Jorn Donner) and a film institute, Suomen Elokuva Arkisto, functioning as a bourgeois showplace. Denmark, which has a film museum, a government film foundation and subsidies for commercial film producers has none the less produced only a few scattered independent films such as Gress Wright's *Boxiganga*, with the original La Mama group from the United States.

France

Surprisingly, France, the traditionally film-mad country, where both film and the avant-garde found their first home, had hardly any independent 'underground' film-making activity in the 1960s. To an outsider this seems strange, in view of the fact that in the late 'fifties the *Nouvelle Vague* was born in France; that the country has the world's largest and most controversial film archive and museum, the Cinémathèque Française (founded in 1936); that Paris has more small cinemas than any other city in the world; that the French produce some of the best 16mm cameras in the world,

F

the Beaulieu and the Eclair, plus some of the best lenses (the Angineux range); that Paris has always been the home of many film artists; and that, above all, France is in the forefront of film history.

Some explanation for all this can be found in the fact that the French film industry is considerably more open to newcomers than in other countries and individuals have been able to get credit for making a film providing they go through the right channels. The French film industry is constantly changing and has always led the world's commercial film industry in revision and adaptation. For example, during the French student uprising in May 1968 the 'Estates-General of the Cinema' was established. Its objective was to make cultural life (and therefore the cinema), which is essential to the life of the nation, a public service. It put out six main demands:

1   Destruction of the monopolies; the creation of a single, national organization for the distribution and exploitation of films, taxed directly in the cinema. Also the creation of a national technical organization (laboratories, studios, film stock, etc).
2   Auto-gestation with the purpose of struggling against the bosses, petrified systems and bureaucracy. Officers of all levels were to be elected for a limited period, controlled and recalled by those who elected them.
3   The creation of self-governing production units which would not be subject to the capitalist profit motive.
4   Abolition of censorship.
5   The integration of audio-visual education into the framework of the revitalized educational system. Auto-gestation by teachers and students, open to all social classes.
6   Tight union of the cinema with self-governing television independent of the government and of money.

Though hardly any of these points were actually realized, it is important to notice how far members of the French film industry were prepared to go in order to initiate change. It is especially important to note that the political structure in France, chiefly during the de Gaulle regime, has inhibited personal, independent film activity. The environment has been so politically claustrophobic that all independent film-making, especially that concerned with the May uprising, tended to aim for direct political expression, often in the form of 'newsreels'. The 'newsreel' concept began in the United States with the growing protest movement against the Vietnam War and spread to other countries where domestic political protests were taking place. 'Newsreels' became records of sit-ins, protest marches, other political expression and police action, but they also showed how to organize a protest and gave witness to the size and strength of the movement in sympathy with the protest. They also tried to show what was ignored by the national media. More recently Godard has established a group called Groupe Vertov and Chris Marker one called SLON. 'Newsreels' have often been distributed by film-makers' co-operatives, but on the whole European distribution has been handled by specialized and more politically oriented groups.

The French government has, in recent years, been afraid of the film as a weapon. It has tended to censor films strictly and very inconsistently (by issuing, not issuing or restricting a *visa de contrôle*, which every film must have before it can be shown). Censorship (which is, of course, present in most countries except Denmark) has been strictest for films that show France, her current government or her authorities in a politically or socially undesirable light. It has even been known to restrict films that seem 'too abstract'. France is also of course a Catholic country and a great deal of censorship has been based on Christian morality (though this problem has been even greater in Italy). Films shown in clubs in France are considered as public and therefore do not go uncensored, though 'private' showings are freer. 'Private' means within a private dwelling that is not open to public entry, and this of course is where many independent films get shown. Many of the censorship codes enforced during the de Gaulle era put a taboo on drugs and other activities that seemed to be directed against middle-class and nationalistic values. Many films that challenged these values were totally banned. Then, too, 'underground' film techniques indicated how easily a film can be made. Given the great propaganda power of films, easy film-making was a thing to be avoided. (This attitude also exists in many other countries, including Britain.) Even the antics and happenings organized and enacted by Jean-Jacques Lebel & Co. were axed by the French authorities. Though this atmosphere did not allow any free, independent cinema to develop, a few personal films did get made, including one by the actor Pierre Clementi and Marcel Hanoun's subtle and intellectually precise film *L'Authentique Procès de Carl-Emmanuel Jung*. More recently a very strong line of newer French films has appeared: I refer particularly to the films of Philippe Garrel, like *La Cicatrice Interieure* or *La Revelateur*.

West Germany

Among the European countries (besides Britain) the greatest amount of independent and personal film activity, outwardly at least, has been in West Germany (BRD), with Italy and Austria running up, followed by Switzerland, Holland, Belgium and France.

In Germany (as in Italy and Austria) the socialized structure towards film has been the weakest. In Germany film-makers have come from varied backgrounds in the arts other than the film industry though, more recently, this trend has been changing with such strong influences as the Munich and West Berlin film schools (Hochschule für fernsehen und Film, München; Deutsche Film und Fernsehakademie, Berlin).

A strong re-evaluation of film has occurred, in terms of social/political attitudes as well as in conceptual attitudes. The output has been large and varied, though in the initial stages film-makers concentrated on the exploration of aesthetics and the material of film itself. A pronounced attitude was a less poetic and more didactic style. Technical and tactile sensitivities were developed along with conceptual attitudes to do with the sense of time in film, in what might be labelled 'minimal' directions. Another important phase of German film-making was the alteration and exploration of content and narrative which developed into 'pop' with strong television associations. German film-makers at this time used television in the same way that American film-makers used the Hollywood style and the result has been highly 'minimal' documentary dramatics; hysterical anarchist parodies.

Though independent film work in Germany is diversified – it even varies from one section of the country to another – random generalization makes it possible to divide the activity into three sections. A statement of film aesthetics using structure, form and material constitutes the first section – elements such as time and material fall more easily into painterly terminology and thinking. The second aspect might be called documentary 'pop' parody with strong anarchistic overtones. Such films are social comment as well as entertainment. The range of personal attitudes is wide, ranging from operatic comic strips, for example, to rather pointed and direct social comment. The third section, and the most recent development is social/political film-making in Germany. A major split in German film ideology has become, as in other countries, a source of great argument especially between the film-makers themselves. By the early 1970s 'Sozialischen Zielgruppenfilme' became predominant over other film-making activity largely because of a growing intellectual hostility towards the personal 'art' forms as an elite bourgeois activity. This feeling exists not only among German film-makers but in many western countries. A split occurred between 'art' and 'politics', chiefly as a reaction to the conservative and anti-liberal political structures that began to form in the early part of the decade. This, of course, is not a new development but has created the greatest fracture within independent film activity. Of course, generalization is neither possible or desirable when talking about the development of attitudes in film. There is of necessity a large amount of overlapping between the attitudes.

The reasons why Germany has so many independent film-makers, as well as being open to ideas and change, are many and varied. There is an increasing availability of equipment in the country and a measure of state support. Also German television networks have been relatively open and encouraging towards film. In many cases television has either shown independent films or paid for the production of these films. The amount of television support, though far from ideal, has been very large when compared with television in almost all other western countries including Britain where, for example, there has been almost no support or interest. Most of the television interest in Germany has centred around the regional network (third programme) where more local interests are involved. The regional break up of Germany has in a sense created different attitudes in film-making itself. The Rheinland region is a good example in that it has strong art centres like Cologne and Dusseldorf and a great number of esoteric and personal films have been made there including those of W. and B. Hein and by the artist Vostell. As a result of the number of active galleries and publishing houses in this area it has become a centre for conceptual and structural art. Cologne television (Westdeutscher Rundfunk) was one of the first television stations to purchase so-called 'underground' films (including up to sixty hours of the New American Cinema).

Hamburg is another area worth mentioning. Here film activity has been highly energetic and diversified, covering a great range of attitudes, though there has been a split between esoteric and political film-making. Werner Nekes, Dore O, Hellmuth Costard, Lutz Mommartz (actually from Dusseldorf), Thomas Struck, Klaus Wyborny, Kurt Rosenthal and Helmut Herbst are among the many film-makers who are associated with this region. Hamburg has its own and very active Co-op (Filmmacher Co-operative) which annually organizes its own film festival called the Hamburger Filmschau. This Co-op is the strongest of the various co-operatives which have appeared and disappeared in Germany. Hamburg television has also shown an interest in independent film activity, providing support for films made by Kenneth Anger and Jonas Mekas, for example, and has shown many of the films.

West Berlin and Munich are two other important centres. In these areas there has been a concentration on both social/political film-making as well as operatic and anarchistic film-making, though Munich has produced more examples of 'pure' and 'minimal' film-making. How much of this is influenced by the Munich film school, where both the social and structural film ideologies seem well established, it is hard to say. Film-makers such as Wim Wenders and Klaus Emmerich come from the area and films like *Bruno – der Schwarze, es blies ein Jäger wohl in sein Horn* by Lutz Eisholz were made with backing from the school. Jean-Marie Straub, who has worked in Munich, must also have brought some influence to bear. 'Operatic comic' films and anarchistic films have been produced in Munich by such film-makers as Werner Rainer Fassbinder who, incidentally, had some support from Munich television (Bavarian). Vlado Kristl, Fritz Andre Kracht and Werner Herzog all contribute in their own way to what is going on in Munich. Berlin film-makers have also maintained a strong trend towards parody and social/political themes in their work, as can be seen in the films of Rosa von Praunheim and Werner Schroeder. The formation of the Film Verlag group has pulled together many of the film activities. Thanks to the existence of the 'Friends of the Kinemathek', organized by Ulrich Gregor and his wife, Berlin has enjoyed by far the greatest exposure to independent film. There is also the Berlin International Film Festival which recently has initiated a young film-makers' film festival.

Any attempt to sectionalize German film activity is almost impossible and probably misguided; there is no single central focus as sometimes is found in other countries. Small centres exist autonomously, as in Baden-Baden where Adolf Winkelmann works. Germany has a great tradition in film, having produced men like Lang, Pabst, Von Stroheim, Fischinger, Eggeling, Richter and Wiene and whether the fragmented activity at present is a positive development is yet to be decided.

Germany, like many European countries, has been influenced by the New American Cinema. Prosperity and the rise of the 'pop' scene has uncovered many new talents and new outlets. The period around 1967-68 saw the growth of independent film organizations like the Filmmacher Co-operative in Hamburg, X-Screen in Cologne and PAP in Munich. X-Screen, which was run by Birgit and Wilhelm Hein, was not a co-operative but was mainly a grouping for the exhibition of all independent films and an attempt to work through co-operatives in other countries as well as in Germany. PAP (Progressive Art Production) in Munich was also not a co-operative in form but was run on semi-commercial lines, exhibiting and distributing along the lines developed by the co-operative movement.

The possibility of creating a European Film-makers' Co-operative was discussed at a Munich Conference and before that at the Belgium Fourth Experimental Film Festival. The discussions were interesting but fruitless. The subject has always provoked mistrust and paranoia. During the Munich meeting, for example, the Italians pointed out that if dissidence existed between the film-makers of Cologne, Munich and Hamburg, how could a European co-operative hope to survive? News from the various parts of Europe was always sporadic and obscure making it difficult to know what was going on. Customs problems, particularly between Britain and the Continent, certainly would not help free exchange. The Austrians said that they had no place in their country to show or distribute films and there was some concern as to whether the Americans should be involved or not. The idea and its discussion, though exciting, dwindled by 1969-70, coinciding with the period in which there was the largest audience interest in independent film. Much of the general interest was created by television which provided not only news about what was going on but films as well. Warhol's *Flesh* was a great success and many young film clubs were formed at the time to show the independent cinema. German magazines such as *Film*, and for a time, *Kino* and *Filmkritik*, discussed both the independent film and commercial cinema on equal terms, which, if nothing else, provided a more natural acceptance and understanding of many of the new films.

Besides the Hamburger Filmschau there are three major film festivals in Germany. The Berlin Festival, like Cannes or Venice, has been almost exclusive in its coverage of the high-powered, international, commercial film industry, though it is my opinion that the young film section might show itself more often as it has in the young film forum in Berlin. The Mannheim Festival (Internationale Filmwoche Mannheim) is traditionally dedicated to first feature films and has been more open to the exhibition of the new independent cinema, though its prize-giving, however, remains a little conservative. The 1971 Mannheim Festival, as was the case throughout Germany, showed a marked swing towards social/political film-making with only a small selection of personal independent films. Oberhausen Festival is given over to short films and has been more popular among the independent film-makers for this reason. Traditionally it is ambitious but conservative. During the 1968/69 festival, for example, there was much concern, and controversy, over the lack of new independent films selected to be shown. As a result many independent films were shown but trouble persisted and the festival was virtually closed by student riots. Oberhausen was affected at this time by the intense political unrest in Germany and as a result personal film-making was over-shadowed and there was overemphasis on Sozialistischen Zielgruppenfilme.

Austria

Meanwhile over in Vienna there has been a more revolutionary group comprising the Austrian Film-makers' Co-operative. The group has had a rather unusual approach to film-making – equivalent in spirit to the Fluxus Group in New York – and is closely linked to the Institute for Direct Art in Vienna. Its film activities range from sophisticated editing to the total 'happening' (known as *Materialaktion*). The human body is treated as a material and, as the name implies, action – any action – becomes the material for a film. Thus film itself is also material. Action, when filmed, is transformed into a new action. Such action is a prime facet of 'direct art'.

This particular group of Austrian film-makers works strongly in this direction, their group character being painter/happening artist/film-maker/friend. The group includes Otto Muehl and Günter Brus, whose main field is *Materialaktion;* Kurt Kren, Hans Scheugl, Ernst Schmidt, Gottfried Schlemmer, Peter Weibel and Valie Export all concentrate on film and expanded cinema. The experience of their actions often results in films and events that please or horrify, even to the point of nausea, but none the less do confront an audience. A letter written by Birgit Hein describes a *Materialaktion* given in Cologne by Otto Muehl and using a girl and two boys:

The atmosphere was very strange, sometimes it was so quiet you could hear a needle fall. From time to time, when the tension grew, people all of a sudden lit their cigarettes; sometimes they gave short laughs as to free themselves. Muehl and the others were naked during the whole action. It would take too much time to describe everything. The end was that Muehl opened his white pants, and the head of a live hen came out. He slowly took a big knife and then suddenly cut off the head. The blood dripped on the naked body of the girl lying at his feet on the floor. He took out the whole body (of the hen) and laid it at the vulva of the girl. He poured red juice all over her so that she looked as if covered with blood. Two days after, the papers tried to make a bad mood against Muehl and his 'dirty' actions, but luckily, until now, no serious reaction has come from the public.

This type of *Materialaktion* is the basis of a good number of Austrian films. Kurt Kren takes such material, as does Ernst Schmidt; they then re-edit it into their own kind of action. Muehl's *Materialaktion* was the basis for Kren's films *Mama and Papa* (1969), which merged nudity with food; *Leda and the Swan* (1964) involving feathers and food swimming together to form flesh; *O Tannenbaum* (1964), with nudity decorated like a Christmas tree; or *Cosinus Alpha* (1966), with its changing colours and transformation of flesh. Ernst Schmidt used another Muehl *Materialaktion* in his powerful film *Bodybuilding*, which, unlike Kren's films, includes strong sound and juxtaposes white frames to contrast the colour transformation of the body. Kren's strength is in his editing and he often creates very poetic and dramatic moods, as in *Self Mutilation* (1965), based on an action by Günter Brus, where the human form and face move and are transformed like dough – slowly with the feeling of tincture in black and white; or his *Ana* (1964), also based on a Brus action, where the black and white abstractions almost look like a Franz Klein painting in motion.

These Austrian films are not only based on 'happenings' but also produce other actions on their own. Kren, who is probably the most prolific of the group, incorporated pure visual experience into his *Neg/Pos* (1961), where the editing juxtaposes opposite views of the same object to form a visual pattern. Then, in a strong wartime reminder, his *Schatzi* (1968) shows, from fading, to flickering, to full image, an old German officer standing over a battlefield. The image is a still and as the film continues it gradually reveals this image of past Fascism. Kren worked in the Österreichische National-Bank until he was sacked for running a 'shit-in' at the university; he is a short, lovable, old-fashioned type of guy who loves his beer and his films. He wrote about one of his films; 'The next week I'll finish a new film: "16/67 – 20. September". It is very dirty being about eat-drink-piss-shitting. Many friends will hate me after having seen that film. Sorry. It had to be done!'

Tappkino VALIE EXPORT stellte in München ihre revolutionäre Erfindung vor: das Tast- und Tappkino. Auf dem Bild VALIE EXPORT mit Peter Weibel. ¡Mehr über das Tast- und Tappkino auf Seite 14, Daten und Filmografie von Weibel und VALIE EXPORT im «Katalog des unabhängigen Films» im Anhang dieses Heftes.

Terms such as 'expanded movies', 'object film' and 'action film' apply to many of these Austrian films where 'actions' combined with film – in the same way that sound has traditionally been combined with film – become an integral part of the whole film. Peter Weibel and Valie Export adopt this approach. To describe the films would be useless, since they do not exist without the action. An example here is Valie Export's 8mm film *Ping Pong* (1968) which has an animated dot that jumps across the screen (left to right). Against this (projected on to a wall) she plays real ping-pong, hitting the ball against the wall to try to hit the moving dot. Even more extreme is what was claimed to be the first tactile film (which the German magazine *Film* called *'der erste Tapp- und Tastfilm'*). In Munich in November 1967 Valie Export fixed a box over her chest with a curtain in front, like a small puppet theatre. Weibel, with megaphone, and Valie Export, with box, went into the streets and announced that anyone could experience this new film – by reaching through the curtain and having twelve seconds to experience Valie Export's breasts. Again in Munich, Gottfried Schlemmer showed a film where the audience of film-makers knew exactly how long to stay out of the cinema, yet while doing so experienced the film. This was *8h01-8h11*, a 10-minute film of a clock running continuously for ten minutes. Everyone waited outside looking at their watches for ten minutes and then went back in.

In terms of environmental experience we have Hans Scheugl's 16mm 6-minute film of toilet-wall graffiti, *Sugar Daddies* (1968), which is projected on to an actual lavatory wall. Scheugl's films are, however, generally less bombastic and attacking than this and adopt an attitude of transforming reality into something new by way of film. His film *Wien 17, Schumanngasse*, which consists of one continuous take down a street, runs for as long as it took to go down the street. By watching this action in the form of a film we really do feel that it takes on a new reality. With his *Hernals* he takes a single documentary action, films it from two camera angles and then inter-cuts them together. The result is two truths at once, creating a new truth and experience (and following, in part, the aim of the Cubist painters). Ernst Schmidt's 16mm 21-minute *P.r.a.t.e.r* (1966) follows this idea, but uses different images and camera techniques. Here a shredding of realities makes a strange new reality (like a collage), combined again with the intoxicating sound poetry of Austria's Ernst Jandl.

Although *Materialaktion* is the basis of a large number of Austrian films, this is by no means the whole story. Of course, many strong films have been created in this way, such as *Bodybuilding* by Ernst Schmidt which incorporates a striking soundtrack, and juxtaposes white frames against the colour transformations in the images of bodies. Kurt Kren, also, has produced some fine films of this type, including *Mama and Papa, Leda and the Swan* and *O Tannenbaum*. Kren, as a film-maker, has extended himself fully in his work particularly as far as his editing is concerned. Of the Austrian film-makers both Kren and Peter Kubelka have a highly precise concept of film editing in which the force of time between two image movements becomes crucial to the statement being made. However, Kubelka's work shows a different facet of the Viennese film scene and he is not part of what constitutes the Austrian Film-makers' Co-operative. Instead he has been strongly associated with the New York Co-operative and he is one of the original five members of the selection committee for the Anthology Cinema in New York. In 1964 Kubelka, along with Peter Konlechner, found the Osterreichisches Filmmuseum as a major outlet for films in Austria. The Filmmuseum, together with the activity at the Co-operative, has been the essential place where much of the independent cinema finds an outlet. Before this there was little concern or interest in the avant-garde and independent film activities. Austria has no major film industry and offers no government support for film-making. The Osterreichisches Filmmuseum is a private concern and there are few other possibilities in the country for distributing independent films. The Filmmuseum, however, does receive a small subsidy from the government.

The Austrian film-makers (like many in other countries) produce situations that function conceptually in the vein in which the Cubists and the Dadaists flourished, and even work with Vertov's idea that film is the alteration and juxtaposition of images and associations, to 'find the correct and necessary line among the millions of phenomena'. These phenomena are the actions and the material chosen. This association creates a response that is direct, and thus, in the 'sixties, we have destruction themes or the sensual themes of bodies, food and violence, which may represent a reaction to the claustrophobic restrictions in today's societies. Contemporary Austrian society is particularly conservative, so reactions to it become more vehement. In a way they are forms of social awareness; in another way they create involvement. The act of doing, the act of experiencing and the act of being involved can be taken as the art of living the moment that is happening. Once, in an extreme case, the whole Austrian Co-operative ended a programme by uncovering a screen made out of metal foil in which fireworks had been placed. The Co-op members lit the fireworks and the unsuspecting audience found themselves viewing a broadside of Roman candles. Quick exit.

Kubelka has been very influential in Austria, being one of the first to bridge the gap between American and European film-makers; he has in this way increased general awareness of many of the newer films. As a film-maker he is also one of the most sensitive and precise. His presence as codirector of the Filmmuseum makes it one of the most encouraging places of its kind in the world. As a film-maker and as a personality, his influence has been great and has provided an essential link between independent film-making in Europe and in America. He has been on the committee of the New York Co-operative and, of course, has had his films distributed there. He has also lectured in the United States and in England.

Kubelka's attitude is to treat film as a piece of architecture and he spends long years patiently structuring and building up his films. His most brilliant film, *Unsere Afrikareise* (Our Trip to Africa), is a 12-minute film that took five years to make. Each frame and each sound is precisely worked out and combined to create a flawless structure. (He managed to memorize about eighteen hours of sound tapes and all the frames from three hours of film footage.) The film is a sardonic view of a 'white man's' pleasure-seeking safari into Africa, the maker's attitude being emphasized by the articulate photography and the precise editing. Jonas Mekas said once: 'Kubelka's cinema is like a piece of crystal, or some other object of nature: it doesn't look like it was produced by man; one could easily conceive that it was picked up from among the organic treasures of nature.' He began making films in 1952, his first being *Mosaik im Vertrauen* (Mosaic in Confidence), a portrait of his native Vienna, which he finished in 1955. On this early film his cameraman was Ferry Radax, another prominent Austrian film-maker (whose films include *Sonne Halt!, Am Rand, NDF-Report* and *Trigon*). In 1957 he made *Adebar*, a filmed dance, lasting 1½ minutes and made of intercut negative and positive images, mingled with freeze frames that punctuate the action. It is intended to be seen at least twice. His *Schwechater* (1958) must also be seen more than once. Originally sponsored by the Schwechater Beer Company as a commercial, it ended up as a 1-minute film that the company rejected. It represents a precise inter-cutting of five different image sequences, each of which was cut into shorter lengths and then reassembled into a metric pattern. Later on, the beer company did want the film after all. His *Arnulf Rainer* (1958/60) is a non-image film, built on a pattern of black and white frames, also structured metrically. Kubelka has said about his work: 'I take my time. . . . I feel that when you work all your life and when you really want to see and feel and communicate, and you produce something that speaks – there is no time limit, and one minute of film is enough. . . . The real statement which I want to make in the world is my films. Everything else is irrelevant.'

Italy

The appearance of the New American Cinema had an effect on most inde-pendent film-making in Europe but it particularly affected the Italians. It was at the same time as the 60-hour New American Cinema programme sent by Jonas Mekas was touring Europe, in May 1967, that the Co-operative Cinema Indipendente (CCI) was formed in Naples. From this it spread into a tripartite structure with the main centres of activity in Naples, Turin and Rome. It was formed as a sort of melting-pot for scattered, independent film activity, which had mainly been going on in and round these three cities. Though when it was formed it established a formal organizational structure, it was held together solely by a strong sense of comradeship among its members. Like many of the other European co-operatives, it began with a great flurry of activity. By 1968 it claimed to have thirty film-making members with films that had reached an audience of twenty thousand people. Under the influence of the May 1968 French student uprisings and the subsequent student uprisings in Italy, the formal organizational body of the CCI disintegrated because of what has become the classic argument about 'art' and 'politics'. Yet the primary bond of friendship and co-operation remained, as did the actual film-making.

The CCI represented an important contact between the independent film-makers of Italy, most of whom came into films from painting and literature. 'We are all very much influenced by our friends' work and [are] very rapidly developing new experiences and approaches – a process which would have taken longer if we had all stayed on our own,' said Massimo Bacigalupo, one of the film-makers involved in the CCI. Earlier independent film activity in Italy had caused very little stir. Very little, for example, is generally known or seen of the films of the Italian Futurist school made in the early 'twenties, and many contemporary efforts seem to have been overshadowed by a thriving and influential film industry. Yet the impact of the Italian Neo-realist films, which began in about 1943 and included Rossellini's *Open City* (1951), had a liberating effect on the rest of the world's cinema, influencing the French *Nouvelle Vague,* the British Free Cinema and eventually the New American Cinema.

The Italian cinema industry has produced directors like De Sica, Fellini, Antonioni and Pasolini among many others, as well as making vast 'epics' and 'spaghetti westerns' *à la Hollywood.* This diversified industry has obscured much of the independent activity, though it has put the independent film-makers in a position reminiscent of the beginnings of the New American Cinema. The presence of a strong and active industry, as in Hollywood, possibly caused the independent film-makers to pursue film in a more personal and fluid way, in a way that is far removed from a general appeal and instead related to subjective expression, symbolism and comment of the kind more often associated with painters.

The new independent Italian cinema has indeed tended to work a great deal with the meaning and poetry within images. It has turned to fantasy, symbolism, montage, superimposition and studies of everyday things and the makers have worked in personal styles that are very different from their own commercial cinema, though this, as we have seen, is already quite broad. (Anyone in Italy who forms a legal film production company can get government financial aid and this obviously allows more individuals than elsewhere to make the commercial productions they want to make.) The independent Italian film-makers generally work with less complicated equipment than in other European countries, using a great deal of 8mm and Super-8, and they have a strong 'home-movie' attitude. This simplicity of equipment puts more dependence on the image, whose meaning becomes the content. It also gives their films a naïveté and a sense of ease that is closely related to everyday life. It thus has much of the feeling found in the early stages of the New American Cinema, breaking down the technical mystique and making it seem that anyone can make a film. This closer affinity to the New American Cinema gelled in 1967 when the NAC film exhibition arrived in Europe, bringing together much of the independent film-making that had been going on since at least 1963. It was at about this time that the work of Bruno Munari, Marcello Picardo, Roberto Capanna, Giorgio Turi, Mario Masini and Antonio Vergine came to life. Munari and Picardo worked at a place called Monte Olimpio, where at least fifteen films were made, including Munari's *The Card Players*, after the Cézanne painting of the same name. This film consisted of the static image of the card players, with the only movement the smoke from their pipes. In the last sequence, with the main image still static, the player lets a card drop to the floor. Of the other makers, Masini made *Il Sogno di Anita* (Anita's Dream, 1963) and *Immagine del Tempo* (Impressions of time, 1963); Capanna and Turi made *Il Fachiro* (The Fakir, 1963) in a *cinéma vérité* style and then *Voyage* in 1964, while Antonio Vergine made the oldest film in the original CCI catalogue, *Cronache* (1963).

With or without any other influence, five other film-makers appeared between 1964 and 1965: Mario Schiffano, Luca Patella, Silvio Loffredo, Mario Ferrero and Alfredo Leonardi. It was Leonardi who became the spiritual leader of the independent Italian film-makers, their main spokesman and one of the main protagonists of the CCI. He is also one of the better film-makers, as well as being a writer. He made his first short film, *Indulgenza Plenaria*, in 1964. His interest and involvement with the theatre led him to spend some time with the Living Theater and he shot and collected enough film material to make his *Living and Glorious* (1964). His wanderings round Stockholm resulted in *Stoccolma un Giorno* (A Day in Stockholm, 1965), which was followed by *La Festa Ambigua* (The Ambiguous Festival, 1965), *Musica in Corso* (1966) and *Noi* (Us, 1966). It was not until the end of 1966 that Leonardo made his first longer and maturer work, *Amore, Amore* (Love, Love), with Mario Masini helping on the camera work. *Amore, Amore* begins to express in visual terms a particular aspect that is found in much of Leonardi's work: a composite series of analogies and oppositions put into slow rhythms. The images are taken from everyday life or from particular events (such as experiences with the Living Theater) and many of them maintain the 'home-movie' atmosphere or else offer a type of random seeing. The accumulation of this type of sequence gives his films a rather unusual and surprisingly strong feeling of fluidity, as if one were watching a thought process. Though these feelings are to be found in many other independent Italian films, they are the prime aspect in Leonardi's work and become more noticeable in his later films, particularly in *Organum Multiplum* (1967), *Se l'Inconscio si Ribella* (If the Unconscious Rebels, 1967), *Libro di Santi di Roma Eterna* (1968) and in *Le N Ragazze Piu Belle di Piazza Navona* (The N Most Beautiful Girls in the Piazza Navona, 1968). This latter film is more like the reception of watching and wandering. As he sits and relaxes in the Piazza Navona, Leonardi's eyes, through the camera, wander and watch the people, just as anyone might sit, on any warm day, in any square or park watching other people.

Leonardi's particular feeling for the New American Cinema won him a Ford Grant to spend a year in America to acquire first-hand knowledge of films and film-makers so that he could prepare a book on the subject. He returned to Italy with a 70-minute film called *Occhio Private sul Nuovo Mondo* (Private Eye on the New World, 1970), which was shot in Super-8 in diary or notebook style. This diary style runs very close to the mannerisms found in personal diary writing, in that it visualizes the particular things that interest or affect the fim-maker's own life.

The parallel with the New American Cinema is visible not only in the Italians' interests in that movement but also in their use of various fantasy, personal, diary or allegorical styles. They do not copy any of these styles; they merely have a similar conceptual relationship. The allegorical style is dependent on image content and the use of mythological or iconographical characters, ranging from vampires to biblical figures. By the beginning of the 'seventies this mode had found its way into larger, more commercially orientated Italian productions. An example of this is Franco Brocani's *Necropolis*, which contains Viva, the Warhol-styled superstar, and Pierre Clementi, and uses such allegorical character types as Frankenstein and the Moon Man.

The greatest exponent in Italy of beautiful and dreamlike fantasy films is Antonio De Bernardi. De Bernardi, who lives and works in Turin, is one of the best examples of the devoted and sincere film artist, who puts all his feelings and efforts and the money he has earned (by teaching Italian literature) into his work. He works almost exclusively in 8mm and has developed this small gauge into a spectacular, expanded and exploding format. Most of his films are in colour, with sound (note to the ignorant: it is possible to sound-strip 8mm film magnetically). They go beyond the single-screen effort, for two to four screen projections are part of a fantasy world woven from exotic, bizarre, nightmarish and beautiful people who, besides unravelling in linear fashion on the single screen, overlap and form a web of scale and movement in multiple projections. The projections are not just side by side, for the different screens are also arranged in flower-like patterns in which part of one screen is superimposed on to part of another screen. His first film, made with Paolo Mensio, was *Il Mostro Verde* (The Green Monster, 1967), a two-screen film with, in this case, the two shown side by side. His other films, which contain the same strong subjective fantasy (in De Bernardi's case, the moods are described to a certain extent by his titles) include *Il Vaso Etrusco* (The Etruscan Vase), *Il Bestiario* (The Bestiary), which is for three or four screens and is still one of his best; *Il Sogno di Constantino* (Constantine's Dream), for three screens; *Lune e Pienessa* (Moon and Fullness), for two or three screens; *Le Vestitione* (The Vestments) and *Dei* (Gods).

Also working in Turin, with De Bernardi, are Pia Epremian and Mario Ferrero. *Doppio Suicidio* (Double Suicide), *Antonio delle Nevi* (Antonio from the Snow), *Proussade* and *Medea* are Epremian's best-known films. In them she keeps a soft, almost meditative romantic fluency, while Ferrero strives towards more intense and concentrated imagery. His 16mm 9-minute film *Vep* (1968) is nothing but a series of long views of a man in a bath, the cycle being repeated until a girl appears at the end. *Schermo* (1968) follows a similar conceptual structure, and in the 8mm *Luci* (1967) or the 16mm *But Me No Buts* (1967) he continues a static use of the camera. Ferrero also ran *Ombre Elettriche,* the Italian underground cinema magazine.

To document all the independent Italian film-makers would produce a mere catalogue, though a quick cross-section may give some idea of the scope and attitudes found among them. Many came to light when the CCI was formed, such as the painter Gianfranco Baruchello, who has made quite a few films, including *Costretto A Scomparire* and *Perforce*. His films go in for symbolic imagery, as in *Perforce*, where a man puts dolls into loaves of bread to make sandwiches; he puts the sandwiches into sacks; the sacks are carried by children and then thrown into the water; and a nude Negro boy floats up from the water like a sack. On the soundtrack we hear chanting. In quite a different vein, Baruchello also made, with Alberto Grifi, *La Verifica Incerta* (The Incertain Inspection, 1961/64), a hilarious inter-cut collage film made up of cliché sequences from Hollywood films, mostly westerns and period pieces. In a similar collage style, though with a pointed social comment, is *Scusate Il Disturbo* (Sorry to Disturb You) by Giorgio Turi, which is built up of inter-cut television images filmed from advertisements, newsreels, plays and films.

Meanwhile Luca Patella strives for soft, diffused filmed visions, formed like short visual poems. In his 10-minute *Tre e Basta* (Three is Enough) he treats cars this way, and his even shorter film, the 3-minute *Passaggio Misto* (Varied Landscape), is a simple, soft fade in and out between an eye (filmed) and a misty tree in a landscape. Adam Vergine, who is related to Antonio Vergine (*Cronache*) and Aldo Vergine (*Irene*, 1960), made *Espiazone* (Es-pi'AZONE, 1968) and *Ciao Ciao*. *Ciao Ciao* was shot with an 8mm camera but is projected as 16mm. The result is a quadruple image: four images appear at once, the two on the left moving forward while the two on the right move backwards. The left-hand images are of a girl coming forward and generally moving about and waving hello, while on the right she is waving goodbye.

Guido Lombardi has transformed the diary-type film into more than mere notes. His *Sviluppo Nr. 2* (Development 2) is everyday subject matter interspersed with alternative flicker imagery, while his *A Corpo* roves through domestic scenes, including tubes of toothpaste, with quick cutting and hand-held camera movements. His *Si Prende una Ragazza, una Qualunque, li a Caso* is built up on alternating frames going back and forth $(1+2+1+2+1+2$ etc.) of a picture of a boy and a girl taken from a magazine, with occasional glimpses of a home-movie of an Italian family round the dinner table.

The calm and pleasant Massimo Bacigalupo (who wrote to me: 'This book of yours must talk about all the greatness involved! hope it won't make any sense whatsoever! ') has made such films as *Quasi una Tangente, Ariel Loquitur* and *60 Metri Per Il 31 Marzo* (200 Feet for 31 March). This latter film is based on a newspaper description of a police action and uses actual words cut out of the article and filmed; in Bacigalupo's words, it is 'an attempt to find a ground pattern within the day's reality'.

Finally, we have *Le Court Bouillon* by Silvio and Vittorio Loffredo, a collage made out of old films, films by Umberto Biguardi, who made *Motion Vision* (1967) with Alfredo Leonardi; Mauro Chessa (*The Time of Mutation*); Renato Doghani (*Mescal, Lei In*); Nicola De Rinaldo (*Francesco dell'amore*); Tano Festa (*Write a Love Letter, E tu che ne sai dell'America, Fotografare e Facile* – Photography is Easy); E. and R. Centazzo (*Topografia Nr. 1*); Franco Angeli (*Giornata di Lettura* – A Day's Reading) and Pierfrancesco Bargellini. All these are among an even larger array of independent film-makers spread informally round Italy.

The most familiar place in Rome where most of the independent films, Italian and foreign, have been screened is Filmstudio 70. Film shows have also been held at the Union Culturale in Turin, the Club Nuovo Teatro in Milan, and in a few art galleries like L'Attico in Rome or the Bertesca in Genoa. But then, the Italians have always had more film festivals that have been responsive to the new and independent cinema than any other country. The Pesaro Film Festival (Mostra Internazionale del Nuovo Cinema) was one of the first forums (after the Experimental Film Festival in Belgium) for the new cinema and took, in 1970, Glauber Rocha's statement which ends by saying: '. . . the *new cinema* sets itself apart from commercial cinematography which, as an industry, is committed to untruth and exploitation.' Beside Pesaro, there are also the Bergamo, Venice and Florence film festivals, which have also given space to the new cinema, while the 1970 Venice Biennale, one of the largest art fairs in the world, had seminars and film shows on the 'underground' cinema. Press interest in the film, including the independent and 'underground' cinema, is quite considerable in Italy and journalistic coverage even reaches into the architectural magazine *Domus*, which discusses the Italian and American independent film movements.

It would be interesting to know what effect, if any, religious censorship has had on independent film-making in Italy. There does not seem to have been any strong religious or otherwise censorable material in the majority of the independent 'underground' films, though in the commercial Italian cinema religious attitudes become more apparent (for example in the films of Pasolini or Fellini). Instead, an obvious 'family life' atmosphere is portrayed in Italian films, a feeling for friends, family, ramblings and day-to-day activities. But the Italian can be as political as the next man and when the French student uprising took place in 1968 the young Italians rose up as well. Even the festivals and the Biennale were hit by left-wing protests and there were marches (with the 'Book of Mao' held high) all over the place. As in other countries, the film-makers soon began to join the political movements. This, of course, was the cause of the initial split in the CCI. Occasionally different film groups would be formed to increase political activities, such as the Cinema Militante. Film-makers like Ferrero and Lombardi began to make films with more direct political elements, but Leonardi had begun to bridge some of the political and poetic gaps even earlier, in 1967, when he worked on *Cinegiornale*, a film journal that pointed to the contradictions in the national press. On returning to Italy from America, Leonardi wrote in a letter dated 7 March 1970: 'I found the Co-op's situation in Italy pretty much the same, except for a stronger political interest in some film-makers, including myself. There are a few good new films by Lombardi ("C"), De Bernardi, Baruchello, etc.'

Even though the strong formal organization of the CCI had broken up, twelve of its members joined together as a sign of friendship to make a collective film. Finished in March 1969, this was called *Tutto, Tutto Nello Stesso Istante* (Everything, Everything at the Same Time) and the film-makers were Bacigalupo, Bargellini, Baruchello, Chessa, De Bernardi, Epremian, Leonardi, Lombardi, Meader, Menzio, Turi and Vergine.

G

Switzerland

Co-operatives and independent film activity have appeared in Switzerland with such film-makers as Hans Jacob Siber, Klaus Schönherr and Dieter Meier. Very few other Swiss films have travelled beyond that country. It was not until 1969 that a festival directed mainly towards 16mm films was started. This was called Festival International de Cinéma Nyon and among its first judges was Gregory J. Markopolous.

Of the known Swiss film-makers, Klaus Schönherr has been the most active. In style (not content) his films are reminiscent of some of the earlier New American Cinema film-makers, in particular Markopolous, Brakhage (Brakhage has had the most pronounced influence on almost all European film-makers) and bits of Ron Rice, though never quite hitting the same strength as any one of these film-makers. Schönherr's *Gedanken beim Befühlen einer Mädchenhaut* (Thoughts on Touching a Girl's Skin) is a 25-minute film made up of poetic colour views and studies of a pretty girl, mostly of her face and often done with superimpositions. It is a film portrait, with Bach on the soundtrack. His other films (many with long-winded titles) include *Thaler's, Meier's, Sadkowsky's life in the evening* (1967), *4 Minuten Nachmittag* (4 minutes in the afternoon, 1967), *Das Gesicht der Alten Frau, die Suppenterrine, Vreni Keller Spricht und der Popo der Madam* (The Old Woman's Face, the Soup Tureen, Vreni Keller speaks and Madame's Fanny, 1967), a montage film, *Play* (1967), *Sonate* (Sonata, 1968) and *Autoportrait* (Self-portrait, 1967). They are in 16mm. Schönherr has also run the magazine *Supervisuell*, which was supposed to disseminate European co-operative information, though its earlier issues kept within a very limited circle.

One of Dieter Meier's films, *Klaus Schönherr isn't Making a Film in Someone's Room on Sunday Afternoon* (1968) follows the easy-going ramblings and superimpositions found in Schönherr's own films. The first ten minutes are taken up with a street scene with a parked car. When the car drives away, a double exposure of it as it was when it was still parked remains, creating a ghost-like image. One of the nicest things Meier has done was to stand for about a minute in front of the light from a projector, with a screen behind. Both Meier and Schönherr have had strong contacts with the German film groups, with whom they work closely, particularly with X-Screen and PAP, of which Meier is coorganizer. Schönherr wrote once that in the Swiss Co-op '. . . they have no good films at all, and usually pay nothing to the film-maker.'[3] Maybe there is no co-operative at all, just a few film-makers. Who knows the whole truth? To quote Schönherr, in *Supervisuell 4*: 'Blah, blah, blah, blah, blah, blah, blah, blah, blah, blah, blah, blah, blah, *blahblah,* etc.'

Australia

The concept of film-makers' co-operatives has also reached the Pacific and then swung back to North America, the most active places being Australia, Japan and Canada. The Australians first formed a group called Ubu Films (after Alfred Jarry's *Ubu Roi*), which functioned like a film-makers' co-operative, and then later became a base for the Sydney Film-makers' Co-operative which works as an active meeting-place, a distribution agency, and catalyst for independent film-makers. The Australians have produced a fair number of independent films, with a particular tendency towards dramatic parodies, a narrative interplay style or a documentary style – at least in those films seen outside their own country. A few have, however, broken further away from these styles, often into personal, poetic and abstract films, the more prolific film-makers being Albie Thoms, David Perry and Garry Shead.

Thoms, who up to now has been the best-known of the independent Australian film-makers, has also been the most productive, varying his roles from director to producer to script-writer. His film *Bolero*, which uses Ravel's music as the sound, is a continuous 15-minute slow zoom up a street until it reaches a girl at the end. Conceptually it is similar to Michael Snow's immensely powerful 45-minute *Wavelength,* and both films appeared during the same Fourth International Experimental Film Festival in Belgium. Though *Bolero* is probably one of the best examples of this minimal film style, it lacks the subtle and engrossing form found in Snow's work and its purity is spoiled by the use of sudden and impatient 'jump' cuts to reach the girl's eye at the end. Among the fifteen other films Thoms had made by 1970 there is *David Perry* (1968), which consists of exposed and unexposed pieces of film, edited and hand-coloured. The exposed pieces are offcuts from other films, the final shot being of the film-maker David Perry. Thoms's *Marinetti* (1969) is a feature-length film inspired by the Italian Futurist poet Marinetti. John Mathews described the film:

> Thus Thoms began with a conceptual framework [Marinetti's manifestos] expressing certain polarities, and resting firmly on a cyclic progression from an abstract synthesis of light and sound, through tonal values that oscillate from the particular to the general, from portraits of those involved in the film to the city that swallows them, to a final abstract analysis that strips the image of all irrelevant material. We are left with a white light-filled screen, the complement of the dark screen we started with.

Another tendency among the Australian independents is to produce autographic or non-photographic 'hand-made' films. This method includes scratching, painting and pasting on to film (similar methods to those used by Len Lye or Norman McLaren), or punching holes into it. *A Tripartite Adventure in Redfern* (1968), made by Albie Thoms, Aggy Read and Susan Howe, is a 3-minute film combining scratching, hand-colouring, sandpapering, filing, grinding, biting and chewing of the raw film stock. David Perry's *Puncture* (1967) has circular holes punched directly through the film, while his *Halftone* (1967) was made by enlarging half-tone dot patterns (normally used for the graphic printing of photographs) and printing them on to the film. Perry has also made some more descriptive animated films. All in all there is a fair amount of new film activity in Australia, though by no means as much as in other countries. The styles range from the freer methods used by Thoms to the solid art documentaries of Arthur and Corrinne Cantrill. However, the overall impression is one of a struggle to find a more positive and committed direction. There seems to be a time lag and a degree of isolation, plus an influence from the older British documentary school on both film-making and creative thinking. Australia does not have a large internal film industry. Many of the problems seem to come from the country's rather insular and conservative Establishment, which has tried to maintain a cross between a Christian ethos and a Victorian British ethic. This has resulted in strong control both over the type of film entering Australia and over the kind of film leaving the country. By 1970 pressure from internal groups had unfortunately had the reverse effect of getting more internal controls put on films.

Japan

In the West, especially in Western Europe, even less is seen, or even heard, of the films and film-makers of Japan. Very few commercial Japanese films reach western eyes and ears (though it must be remembered that only about 25 per cent even of the commercially-made films in the western countries ever reach Britain). One hears of or even sees the work of a few Japanese directors such as Kon Ichikawa, Akira Kurosawa, Yasujiro Ozu, Masaki Kobayashi or Hiroshi Teshigahara, and more recently Taramaya. This, along with the more recently known animated work of Yoji Kuri, is of superb quality. Much more is apparently going on in Japan, but the material hardly trickles out. Recent showings of numerous Japanese animated films reveal a quantity and a quality complementing much of the best of the western output. Much 'live-action' and 'experimental' film-making has also been going on for almost as long as in the West.

Curiosity about Japanese films strengthened during the Fourth International Experimental Film Festival, when Koji Wakamatsu presented *The Embryo* (1966). This depicted the sadistic torturing of a girl (tying her to a bed, cutting her with razor blades and so on) and the effect upon the western audience was such that it caused a good number of them to charge at the screen and try to stop the projection. Wakamatsu's statement about the film ran as follows:

> The reason why I have chosen 'The Embryo' as our entry to the festival is to let you know the level of Japanese experimental movies produced since last year. 'The Embryo' was produced as a drama movie of such a strong sadistic touch that it has never been shown before the public. I want very much to let the world know that such fantastic films are being produced in Japan one after another.

Wakamatsu is not completely right, since various pieces of information still indicate that a considerable amount of more truly experimental and personal independent film-making has been going on in Japan.

In March 1968, the Japan Film-makers' Co-operative was formed in Tokyo. Its first committee consisted of Takahiko Iimura, Kenji Kanesaka, Jushin Sato, Nubuhiko Ohbayashi and Ronald Richie and its 1969 catalogue listed the work of about forty-five different film-makers (of these, eight were not Japanese, or even resident in Japan, but were primarily from the New American Cinema group). The Japan Co-operative followed the same policies as its New York counterpart. A few of its members had previously belonged to an organization called Japan Film Independent, which was created in 1964. When some Japanese experimental films were shown at the Museum of Modern Art in New York in 1966, Ronald Richie wrote: 'Japan is the country of the *haiku*, that terse and inner statement the meaning of which must be inferred – communication is less important than consideration. The Japanese experimental film – in evidence since the late 1920s – is traditionally intended for no audience at all. It is an object, like *ikebana*: something to admire, something to disregard.'

Because of the limited cultural exchange with other countries (the greatest contact has been with America) the films from the independent Japanese cinema (*ziyuu na eigakan*) are rather difficult to see and therefore difficult to talk about. The films of Takahiko Iimura have been the most available in the West, mainly because he lived in New York for a while and was associated with the Film-makers' Co-operative. He then toured Europe, depositing a few of his films with the co-operatives in the countries he visited. His own films vary in style, showing a versatility of thinking and working and films varying between 8mm and 16mm. His first film *Ai* (Love) which dates from about 1962, was originally shot on 8mm and then blown up to 16mm. It is a gritty and swarming film, full of grain and contrast, of a couple copulating. Much of it was shot through a magnifying glass (over a short focal-length lens) and the effect is wildly abstracted, with the movements of the pubic hair looking like ants pushing blades of grass and the actions making us feel that we are standing on Gulliver's face or leg. The soundtrack was recorded by Yoko Ono. Some of Iimura's early work involves filming old prints and engravings. *De Sade* (1962) for instance, is made out of eighteenth-century engravings, while *Ukiyo Ukare* (Peep Show, 1964) has close-ups of erotic Japanese prints. He goes into abstract colours in *Iro* (1962) and into surrealistic attitudes in *A Dance Party in the Kingdom of Lilliput* (1964). *Lilliput* is made up of simple sequences, like chapters, each with its own title and containing simple actions or poses. It is about a man whom we see in profile, head on, naked, running upstairs, like a dream or a strange Kafkaesque comedy.

Iimura's main forte is really the erotic. *Onan* (uncompleted coition, masturbation, 1963) is about a man who burns holes in nude pictures of girls, runs into the street in his underwear and meets a girl. *Sakasama* (1963) shows the feet and thighs of a woman, upside down, the neo-Dada attitudes in this film seeming to be related to the work of the New York Fluxus Group. Iimura's film range continues with *Virgin Conception* (1968), one of his strongest erotic films, which he describes as a camera experience with a girl, while *Flowers* consists of poetic superimpositions and a strange orgy set against a New York setting. There is also *I saw the Shadow* (1966), made only of shadows, and *Summer Happenings, USA* (1968), made while Iimura lived in the United States and treated as a newsreel/documentary film. A list of all his films would fill a couple of pages of a catalogue. Yet he is only one of many, and from his impressive list we can assume that the other independent Japanese film-makers have been very active.

Canada

Like many of the countries already mentioned, Canada has a growing independent and 'underground' cinema. For a long time she has had the great cultural problem of being caught in a crossfire between her giant and influential southern neighbour, the United States, and her Commonwealth mother, Britain. This is also a sprawling country, with a relatively small population and, on its eastern side, a bilingual culture. Many activities, especially in the arts, that have occurred in the United States have been quickly shunted up north, and this has obviously affected any indigenous growth. The presence of nearby Hollywood has meant that there was no real need to develop a similar film industry. Since Hollywood so readily ploughed its goods into the country, the Canadians took to developing a film system more akin to the British.

John Grierson, and later Norman McLaren, both from Britain, have built up the dominant National Film Board of Canada. Its emphasis has been on short to medium-sized films rather than on feature films, with the content being treated generally in documentary and animation styles. It has produced some superb films in the documentary style, but it is in animation that the Board has been most creative. Thanks initially to McLaren, who is one of the most advanced animators around, the Board fostered the development of many other great animators, and has given Canadian animation a special place in world cinema.

Yet many new and independent film-makers have managed to break away from the omnipresent National Film Board. In 1970 the Canadian Film-makers' Distribution Centre (Toronto), Intermedia (Vancouver), Co-operative des Cinéastes Indépendents (Montreal) and the London Film-makers' Co-operative (London, Ontario) combined their activities and distribution (with the help of money from the Canadian Film Development Corporation). As with other countries, independent film activities and shows have been scattered and generally confined to universities and a few art galleries. The Underground Film Centre in Montreal has also shown independent films regularly and was responsible for organizing a Canadian

Underground Minifestival, which travelled through Europe. The film-makers represented on this tour were Michael Snow, Martin Lavut, Clovis Durant, Joyce Wieland, Morley Markson, John Juliani and Bob Cowan.

Many new film-makers in Canada, again as in other countries, have come from the other arts. Michael Snow has not only become one of the most important of them, with his *Wavelength, New York Eye and Ear Control, Standard Time, One Second in Montreal* and so on, but is also one of the leading avant-garde sculptors in Canada. Joyce Wieland, another leading figure in Canadian art, is one of the most advanced and influential film-makers (*Rat Life and Diet in North America, Water Sark, 1933, Sailboat, Catfood*) while Bob Cowan (*Child, Summer Dance, Evocation, Soul Freeze, Rockflow*) formerly studied painting. (All these film-makers are associated with the New American Cinema group and have also spent much time working and living in the United States.) Other film-makers are Larry Kardish (*Slow Run*) and the independent animator Al Sens (*The Playground, The Puppet's Dream, The Sorcerer, Once or Twice Upon a Time*).

The Canadian cinema has recently begun to show signs of change, as is indicated by the work of men such as Allan King (*Warrendale*) and has been very active in such areas as the 'expanded' cinema. Expo '67 in Montreal became the fairground for all sorts of experiments in expanded and environmental cinema and, along with Czechoslovakia, Canada is showing great technical progress in these areas. Canada, being in a more fortunate position politically, has of course progressed even further.

Information on the new, free, independent cinema has so far been random, personal and often vague. Though the details I have given here are by no means complete, I have tried to indicate some of the directions it has taken, particularly on the personal or so-called 'underground' level. There are levels of film-making and directions that have hardly been whispered about (such as greater detail on the technical developments in expanded cinema, multimedia, etc). There are other areas, such as the developments in the commercial cinema, that have been and are being well covered by other documents. There is film activity in other countries that has not been mentioned, or barely mentioned – for example in Belgium, Spain, Portugal, India and the Latin American countries.

Documentation of the independent and 'underground' cinema and all those making films in it is a near impossibility at this point. So much of the activity is still in a state of flux and change, with some of it going in commercial directions, some into esoteric exercises, some replacing paintings, some just disappearing. Even within one's own country it becomes difficult to find out exactly what is going on. Anything that is alive is by definition changing. As with many of the arts (or any activity, for that matter), individuals often pursue their interests quietly, in little corners, being content if just a few friends see what they have done. Personal motivations, personal interests (or frustrations) and personal experiments have led many individuals to make personal films, as others might paint or write poetry. No one knows how many there are, or how good they are. Few ever get seen or heard. One keeps bumping into people who are making films, or who have made films. Some slip away again into obscurity. Some lack confidence. Some lack conviction. Others are frightened. Others think film-making means being 'professional'. Others make films just to be part of a group; but there are others who make films with sincere conviction and belief in what they are doing. Some of them try to give greater life and existence to their work. Some of them make it; but even more of them get swallowed up or destroyed.

So the documentation here merely indicates a process. It is all history. It does not show all that is going on, or that has been going on. Nor does it indicate what will be going on. Processes will continue; the results, effects, names and places will aways be different.

Part Two

4 Memories of Films and Film-Makers

Introduction

To discuss a language that is primarily visual, or that uses visual data with auditory means, by means of another language – the word – is both dangerous and difficult. This is the case not only with films but with painting, sculpture, dance or music, especially when these are not essentially narrative or literal. One can only try to evoke a sense of the visual experience. Like painting, not all films are verbal, and they can therefore escape words. With words, it is possible to search round a particular image: with technical information, with descriptive translations, with opinions, with comparisons and with a film-maker's statements of intention. But words cannot create the same visual effect, the reality and complexity of the thing itself.

In a review of a traditional film there is usually a brief synopsis of the film's story – its plot or narrative. The critic will probably make some comparison with another film or with the director's previous films. He may then give an 'opinion', using a variety of adjectival labels, giving general references to something else and imparting a sense of his own arrogance. One, for instance, went: 'Lethargic thriller which follows the familiar Boileau-Marcejac blue-print of sombre mystery with supernatural overtones and a surprise twist that comes as little surprise.' Another: 'Extensive cuts leave a few gaps in the narrative, but this is so dull that it hardly matters.' A more positive criticism ran: 'For what is obviously a low-budget production, this is a splendid piece of hokum, with good sets and photography and a lively pace.' What do they say about seeing? And what if you do not know the Boileau-Marcejac blue-print? Because the film seemed 'low-budget' it was all right, but supposing it had been a costly production? And what constitute 'good' film sets and 'good' film photography?

These criticisms relate to a traditional narrative film. But how do you express in words your thoughts on films without traditional narrative, or with no narrative at all? And what do you say if these films also have no commercial pretensions and do not use traditional techniques? One would expect or hope that the critic, like any other viewer, would approach the subject open-mindedly. Since the critics of the new independent cinema can find no neat labels and no points of reference, they slate its films almost as a matter of course. They have no time to see or to think, but simply record their disgust or dismiss them out of hand as dull. The potential viewer is not encouraged to judge a film for himself. Once, at a film show given at the University of Essex, a man exclaimed that he could not understand the films shown because nothing had been written about them. He therefore rejected the films until he could find some labels. 'Labelling is the perennial human substitute for thinking,' writes Susan Sontag; and for feeling, I might add.

To criticize criticism is a circular process. It is not enough to say 'you know what I mean'. We are not that free yet. Books like this one are being and have been written about the independent cinema; even more books have been written about the traditional cinema; far more books have been written about seeing and the visual arts. It is a shame that we cannot see films very easily, for only by seeing them can we begin to understand them. I am a film-maker and I should like you to see the films, experience the films, feel the films, and hopefully to understand and enlarge your vision. As this is a book made up of words, I have to use words as points of reference to conjure up something concrete about seeing. It is important to consider that in these personal and independent films two factors interact: one is the effect of and development from the traditions of the commercial cinema; the other is the development and exploration of film through the ways of seeing that have evolved through the other arts – painting, sculpture and music. Some films and film-makers tend to adopt one attitude or the other; others attempt some meeting of the two. The tendency in the material discussed here is to develop the attitudes inherent in the arts.

It is from this rather fluctuating viewpoint that many of the films considered should be seen – not as a strict comparison with films of the past, or as a comparison with commercial films. Many independent films do not compete with films produced by the cinema industry, but instead run parallel to them. Admittedly it is hard to look at 'a film' without immediately referring to 'the film'. The hundreds of films many of us have seen among the thousands made, plus the dozens of books about them, become a guide as to what films should be about. Yet there are no rules, and anything is permissible. It is interesting to point out here that a large number of the greatest directors and film-makers who laid the foundations for what has become the traditional and commercial cinema turned to film from a variety of other activities. For example, Robert Wiene (*Doctor Caligari*) was a painter; Fritz Lang a painter and architect; Friedrich Murnau a painter and art historian; Sergei Eisenstein an engineer and a theatre director; Dziga Vertov a medical student; Vsevolod Pudovkin a chemist; Alexander Dovzhenko a schoolteacher and painter; Vittorio de Sica an actor; Luchino Visconti a theatre director; Federico Fellini a cartoonist; Robert Flaherty a miner; and D. W. Griffith a writer.[1] Yet many innovatory film-makers (some independent) have come from within the film industry or have been trained in film schools (one example is Andrzej Wajda, who went to the Polish film school before making such films as *Kanal* and *Ashes and Diamonds*). Their films stem from the traditional film and they have often produced quite personal films in this context. However, few go beyond the points of reference established by the film industry. At best only a few are able to refine and truly develop the film as a wholly individual entity. Directors like Godard and Antonioni (interestingly enough, both were once film critics) have uplifted the film's points of reference to a new dimension, which many a viewer and critic, clinging to the past, are unable fully to grasp.

Interest in film as material and as a medium seems constantly to involve the artist, especially when it is available to him. Whether the writer turns to film as a strong outlet for social comment, or the painter for the possibilities it affords for putting image into a time/space continuum, each begins to transform its points of reference. They no longer use the film as a commercial commodity but as a personal initiation.

The 'arts' have tended to be restricted to the few who choose to work in them (or to be an investment for the rich man). Film, on the other hand, has been projected as a mass-communication and entertainment medium. With the other 'arts', such as painting, the viewer has to transport himself into the image. Film traditionally does this for him. The newer independent films incorporate the aesthetics of the other arts with that of film itself. Film can examine, explore, enlighten, entertain or bore. It can persuade, perceive or dwell in poetics. It is a highly malleable material and has the potential to reach the creative and social conscience of a people's culture. Since film provokes extension and association, uses time, movement, space, rhythm and colour and alludes to an individual's physical realities and to his dreams and fears, it can use the elements with which artists and poets have always been involved. Films are the continuation and extension of creative material.

Many of the new films are sincere efforts at expressing feelings, ideas and visions – some by means of abstraction, some by means of technology, others by means of environmental features or narrative and documentary exploration. There are successes and failures among them, but film-making is a human activity that demands as much attention as any of the other arts. It is not restricted to a handful of people, but occupies hundreds throughout the world.

When I began to make films in about 1958 I had never heard of the so-called 'underground' and I had never seen any of its work. Perhaps it did not exist then. I have since discovered, however, that independent films have a history and that many films were already being made at that time. I have now made a few films myself and have seen many others. I have met many film-makers in the interim and I suppose many started the way I did – not all, but many of them. There is no precise explanation as to why we did so, nor any specific reason why we all do what we do. The environment was right and much of the equipment was becoming more easily available. This latter point is important, because film usually depends on expensive equipment, on film material and laboratory-processing bills. The equipment now became more accessible, at least in New York, and there was out-of-date film stock to hand. Like many others, I discovered a lab on 43rd Street that did the processing somewhat more cheaply than other labs. No one really thought much at that time about big productions or fancy equipment. A camera that worked, whether it was 16mm or 8mm, and a roll of film were really enough. Imagination runs free without technical hang-ups.

I suppose there were other things that led us to films. Many of us had been virtually weaned on the movies; it was a language that was as natural as that of comics and advertisements. I had studied design and painting and most of the other film-makers, then as today, in America and Europe, were painters, or maybe writers, sculptors or possibly photographers. In any case, there seems to have been a positive link between our thinking, inclining us towards films.

I have seen so many beautiful films that it would be impossible to mention each one of them, and there are so many film-makers, too, that only a list of several hundred pages could include them all. In 1967 the New York Film-makers' Co-operative catalogue listed about 840 films – after only four years of activity.

> The questions 'What is length?', 'What is meaning?', 'What is the number one?' etc., produce in us a mental cramp. We feel that we can't point to anything in reply to them and yet ought to point to something. (We are up against one of the great sources of philosophical bewilderment: a substantive makes us look for a thing that corresponds to it.)
>
> From *The Blue Book* by Ludwig Wittgenstein

I saw one of the finest of them during the Fourth Experimental Film Festival in Belgium in 1967. This was Michael Snow's *Wavelength*. It was shown on a large screen, and at that time part of the soundtrack was still on tape. The film is a continuous zoom through a room, taking forty-five minutes. But it is not as simple as that; rather it is a spatial movement, a flowing movement through a visual space. Four incidents occur in the film at intervals: a bookcase is moved into the room; two girls listen to the radio (which plays the Beatles' 'Strawberry Fields'); a man comes in and falls to the floor; a girl enters and telephones someone to say that the man is dead. These incidents punctuate the space, and in doing so strengthen, by their contrast, the spatial and time structure that constitutes the film. These human events have no story, they are part of life. The whole emphasis is upon the time and space factor. Throughout the punctuating actions, the movements overlap visually and the colours overlap and change. It is hard to explain this in conventional terms. At certain points during the film's time, though seemingly not at any particular time, the image of the room returns to an earlier point, maybe seen a minute or two earlier, and then goes forward again, passing itself. The room across which the film is shot at the beginning is an 80-foot loft in New York (a clear, open space ranging from 80 to 125 feet long, maybe 25-30 feet wide), one end of which looks towards four windows at the far end. The camera zooms towards the wall space between the two middle windows. The overlapping of the image, like a superimposition, causes the colours to mix, creating a whole series of subtle changes. The film is not merely time as movement but time as change.

The change occurs not only in the movement and the overlapping but in the change from day to night, as seen outside the windows, and in the varying degrees of daylight filtering in through the windows, or in the lights inside when it is dark outside. All the time the image is moving (or we, the spectators, are moving via the camera). Part of all this, and vital to the structure, is the sound. While the visual movement is across a space, from a wide field of vision to a narrow one, the sound is an auditory movement made by an electronic sine-wave from its lowest to highest note. The sound moves from fifty cycles per second to twelve thousand per second in forty minutes, though the first five minutes of the film have only normal street sounds.

The visual movement crosses the room to the wall between the two windows, focusing our vision on to a picture on the wall. All the time the sound's pitch is closing in on our auditory senses. Gradually, again with overlapping, the picture on the wall becomes the only image. It is a photograph of ocean waves. That is all we see, and it contains the infinity of the ocean. We have moved into a new space outside. The sound reaches its highest pitch as we move into a subjective continuity of space through the ocean waves.

When I first saw this film I was totally overwhelmed. I experienced a feeling of being within a sculptured space of movement without physically moving myself. I found myself exhilarated by the sensation and the experience, and no matter how many times I see the film it still has the same effect upon me, yet with more subtleties.

During my second viewing of *Wavelength* I made the following notes:

inside room
windows
traffic sounds
view of traffic going past

yellow flashes, orange, blue
 (whistles in audience)
two people walk into room
sound track of steps
Beatles, etc., living is easy, etc.

red, orange, bluish

girl goes away

sound on
hum

the other people on screen
go, no traffic
humm
room dark, flash
only windows show

yellow, brown room
black and flash
hummm
flash
yellow windows
hummmm
camera in flash
flash
to blue, yellow, red, magenta
hummmm more
intense
traffic on
hummmmm intense
flash red
red no image
magenta
light
no traffic
yellow, brown, orange
neg?
more brown flashes
hummmmm sharper
back to brown, yellow
move in
interior dark, light
hummmmmmmm change
pink flash brown
hummmmmmmmm intense
light blue, white frame
light windows yellow green
hummmmmmmmmmm
dark window
moving in
sound sharper
interior lit from inside
camera in
pink white yellow lighter room pink
sound intense
room blue, normal
sound intense
pink, red, normal white
light outside
body
body falls
move in
double image
to normal, red flashes
hummmmmmmmmmmmmm
flashes of pink many times
hummmmmmmmmmmmmmm sharper

room yellowish
flash yellow
flash yellow
flash yellow
greed red
car goes by
camera in
   (shouts from the audience)
same image window
buzz flash buzz
sound still more intense
move in windows
girl comes in
on phone by window
sound intense
I just got here there is a body . . .
what shall I do
goes away
double image
girl on phone
same interior flashing together
goes away
sound loud sharp intense
move in
flash same
sound intense
hummmmmmmmmmmmmmmmm
normal, double, flash
sound intense
move in
extremely loud sharp sound
green and fading
green fading
sound intense
magenta cast
red pink flash double image sometimes
sound—intense
on and on . . . move in
picture between windows
water
goes to the water
sound up
hummmmmmmmmmmmmmmmmmmm
zoom in
louder
water
move in, in and in
wave
water
in, in

H

> change in hum
> fades
> as unsharp
> white screen

Snow has himself said of *Wavelength*:

I wanted to make a summation of my nervous system, religious inklings and aesthetic ideas. I was thinking of planning for a time monument in which beauty and sadness of equivalence would be celebrated, thinking of trying to make a definitive statement of pure Film space and time, a balancing of 'Unison' and 'Fact', all about seeing. The space starts at the camera's (spectator's) eye, is in the air, then is on the screen, then is within the screen (the mind).

Michael Snow was born in Canada in 1929 and trained as a sculptor in Toronto. He made his first film in 1957, but before that was a painter and also a jazz musician. The contemporary artist no longer isolates himself on the narrow, single-lane road; he is more like someone riding on a highway on which many lanes travel in the same direction. He can switch from one lane to the other, depending on his particular condition. Picasso opened up this road and drove over the place. The tie of some film-makers with the arts is further apparent in their references. Michael Snow refers to *Wavelength* as 'much more like Vermeer', though he considers that his work is representational as Cézanne's 'work was representational'.

In 1960 Snow began a series called 'Walking Woman', which was probably the earliest example of fixed-image work. The Walking Woman was a stylized silhouette of a typical city working girl and he applied this image in every conceivable way, from rubber stamps to a large, sculpted stainless steel piece for Expo '67 in Montreal. The Walking Woman appeared in various stages, from naked to dressed, and in Snow's earlier film, *New York Eye and Ear Control* (1964), had a jazz track to match. *Eye and Ear*, though in a sense sculptural, is closer to Cubist art. It inspects and is objective. After *Wavelength* (which won the Grand Prix at the Fourth Experimental Film Festival in 1967), Snow went on to develop and explore his sculptural perception of film. He said that he wanted to make a film that has no explanation. He made a film, not quite without explanation, but without any words in its title. To you, the word-reader, it is called I——I (1969). This film is structured on a continuous back and forth (and later up and down) camera pan. Here Snow is working again with the notion of a fixed space and the space in which the film occurs is a room. The movements of both the camera and what happens in the room (as seen in the film) constantly play up the sense of opposing forces. The room is fixed but change occurs within and around; it is a typical American-styled country school room. After the light goes on, the camera begins to pivot back and forth across the room. At the end of each movement there is a click on the sound track. The camera movement changes and begins to slow down. Activity begins within the 'scene' – a girl sits down on a chair and then disappears after a few back-and-forth pans; people play ball in the room, a man washes the window and the light outside changes from sunlight to dusk. The time and change surrounding this fixed unit of space is constantly restated by the life variants contained within. The speed of the camera movements alone alters the fixed space into new senses of space. Movement itself remakes images. Movement also occurs by the passage of objects one to another and the appearance and disappearance of people. Each activity is intensified. A girl on one camera pass (pan) stands by a window and then after a few passes she is by the window near the door. A man enters, closes the door and kisses the girl, all of which goes on while the camera maintains its back and forth movement. This movement is not only with the camera but between the objects and subjects within the field of view. A girl walks outside past the window (there are voices talking at the same time on the soundtrack) and within another camera movement one sees the same girl inside the room sitting on a chair in the foreground. During another time in the same space – classroom – it is full of people with the camera still moving backwards and forwards. After two camera passes the room is empty again. Later three more people are in the room with more voices on the soundtrack. The back-and-forth camera movement is continuous. A crowd of people then appear by the window that is nearer to the camera and in this crowd two men have a mock fight. After this there is a jump cut but the camera continues its movement and there are more voices heard after which the soundtrack speeds up with a mechanical noise. With this the back-and-forth camera movements also speed up and four minutes later become even faster. A man walks in and goes by, at the same time a woman walks the other way and they pass. A counterpoint is made in what is the frame and what is outside the frame; movements and counter movements emphasize space. The back and forth movement of the camera by this time is faster. Someone is sitting in the room but disappears after a minute or two like a sculptured Méliès. The room becomes a blur, the still faster movement has only natural and organic fluctuations in its high speed. The image now is like looking out of the window of a high-speed train racing along. Then suddenly the movement is up and down. This occurs roughly 30 minutes after the beginning of the film. The image which was once a room now has the appearance of paper being turned quickly out of a giant printing press. The pace then slows down until there is the impression of slipping frames. Gradually this image is recognized as the image of the classroom window. The movement up and down becomes slower. The camera movement is from the light on the ceiling, past the window and down onto the floor and up again. As the movement slows down a policeman appears in the window and then disappears almost immediately. The end of the film is a multiple imposition of many of the movements that have been seen in the film. It is the summary or recap of the 'structural' drama, and the film is a drama of seeing; it is a drama caused by oppositions. Ask to see I——I, 48 minutes in colour at your local cinema. Snow's later 90-minute, 360°, *La Région Centrale*, square-roots the film space and time.

I have not had the chance to ask Michael Snow about the previous film but I was able to talk to him about *Wavelength*. When I asked him, for example, how much of the textures, (colour overlaps etc) were planned, he said that they were not exactly planned but that he set up a container in which it all could happen. He was against the idea of making works of art if the exact outcome was known beforehand.

Whether one agrees with this idea or not the fact remains that this particular process produces indefinable results. Many aspects of the process are certainly indeterminate and operate with chance but there is still an underlying idea and sense of direction which could be called intention. A structure, situation, statement is assured and created which functions as a container or a framework. Discoveries are made and it is in these discoveries that the piece develops. The realities that form themselves are tangible, whether they are directly intended or within the materials used for composition.

In an allegorical sense film-makers function as alchemists. The process of making, regardless of the individual types of film-makers, involves a striving towards a transference of material and objects into a tangible form. The result is the film. The properties of either the original concept, form or object are made into an independent end product. As with the alchemist, each particular property possessed by original matter, and every form it can assume, and every desired effect it can exert is personalized, into its own special substance; an independent substance. In this way the allegorical relationship between alchemist and film-maker is not as unlikely as one might think. Each takes an attribute of a given commodity and finds a composite form. Out of the sum of these elements an assumed body is built and within the mixture is the secret of change. The film-maker, like the alchemist, can by his own actions bring about the changes and the result is perceived film which possesses its own character – it is discovered. Many critics of the film shout down this often unplanned alchemic discovery process, but one must turn a deaf ear to them as they turn a blind eye to film. If ever a film was made by a wide-eyed alchemic film-maker it was made by Ron Rice.

Ron Rice and I swapped film reels once and I suppose this made us film brothers. He was one of the strongest and most important of the New American Cinema group, but unfortunately he left only three complete films and one incomplete one when he died from pneumonia at the end of 1964 while he was living and filming in Acapulco in Mexico. He was only twenty-nine and left a wife, Amy, a kid and a few great films. Ron made his first film, *The Flower Thief*, in 1960. It was made in San Francisco and Ron brought it to New York where it stirred a few minds – at least among some ,of the other film-makers. It starred Taylor Mead (a vital member of the New American Cinema) and was dedicated to the extra unknown man (called the 'wild man') who was kept on old Hollywood film sets to 'cook up' something when all else failed. He once wrote: '*The Flower Thief* has been put together in memory of all dead wild men who died unnoticed in the field of stunt.' The film is slow, gentle and dreamy, set in a no-man's-land.

In 1962, still before *Chumlum*, Rice made *Senseless*. It covers a journey to a contemporary land of Oz, in this case the marijuana fields of Mexico. The journey is made up of filmic exploits and themes of playful scenes and more dramatic ones. And so it goes, from the road to the bullfight, to the fields, to make the biggest joint ever. Rice's incomplete film, *The Queen of Sheba Meets the Atom Man*, looked into a different realm. *Chumlum* was his real dream, whereas *The Queen of Sheba* seemed to be directing his magnificent outrage forwards. In a note on the film's first screening he says: 'This is a wild man rough cut like no Hollywood director would dare show the public for fear of having his ideas stolen. We defy anyone to copy our style. . . . This is your opportunity to help challenge the Hollywood stranglehold on morals, expression and art and what have you. Dig us.' Taylor Mead again stars in this film, as a thin hero dragging in a drumful of narcotics. Here also is the vast and massive nudity of the vast and massive Queen of Sheba (all the flesh of Winifred Byran). Between this thin hero and giant woman a series of bizarre and humorous episodes, full of parody and confusion, unravel until all collapse. This Hollywood parody was part of the love/hate relationship with Hollywood that many of the film-makers felt – in some ways like their relationship with comics or Coca-Cola. The title alone suggests this. Ron was not the only one to adopt this attitude, since Andy Warhol was making *Tarzan and Jane Regained, Sort Of* at about the same time. Here the reference of the arts gets crossed with the reference of the more traditional cinema. The Hollywood film becomes like all the other glossy commercial objects around. As with the Pop painters, some of whom made films as well, there was an exaggeration, an intensification and exploration of the object. Just as painters blew up the commercial styles of commercialized objects, so film-makers blew up the styles of Hollywood. The characterization and super-romanticization of the Hollywood films became an everyday mental identity for those who had been brought up on them. Included was a feeling of sentimentality towards these films, and their characters, as much as towards comics and adventure stories. This whole generation of American film-makers had strong associations with the Saturday matinées and serials that were dominant at one time (from the 1930s to the 1950s). Superman had stirred many a kid's mind, and all those Hollywood films had developed a feeling for pure, undaunted heroes. These movies had been part of the environment, as much as Campbell's soup. And, of course, they were now all being seen on television too.

The process of making, as Aristotle suggests, is derived from our mental apprehension of the environment outside ourselves and through the perception of external objects. Hollywood movies as the object, the styles and stars of these films became for many the shape of thinking. But the undaunted heroes and stars were also the mystery of life. They were there and real, yet were an unreality. It was like emptiness and plenty at once; an absurd reality. So the absurdity that seems present in Ron Rice's *The Queen of Sheba Meets the Atom Man*, or in many of Andy Warhol's films such as *Tarzan and Jane Regained, Sort Of*, or in the films of George Kuchar, is often a comment on the absurdity of the commercial Hollywood film. All these films, however, in their exaggeration, become individual entities with their own aesthetics, and form an affirmation of the life round us; poetry with a tender ridicule.

Within the New American Cinema this Hollywood reference constantly appears, in films and film titles, down to the making up of filmstar names such as 'Ingrid Superstar' or 'Mario Montez' (from Maria Montez), though the comparison is valid only in so far as Warhol's painting of Marilyn Monroe has to do with Marilyn Monroe herself. For obvious reasons, not much of this Hollywood reference ever developed in Europe as it did in America. What did develop was the reference to America itself, and when the Hollywood film came to be used there seemed to be a tendency to use bits of Hollywood film, not to create them. One good example is Werner Nekes, possibly the most prolific of the newer independent German filmmakers, who used an 8mm Tarzan film he picked up in London to make an influential film entitled *Operation Tarzan Kampf mit der Gorilla*, complete with Tarzan bellowing on one track.

This idea of using actual bits from shot films already suggests a different set of circumstances and provides a different kind of film from those that developed out of the culture of Hollywood. Before going further, I should mention one film that shows the Hollywood cliché in its own light. This film, one of the most hilarious I have ever seen, is *La Verifica Incerta* by the Italians Gianfranco Baruchello and Alberto Grifi and is composed solely of intercut bits from hundreds of Hollywood films. It also exposes the empty and stylized pattern Hollywood had developed, whatever the subject of the film. *La Verifica Incerta* shows in its juxtapositions that it does not matter if the Ancient Egyptians attacked a cowboy, or if its thousand Red Indians raced from knights of old; that who was shooting whom, or who said 'I love you' to whom, is of no consequence. All the actions, camera movements and narratives were the same, no matter from which film they were taken. The film is a sort of gravestone for Hollywood.

We look at people; we look at things around us. Men look at women, women look at men, men look at men, women look at women. Everyone is looking – even the blind. Watch the people on the bus; watch the couple kiss in the street; watch the girl with her nice bits bare; watch the man eating spaghetti; watch the drunks having a fight; watch television for six hours; see the wind blow the trees; watch your shadow on the ground; watch the ant carry a grain across the miles of your feet; observe the eyes of your enemy or your friend; watch the kids skipping; watch the lights; watch yourself. You select; you relate, you feel; you ignore; you change and each thing becomes a moment in you. You do it every day. Even those masterful people who consider themselves in control in fact select, change and interpret. They do not do this to what is really there, but to what they see. Film-makers do this through their films, as the painter does with his painting. You watch a film too. Do you always think about what you see or about why you see what you see?

> 'I don't paint anymore, I gave it up about a year ago and just do movies now. I could do two things at the same time but movies are more exciting.'
>
> Andy Warhol

With a film by Andy Warhol things are quite simply as they are. In a film like *Empire* we have eight hours of silent observation. The camera sits still, seeing without thinking. The Empire State Building stands tall, all day, as it has stood every day since it was built. It does not move, only the things round it do so. Warhol gives us this reality, this affirmation of actuality in uninterrupted time. The building emerges out of the morning mist, though it is the mist that moves, not the building. The day progresses, through its black-grey-white-grey-black alternations. It is the purest of films, for it is *time* which is film's quality; it is being photographically actual, which is film's property. Warhol is an artist, perhaps the epitome of a whole generation, or the manufactured artist of a hamburger. He was one of the originators of the Pop Art movement. He is the realist of his own environment, the mirror, where others are merely reflectors.

He accepts this world without question, not the abstractness of it, but the objectivity of it, and the people in it – people are very important – 'people are fantastic' he said. He projects an intimacy with things that we have forgotten or ignored. Industrialized and manufactured clichés are the gods of American society. These gods appear everywhere, just as the Greek gods did in Greece and the Christian God does throughout Christianity. Warhol's painting of a soup-tin had the same commercial, manufactured quality as the everyday object itself, and he painted it as a commercial, manufactured, everyday god. His screen paintings of Marilyn Monroe or Jackie Kennedy project images of mass-media goddesses. We see them over and over again; hear about them over and over again; they are like cases full of Coca-Cola bottles, the same ones over and over and over again, or like the money we see and dream of, bank-note after bank-note after bank-note. The objects are statements in themselves; but do not seek explanations from Warhol – things are simply what they are. You may search for cause and effect, but try not to analyse Warhol; rather, look at the society you yourself live in, wherever you may be. And descriptions of Warhol's films tend necessarily to be slight, but very direct. *Kiss* (1964), for instance, consists of a variety of people kissing – nice, long, real kisses – and *Sleep* (1964) covers 6½ hours of a man sleeping, which is about us and about the man sleeping. Why us? Because there is nothing to watch but us. Then there is *Eat* (1963), which projects Robert Indiana eating for 45 minutes, or *Henry Geldzahler* (1965), a 100-minute portrait of Henry Geldzahler smoking a cigar.

As I have said, it is not just the films that are important, but our relationship to them. Some films, by their associative values, make very strong poetic comments. In *13 Most Beautiful Women* (1965) Warhol shows us the faces of thirteen girls. They face the camera; we look at them. Are they beautiful, the most beautiful? (They are!) But there they are. Thirteen totally different kinds of looks, thirteen totally different girls, thirteen individuals, and one tear. During *Couch* (1964) Warhol shows six sequences of about five minutes each, each sequence being a straight full-face view of a couch, and six cameos from the photo-album *à la* Banana Factory-style. With *Poor Little Rich Girl* (1965) the camera watches Edie Sedgwick getting along with her inheritance, moving, with nothing to do, out of focus. She has nothing to do, and nothing much 'happens'. And you think, 'poor little rich girl, your life is so blurred with nothing to do.' This is not just an American boredom, you can see it anywhere where there is a rich class. Warhol's film repertoire, as I mentioned earlier, includes the development of Hollywood as the object, starting with *Tarzan and Jane Regained, Sort Of* (which was actually filmed in Hollywood). The constant sense of the manufactured Hollywood cult of stardom and publicity is the actuality that Warhol himself began to employ. He has created his own cult with its own superstars (Ingrid Superstar, International Velvet, Nico, Ondine and Baby Jane Holzer) and its own publicity. His studio is simply called 'the Factory'. These children of the American multiplicity of tin cans and Hollywood Romance made their 'camp' mirror their own environment, using the manufactured cult names as their own and forming a sound/electronic group called the Velvet Underground. In this way the 'camp' or 'in group' cult of Warhol became their own product by the obsessive play upon the artifacts of the commercial propaganda of the Hollywood cult.

In *Screen Test* (1965) Warhol shows the 'underground' superstar having a 'candid' Hollywood-style screen test. In *Hedy* (1966), Hedy is played by Mario Montez, who is of course a man, and he therefore makes a superstar-woman. *Hedy* is a Hollywood play, full of scenes and takes and talk. ('Mr De Mille said I am the most beautiful woman in the world,' says Hedy.) In the courtroom scene Hedy is accused of making pornographic movies. Thinking she looks too old, she has her nose altered – and then thinks she looks too young. She leaves hospital and starts to sing as in a musical – to the tune of 'Young at Heart' – and so the film goes on, exploring and exaggerating. Hedy refers to herself as 'Mrs Lamarr', thus pointing even more closely at the Hollywood cult and the star system. Similarly, *Harlot* (1965) again has Mario Montez as the Jean Harlow-like superstar. *Harlot* is a fixed image of four people – two on the couch and two behind the camera. Mario, sitting on the couch, eats bananas continuously. The sound over the image is a conversation between three people (Ronald Tavel, Harry Fainlight and Billy Linich) off camera discussing the scene before us. The conversation is apparently random. Tavel: 'Look at her jewels, what would you give to be that cat right now?' Fainlight: 'Banana head.'

Yet Warhol's films are technically beautiful and well made. Though he has many people to help him with the camera lighting, such as Ronald Tavel, and often with scenery, it is he who motivates it all. To some extent he seems to be ultra-conscious of teaching us. The out-of-focus lens is used almost literally to show the blurred and dull life of one girl in *Poor Little Rich Girl,* while in *Camp* (1965) Warhol uses intentionally bad camera work, zooms, pans and all the standard tricks in a film that represents a gathering of 'in' 'underground' stars in a kind of revue. Here the consciousness of technique is apparent in the total neglect of technique. He does not edit. When a film reel ends, you see it end. If Kodak put perforations in the film you see the perforation. Things are shown as they are shot, with the sync-sound films. The sound is recorded as it happens, with off-screen talking and the noise of the running camera. But I can hear some people shouting that it is not 'professional'. What does 'professional' mean? It seems to represent isolated cults that develop in one way only in order to keep themselves safe. Yet all ways are valid if they are possible. Warhol's ways are many, and to list all the films he has made would take up many pages. In one year alone he made fifty-two films, a film a week (though many have never been seen). Some people have divided Warhol's films into different periods: a period for those based on long takes, including *Eat*, *Empire* and *Harlot*; or a period based on situations and 'dramas' from scenarios written mostly by Ronald Tavel, such as *Vinyl* (1965), *Horse* or *The Life of Juanita Castro* and so forth.

Of all these films, the one that became a major catalyst between the 'underground' and the overground is *Chelsea Girls* (1966). I say catalyst because this film uses the uncompromising language of the unemotional, unaltered direct camera, the language of selected *cinéma vérité*, the language of the drama and the language of the new expanded cinema. In many ways, *Chelsea Girls* ties up with John Cage's idea of art as 'an affirmation of life – not an attempt to bring order out of chaos nor to suggest improvements in creation, but simply a way of waking up to the very life we are living. . . .'

Though it is not Warhol's single film masterpiece, it is his major attempt to cause an explosion in film and seeing. It is vital because it sheds the mask that traditional cinema has built for us.

Chelsea Girls deals with people, and it is through people that we reach other people. It is a 3½-hour, two-screen trip through a contemporary heaven and hell. Events occur in various rooms in the Hotel Chelsea in New York and the film reveals a whole gallery of complex or simple people – lesbians, drug-addicts, homosexuals, hard girls, soft girls, sex and social sadists. They pass you, you come into the middle of their scene and go out in the middle. The fragments within each room overlap into the next, thanks to the two-screen, two-image projection. The film develops into the life of a hung-up generation lost in the empty heritage left by the middle-class values of their world. The figures who appear in the film are not actors, and if they are aware of the camera and try to act they are only real people trying to act. In one scene the 'Pope' (played by Bob 'Ondine' Olivo) is taking 'true confessions', pressing questions about God and life on to a girl. This becomes a penetrating free form, offering associations of ideas. The sense of their lives comes across. Later the 'Pope' is alone, the camera is on. There is no one to question. Remember 'the Pope' is only Ondine. He gets bored, or lost. He shouts to off camera – what should he do next? He breaks down and blows up. It is real. Through the simultaneous and continuous rhythm of these lives the camera may wander or zoom in to details: close-up on a hand; momentary glimpses of people; or the camera remains frozen and the people unravel in front of it; or people pass by it; or without anyone in view voices are heard talking to someone in view. The two screens may show different scenes or two versions of a single scene; the sound will sometimes come from one screen, sometimes from the other. The film is black and white. It bursts into colour, then has black and white juxtaposed with colour; then black and white against black and white. You can no longer relax with reassuring clichés. In *Chelsea Girls* the camera becomes Virgil and takes us through an Inferno. Warhol is not there, he is remote and uninvolved. His sole action was to put the camera there. The fragments of lives are blown up, projected and structured in their own film time. It is something that only film can do; the preconceptions come later.

To those who use commercial success as a criterion, *Chelsea Girls* was that too. It certainly made those money-bags jump and many people tried to buy it. That's the way it goes – they ignore it, or trample on it, but if it breaks through, they try to buy it. *Chelsea Girls* grossed $10,000 to $15,000 a week during its run.

Film has many qualities. The simple fixed camera on an image. The image can be human: a face; a hand; even a foot; it can be a tree. When it is captured on film, the slightest and subtlest movement can tell a story. You look at someone, say across a room; he is unaware of you, then you see him clench his fist: he has tensed up. You notice from your window that the leaves on a tree are still; they start to move and you know a wind is blowing. You look

at a face: the eyelids droop slightly, the face relaxes and you sense the onset of sleepiness. The smallest movement can change a whole expression, a whole meaning. When you are talking to someone the slightest change can change the mood and your feelings. Perhaps that is why some people dislike the telephone – you cannot watch them as they speak, so is what they are saying what they mean? Seeing is confirmation. This is film. Even the longest movement is made up of fractions of movement. A single frame flashing past, seen only for a twenty-fourth of a second, leaves us with an impression on our brain. Each has its own meaning. Each movement can be isolated; can be repeated; can be combined with another movement. Each combination of movement can be juxtaposed with a single movement; can be linked with scale, with colour, with direction, with sound, with words, with blank space.

There is a film-maker called Werner Nekes. He is from Hamburg, he is married to Dore O who made *Alaska* and has worked with Nekes on other films. As we have seen, he is a very prolific film-maker, and also a painter. He once told me that he wanted to make films in which the audience would have no points of reference for what they saw. He wanted to put them into the position of being like children again, so that they could see in a fresh and uninhibited way without the intellectual patter, the filters and the pseudoisms. So in his film *Jüm-Jüm* (1967), made with Dore O, he uses a fixed camera and a simple movement – a girl on a swing, seen in profile. The movement develops by fragmentation. Normally the movement of someone swinging is a simple back and forth arc. By fragmenting this simple arc one creates pieces of movement, which become separate movements. These fragments are juxtaposed to form a new relationship. We know that if someone is on a swing which is up in the air it will come down in the same continuous arc in which it swung up in the first place. If the film is cut and reassembled – by editing (splicing together) – so that a later part of a movement occurs before an earlier part of the same movement, that normal movement suddenly seems to go backwards and then leap forward. A simple rhythm and movement develops into a new rhythm and movement. The change does not seem as dry and academic as it does when described. In

Jüm-Jüm the girl on the swing flies up, hesitates, goes up and up and back and embarks on further rhythms. Our normal visual association to the swing and the simple arc is broken. The girl on the swing turns into a staccato movement, a light/colour symbol of movement. We become detached from the girl and can see only visual rhythms.

I keep thinking that film-makers use editing in a hundred different ways. For some it is a primary consideration, for some a secondary consideration, for others, like Warhol, it doesn't count at all. In many ways film-editing in film is like the work of a composer. Each frame is like a note, each combination of frames is like a chord. These chords can be composed into a chamber piece, as in Nekes's work, or orchestrated into a symphony, as in Stan Brakhage's. To me there seems to be a great similarity between music and film. Remember Abel Gance's statement: 'Cinema is the music of light.' Think too of the films of Len Lye, Norman McLaren and Oskar Fischinger, who structure their films directly according to the rhythms of music and sound. The rather staccato act of editing can be used not only to break down one movement but to repeat and alternate various thoughts to form a simulated structure. Good examples here are the Italian Guido Lombardi's 8mm film *Sviluppo Nr. 2*, or the American Carl Linder's *Detonation* (1966) or *Skin*, or some of the films of Kurt Kren. Often instead of physically editing the film material, these film-makers edit the film as they shoot.

Let's get back to Werner Nekes. His films vary in the complexity of their visual structure and force and he also tends to use strong contrasting sounds as a counterpoint to the image. His *Schwarzhuhnbraunhuhnschwarzhuhnweisshuhnrothuhnweiss oder Put – Putt* (Black Chick, Brown Chick, White Chick, Red Chick, White or Put – Putt, 1967) is built round a structure that is akin to a sound poem. This structure consists of the staccato sound 'put – putt' and the staccato movements of a chicken pecking at food. The model for this film runs as follows:

Put	Put	Put	Put	Put
	Put	Put	Put	
		Put		
Put	Put	Put	Put	Put
		Putt		
	Putt		Putt	
	Putt		Putt	
		Putt		

The 'puts' are the chicken gradually eating away at the seed. The camera shoots up through a piece of glass, on top of which is the seed and the chicken. At first you see only the seed (the five 'puts'), but as the seed is eaten up the chicken appears (the diminishing 'puts' to the final single 'put'). The 'putt' sound is the chicken without his head in the snow (*one* sudden cut to this). The dying chicken's movements are represented by the separated 'putt putt', until it is dead – the final 'putt'.

Another of Nekes's films contains no editing (remember, there are no rules!). *Gurtrug Nr. 2* (1967) is a split-screen film, requiring two projectors, one with sound, the other silent. The two reels running on the two projectors essentially convey the same images – a crowd of people in a field gradually getting up until halfway through the film the field is empty. Then it all runs backwards and we see an empty field with people getting down until the field is crowded with people. The second reel starts with an empty field, which becomes a crowded one half-way through and empties again. The two projections occur simultaneously, not side by side as in Warhol's *Chelsea Girls,* but one above the other. Instead of the usual rectangle, here the images are a V shape. The top one is a proper V and the bottom one an upside-down V. The two together make an X. The two reels pass each other in the middle where, for just one frame, they are opposite each other.

One young film-maker, talking about how he began making films, explained that he was initially involved with sculptural themes in both painting and sculpture, with, as he put it, 'making objects'. He ended up using linoleum as his primary material. He would lay the lino out on the floor and cut various shapes from it. But he got to the point where he was no longer sure whether the shapes he had cut out or the cut-up bit of linoleum were his 'object'. This confusion forced him to look away, to look out of the window and then back to his 'work'. But he spent more and more time looking out of the window. His perception of the differing realities of 'outside' and 'inside' led him to think about the possibilities offered by film. The change from 'outside' to 'inside' and the movement from one to the other could surely be done with film? His initial intuition was confirmed when he saw Michael Snow's *Wavelength,* a film which, as we have seen, moves through an interior space to an exterior space. It was this film, more than anything else, that gave him the courage to pursue his own interest in film.

This basic attitude towards film results from a simple and direct action (perception) of moving from one point to another. A film is primarily a series of individual images repeated in a constant flux. Even a so-called static image, projected in a fixed duration of time, is repeated, fragmented and transformed by the brain cells. By repeated association the fragmented pieces of one image or an accumulation of different images develop movement. Even the most seemingly alien images can be related by their particular association within the framework of a film. The artist selects an image or images from his own particular world and from his way of seeing. When his particular vision is presented to us, it becomes our particular vision for us; the experience of the artist's vision, in the form in which he presents it to us, becomes associated with our own particular visual process; it becomes part of our experience. This is the way we learn. 'We must learn from others how to see,' said Stanley Burnshaw (quoting J. Z. Young).[2]

The brain is no simple recording system. Many of our affairs are conducted on the assumption that our sense organs provide us with an accurate record, independent of ourselves. What we are now beginning to realize is that much of this is an illusion; that we have to learn to see the world as we do. Perception is no longer understood as a passive relationship between the viewer and what he views. So much does the process involve action on the part of the viewer that elements entirely outside the objects and events before him will influence and sometimes even determine what is seen.

It is often a very difficult matter to allow this process of discovery or experience to occur. A number of explanations have been given for this, on the scientific, psychological or philosophical level. I see the problem as the need to avoid all preconceptions of what something should be. Some people will not act without knowing where they are going, or what they can expect. They are conditioned to the result, thinking they know what it will be. They project results as already experienced into each action they are faced with, and in this way think they know where they are going. Risk, failure or confusion are apparently eliminated. Yet their results merely echo the past. They have a preconception that a particular object should be represented by a particular image. This too becomes a projection of a received or taught symbol, not necessarily a symbol acquired by experience. It is undoubtedly easier to exist in this way, since it avoids change and readjustment, confusion and effort. It also permits control, restraint: you know where you are and you know who you are – at least you think you do, probably because you are static enough to see your whole frozen frame.

Social and religious conditioning constantly diminishes experience by telling you what things are or should be. It narrows and limits experience and separates pieces of life into little totalities; it has separated the mind, body and soul; it has gradually reduced each individual physiological system to a few responses that allow the individual to cope with stimuli (often called nerve conduction). If the number of reference-points is limited, only a few stimuli can be accepted. When large amounts of stimuli are presented, or stimuli that are seemingly alien to any of the response references one has developed, a disharmony or confusion arises. In order to reinstate harmony some simply go to sleep, others become bored, others go away, still others erupt into violent outbursts or maintain a stony silence. When witnessing new films with new imagery, some people completely deny the right of such imagery to exist, calling it wrong or bad or evil. When the reference-points increase, thanks to greater access to the process of experience, the ability to cope with more and more stimuli also increases. Everyone responds differently to a single thing, has different experiences, learns different things, goes in a different direction.

The exhilarating feeling of discovering and experiencing something new is, for me, the greatest form of individual freedom. I have been to many film shows where people leave a few minutes after the beginning; where people mock and destroy the work; and yet at the same shows I have seen people cry because they are moved by the poetry of the experience. The experiences vary: some films make the retina boggle, others offer rhythmic sensations, others are heroic exploits or unravel like a voyage into inner visions.

A film like David Larcher's *Mare's Tail* (1969) is an epic of flight into inner space. It is a 2¾-hour visual accumulation in colour, the film-maker's personal odyssey, which becomes the odyssey of each of us. It is a man's life transposed into a visual realm, a realm of spirits and demons, which unravel as mystical totalities until reality fragments. Every movement begins a journey. There are spots before your eyes, as when you look at the sun that flames and burns. We look at distant moving forms and flash through them. We drift through suns; a piece of earth phases over the moon. A face, your face, his face, a face that looks and splits into shapes that form new shapes that we rediscover as tiny monolithic monuments. A profile as a full face. The moon again, the flesh, the child, the room and the waves become part of a hieroglyphic language.

Mare's Tail is a real 'trip': it flies, swims and moves from point to point; the lines move into shapes which move into orbits and your eyes water with the swirling colours. What each of us can see is more than what we do see. The film becomes one of the most vital penetrations into the experience of seeing, and can be ranged alongside Brakhage's *Art of Vision* as a classic in film perception. Ranging from the abstract to the figurative, it also explores the subjective responses of Larcher himself to his own life and to his personal visual experiences. This is combined with an impressive exploitation of the potential of an expressive, tactile material, a physical exploration that is possible only with the film camera. The list of methods explored in this film reads like a glossary of experimental techniques; it is an archetype of film expression creating a subjective environment. The movement of lines, the slow animation combined with a placid zoom and twist become like fragments of thought. There are also back projections refilmed. The refilmed negative colour film (filmed back on to colour negative) alters the colour subtleties of the film.

Larcher sometimes processed the film material himself, altering the normal methods as he did so and thus creating new textural and visual relationships. The photographed images form an intertextural spatiality set in motion. A good example of this is his film of his two children, Anchor and Karen, dressed as prince and princess, processing through the streets of London (with Anchor carrying a film reel as a sceptre) and then down the wide avenue through Kensington Park Gardens. Shot with a long-focus lens, the children's romping walk seems like a joyous procession of the Magi. This allusion, overlaid with the film texture of toned and sepia cotton hailstones, forms a new world in a new space. The camera chases the children through the gardens with a wide-eyed lens – the cotton hailstones gone – and they disappear underfoot and race out from the side, springing up ahead small, and disappear underfoot again, seemingly drawn by an elastic band.

The image is transformed into rapid, succulent sexual movement: eye, mouth, face, penis, sweat, gestures. The camera focuses on the full stomach of a woman, round and stressed even further with the wide-angle lens. Jewelled hands roll across the tight flesh. A baby is born. Images of other places are interspersed: flocks of birds with birds superimposed, scratching in wild fury, contrasted with turtles, dragged from the sea and lying helplessly on their backs but still laying eggs. We range from the birth of a human being to the death of a fly. As the fly dies it seems like a giant struggling in a spotlight, experiencing human suffering. As the camera soars away, the dead fly becomes finite in a man's world. Black and white; colour, solarization; fragmented movement, pulverizing of emulsion; the long and timeless light of the sun, the moon, a face, a light bulb, and the long endless corridors of man moving forward. A face reappears constantly. Sometimes it is Larcher's face. Or a death mask that splits. A schizophrenic face that looks out, then becomes a profile, then looks in. It comes apart and then is joined together again. It floats and is held. It is thought and then action. The face of a girl: smiling, talking, light and fresh, then greying as if a cloud were passing right through the film. There is also a bat and there is also the light. The light goes on, flashing like lightning, radiates, disappears, flashes and recycles. It is seen, then not seen (in a mirror), but remains in the mind. At another point, a girl is sitting on some steps. You approach. Her legs spread and your hand goes in. Two girls blending their flesh. Fusion; touch lightly; the camera follows, tap, pat, flick, flip, tickle, scratch. One girl prostrate; the eye flying over her, way up, aerial view. A landscape, slightly defused in high-key monochrome with one darker spot. Dive for the spot. In. Safe. A dream, a wish, a truth, an actuality.

Mare's Tail is an important film because it expresses life. It follows Paul Klee's idea that a visually expressive piece adds 'more spirit to the seen' and also 'makes secret visions visible'. Like other serious films and works of art, it keeps on seeking and seeing, as the film-maker does, as the artist does. It follows the transience of life and nature, studying things closely, moving into vast space, coming in close again. The course it follows is profoundly real and profoundly personal: Larcher's trip becomes our trip to experience. It cannot be watched impatiently, with expectation; it is no good looking for generalization, condensation, complication or implication.

Mare's Tail (which was made possible by the unpretentious support of Alan Power) was probably the first British-made film to grope towards this encompassing sense of sure vision, and is one of the best of its kind and size in the world. Larcher has no theories. If he undergoes any influences, these seem to be the 'I Ching' hypnagogic imagery and some of John Cage. At one point on the soundtrack, Cage's voice incessantly asks, 'Am I a butterfly?' from the phrase 'Am I a man or am I a butterfly?'. The question echoes onwards. The real influence, however, is Larcher himself, who roves and discovers his own world, a world without the constrictions of our world. This is the essence of the film and makes it unique. It is a freedom desired by many, feared by most and intellectualized by others. It helps us understand the freedom found in many films made by other film-makers.

Very few films have had such a profound effect on me as Jack Smith's *Flaming Creatures*, made in 1962/3 in New York. I feel that it belongs in the realm of films that become like monuments to visual (and film) language. It is a film made with the kind of honesty that penetrates the false barriers society encases us in, and because of that, it goes deep. Because of that it also provokes the chastisement of the social cross-bearers. For me, it is one of the strongest visual poems ever made and represents one of the few successful translations of fantasy to film. For the police, for the film critics, for the politicians and for the guardians of lies it became the film to crucify. It provoked arrests, confiscation and legal battles, resembling in this such films as *L'Âge d'Or* or *Un Chant d'Amour* or Manet's painting *Déjeuner sur l'Herbe* or Stravinsky's *The Rite of Spring*. Such personal and creative honesty shakes our social stupor and conjures up our fear.

Flaming Creatures moves through a transvestite twilight among the 'lotus-eaters' and the 'dreamers of dreams', through the cult of Hollywood phantoms, through the romance of celluloid, through the 'pop' world of advertising copy, through the symbols of sex, rebirth and sorcery into the amazing world of film. How can we really describe it? Long, hand-scrolled titles. Murky tones, with some figures from an imaginary Saturday matinée serial. An inner world. Old music like an old soundtrack. A girl in Spanish black in one corner of the screen, behind her a beautifully simple, painted background. Her lips smacking lipstick. Then bodies entwined and wrapped in their own abstraction, in their own rapture and their lipstick. Men putting on lipstick, while the camera drifts about. A woman. Legs where heads should be. A face smears lipstick heavily on lips; a penis hangs over one shoulder. The sound of a monotonous voice reading, dry, endless sales talk intoning the benefits of lipstick. A painted face swimming in lipstick moves while the eyes roll in its head. Posed, costumed figures like an old photograph from Morocco; thinking figures from some far-away dream becoming part of the present. Flatly lit, baroque in pattern, decorative grey in film. A sun-bleached, grey-white, sheet-like background. A fly hangs on the sheet. All else sleeps. The fly seems to be hanging eternally in a noon-day sun, waiting untiring, and patient. Then a buxom lady in black races by. The camera holds on the swaying background and a man/woman follows, chasing our lady. He/she wears a white (but sun-greyed) dress; a Turkish-style hat; a masculine face wearing lipstick. The chase continues. He/she catches her, then three figures hold her. He/she from behind while alien men/women suck her sides. Rage, rape and hairy paws; the arched female body screaming. A gloved hand delicately (with thumb and forefinger) reaches for the breast. Untied dress, pop-out breast; rape. The breast, hanging out, in a screaming, dreamy rage, making images that occur only behind the eyelids on a hot day. On the floor, more figures bedazzle and bedeck the frame, and themselves. Up black dress and her legs spread out while the figures hang from her as if for their life. We see it as if it was reflected in a misty mirror, somewhere else looking down. A sandy screaming pit. Figures move in, like chameleons. A rape in a hot snowstorm. The camera shakes, caught

I

in the same storm. A black iron chandelier shakes. The group gropes. The figures become enchanted with fantasy lust, human beings turned into hypnotized myths. A cloud dream and not a nightmare; not hard, but always an opium-high softness. The figures, having assuaged their lust, fall into exhausted sleep. A long sleep. The lady in black, the last remaining person, her breast still hanging, staggers and swoons wearily into sleep.

Still in misty image a grey old woman cuddles the lady in black. An old woman from somewhere else. Is she a vampire? Then from a coffin another creature rises. Struggling at first, a face in a male–female confusion adjusts itself to awakening. This crêpe-paper doll, awake among the other sleeping creatures, writhes to awaken them. A homoerotic, lacy awakening, where the film's frame reshapes like a cloud rising dreamily. So, without morality and without the brickwall rationale that stops others from living, the creatures live again. They move quickly as the blood flows. The whole ensemble moves into a dance, which expands into an intersexual fiesta. Joy of living, no questions asked, as the Spanish dance music plays on.

Flaming Creatures is great, and uninhibited: a film without tension, with no feeling of compulsion, a film that seems to happen of its own accord. A subconsciousness presented and realized, relating to life. We think of ourselves as 'civilized' and rational, but we are still dreamers, creatures of hidden mysteries and feeling. We very often suppress this but when someone or something comes and releases some of it for us it becomes our opium. It relates to those hidden (and feared) abstractions and the unknown composition of our instincts. It is that part that creates our myths; our sensations; our hopes; our weaknesses, but most of all our strengths. We appear to be the only creatures to have this and without fear it becomes our poetry.

Technical eminence as opposed to freedom of expression and content has become in many circles the criterion of a film's value. A set of defined technical values has developed with film because of its dependence upon machinery, chemistry, optics and light. This has blinded viewers and film-makers alike to expression and personality. Technical stylization and values are readily accepted because they put one in a position from which one can easily determine a particular quality. Reaching a presupposed technical level also displays, for easy evaluation, a proficiency that can be objectively equated to achievement (reaching something that is set). Yet creative expression, although not without regard for technical achievement, seldom follows the rules. It goes beyond, around or through them, but it is never confined to them.

The great photographer, Bill Brandt, did not produce his nude masterpieces by following the technical 'rights' and 'wrongs' laid down by the manual. He made his pictures without technical hang-ups and according to the necessity of his expression and particular feelings. The same can be said for almost all great artists. Joyce did not follow the dictates of English language composition, nor did the Impressionists follow the dictates of academic rendering.

Those of us who have studied greatness in the arts and the sciences must be aware of individuals who, having freed themselves from outmoded technical forms, have gone on to fulfil themselves in their particular field of activity. It is my belief that all the technical rules are often maintained by the real professional amateurs.

The quality of the film material in *Flaming Creatures* is part of the expression. The overexposed images, the diffusion, the greyness are as much a part of the people and their features as toes are to feet. If all the so-called technical mastery of Hollywood were introduced the mystery would be gone: the painted backdrop would become a painted backdrop and not the world of Jack Smith. Some people may think that if a film does not have this technical proficiency the film-maker has not worked hard enough; others use technical jargon and skill to set themselves apart and create an ethos. One critic wrote recently that Warhol's films are getting better because they are becoming technically more proficient, and that, to him, makes them more acceptable. Yet only too often this business of resorting to technicalities becomes an excuse for the film-maker's inability to express himself freely, or his fear of doing so.

So Jack Smith has followed up his own particular direction as other film-makers and artists have followed up theirs. And because he did so we have the beautiful *Flaming Creatures*. I believe that this is the only underground film to have been put on trial in New York. At the Third Experimental Film Festival in Belgium it had to be hidden in something like a Walt Disney tin, and was prevented from general showing at the festival (though it was eventually shown privately to the jury). It won *'le prix spécial du film maudit'* and eventually had to be brought back secretly to the United States. Copies of the film are known to have been pirated, while other copies have been confiscated by the authorities. Someone who was giving a course on witchcraft at the New School for Social Research in New York actually used *Flaming Creatures* as an example of the witchcraft myth (ethos). (On hearing this, Jack began to attend the weekly lectures to find out why.) Perhaps he is a magician. He did after all play the magician in Ron Rice's *Chumlum*. But then he also appeared in Rice's *The Queen of Sheba meets the Atom Man*, in Warhol's *Dracula Movie, Camp* and *Batman*, in Ken Jacobs's *Star Spangled to Death*, Bill Vehr's *Brothel*, Naomi Levine's *Jeremelu* and Piero Heliczer's *Joan of Arc*.

After *Creatures* Smith shot *Normal Love*. He never edited it and it has been seen only as rushes. As such it laid the foundations for an epic, camp, cult, pop, fantasy festival. To some extent it is an extension of *Flaming Creatures*, but with remarkable colour, full of brilliance and gestures. Certain scenes and actions have remained permanently in my memory: chorus girls (both real and drag) on top of a cake in a meadow; Beverly Grant with a snake as the cobra woman; green light filtered through leaves; a sunny blue-white Roman bath-like scene; ancient Hollywood decadence relived; a mummy slipping, and flowering, and the chase to rape in the swamp; the richness of the imagery and the strength of the filming. Very few film-makers have ever combined such lucid fantasy with the joy of pageantry.

Jack Smith's vein has sometimes been recreated, in image or in mood, by other film-makers. Sometimes the same context and content have been used, before or after Smith used them, or at the same time. Cocteau, Buñuel and Genet are without a doubt related to him in psychic moods and visual lucidity; Warhol, of course, in the camp element; and Ron Rice with his pageantry. The Italian film-maker Antonio De Bernardi resembles Smith in the way he expresses and elaborates on fantasy. His films (usually on 8mm) are colourful insights into the free-running mind. His images, too, are creatures of his imagination, but they are not the transvestite creatures found in Smith's work. It is more as though part of Dante lived inside his head, and he transfers people in his life into his own *'inferno'* or *'paradisio'*.

Films such as *Il Bestiario* (The Bestiary) (for four screens and three sounds) or *Lune e Piena di Fiume* (Moons and Fullness of the River) (for two or three screens) are only two examples of his personal expression. Many of his films use up to four screens. *Il Bestiario* as the title suggests, takes the form of a fantasy human zoo. It is projected on overlapping screens to form a flower-like pattern, each screen having its images, sometimes seen in close-up, sometimes in long group shots. When projected simultaneously these images increase the surface depth to create an even stronger sense of dream.

It is particularly hard to describe De Bernardi's films, because they are almost totally dependent on a juxtaposition of selected images. The people in the films are painted, decorated, distorted, arranged, lit or grouped according to De Bernardi's personal fantasy. Each of the images presents its own narrative: taken together, with multiple projections on top, the images form a film cosmogony. The titles alone reveal the mythological inspiration that underlies his films and is developed in them. Others, such as *Dei*

(Gods), *Il Vaso Etrusco* (The Etruscan Vase), *Il Sogno di Constantino* (Constantine's Dream), . . . *E i Giardini di Artura R* (. . . And the Gardens of Arthur R) or *Fregio* (Frieze), all made between 1967 and 1969, show the basic mood with which De Bernardi's films begin.

Even more fascinating, almost all of De Bernardi's films come across on 8mm, both in the making and in the projection, and without losing a thing. They are all the richer because they do not depend on superficial treatment but are original and sincere expressions. De Bernardi really is sincere, believing in what he is doing and believing that what he is doing means something. He tries to illustrate Buñuel's statement: 'The cinema seems to have been invented for the expression of the subconscious, so profoundly is it rooted in poetry.' Unfortunately, very few people are able or willing to see De Bernardi's films. Yet during a film show at which only six people turned up he took great pains to make the show just right and when one person said that she liked the films his face lit up with joy.

Like many other film-makers whose work is rarely seen, De Bernardi has to work elsewhere for his living (by teaching literature) and to use his friends, his family and his own meagre finances to make his films. As a person he is gentle; as a film-maker a poet. He began with *Il Mostro Verde* (The Green Monster, 1967) a two-screen colour film on 16mm, made with Paolo Menzio. From there he went on to better things. Of his film *Dei* (a film within time, necessarily endless) he wrote:

GODS, a film within time, necessarily endless. By Antonio De Bernardi, 1968, 8mm, 18f/s, 150' and more.

. . . that dwells in Sardis
but her soul is near us.

And then went down to the ship, set keel to breakers, forth on the godly sea, and we set up mast and sail on that swart ship, it is the film of my life earthly and not. I Antonio De Bernardi living more recently in Turin Where one tries to compose the day. And with the eye the left looking at the high and elsewhere also But always feeling inanity! Oh heart! Oh hope! And it having happened that born at the time of may's end I, here find myself as I must tell the fury of the years thrice ten and one, in via accademia albertina 21, tel. 876455
born of the will to piece together that which naturally shattered and putrefaction accompanies love TO FLY WITHER THE CALL SPEAKS,
it is the flowing of us turbid and almost still large river,
it is music concord to lines and spelling out that is ad infinitum and following the humours,
it is vision from below of that which golden in the high & alive, REACHING THEREFORE THE LIMIT OF THE FLOOD'S OVERFLOW AND DOUBLING THE FIRES OF THE EXCITED
so the marriage of sky and earth hopeless affection and never regained: as I

am going one day thru the roads of greece, the dream was given to me and
the vision I NARRATE THE FABLE, and the becoming
and so gentlemen I ask of you to assist me who little and poor at one time
knocked on every door UNTO THE LAST FRAME FOR THE RETURN
OF THE FIRST
and having I with me in the world my wife Mariella and as companions
those who by the earthly name Massimo-Pia-Adamo I them accompany,
I THEY FORGETFUL – CONCORDANT THIS OUR PASSAGE
and so from the night of times as a long coloured tape-worm Is this present
film to awaken from the black every possible love and so in sweet bouquet
these loves on a red perfumed pyre They all simultaneous in a long agony
burning,
and there come also the names of ANGLEA MARIO LUCIANA
GIORGIO EMMA CESARE LORIS ANTONIO RINA MARI' MINO
SILVIA GABRIELLA MARZIA CRISTINA CECILIA PIERA
SANDRO RENZO LAURA MARCO CARLO ALIDA HEINZ
ELJANA IOPPI ALFIERI ROBERTO GIGI ANNA CLAUDIO
GABRIELE FRANCA OSCAR SERGIO MARA GIGLIOLA PAOLO
IDA LUIGI et etiam Mauro particulare modo
so THE PURE IN HEART AND THE FREE MEN AND THOSE WHO
HAVE GOOD WILL
to these it is dedicated
! FEAR AND HOPE ARE: VISION!

I shall probably find myself accused of rampant self-indulgence with my
exhaltation to poetics – especially in this technocratic age where the term
'synaesthetics' is used for 'poetics'. If I used such a new word, would you
be any happier? Still, I mean those good old real feelings. The feelings
conjured up by *Flaming Creatures* make me think almost immediately of
Genet's film *Un Chant d'Amour*, which occasionally reappears as part of a
programme sold as a sex show, and our perverted society still classifies it as
an erotic film. As with so many films that dwell honestly on personal aspects
of sexuality and in which genitals sometimes appear, it is banished to this
unlawful world of sex; all too often it is subsequently sought after by
drooling gentlemen (and the police). If you have not actually seen *Un
Chant d'Amour*, descriptions of it translate in current terminology as
something verging on pornography or, at least, a sensational and perverted
(abnormal) sexuality. The values that underlie this description still belong
to the realm of ideas which says that you should tie a little boy's hands when
he is asleep so that he can't play with himself.
    Genet's *Un Chant d'Amour* does stir up and provoke these same taboos,
because it treats personal, subjective and erotic imagery without shame and
without fear. To me, the erotic is part of poetry since it pertains to and
comes from love. *Un Chant d'Amour* is a dream of love developed as a film,
the reality of its actions evolving as a filmed dream. *Un Chant d'Amour* is
the homosexual involvement of lonely men: not any men, but imprisoned
men who, in their loneliness and their frustration, find that their only human

contact is with each other and with themselves. The flesh they can touch is their own bodies, and it is through their own bodies that they project their fantasies. In their loneliness they dream and enact the urges of their sex. The viewer, if he is honest, watches and becomes involved in the prisoners' (and the guard's) subjective release. Moving from cell to cell we see a man dancing with a tattooed girl on his arm; two prisoners, using a straw poked between the wall of their cells, sensually inhaling and blowing smoke to each other in the symbolic intercourse of two people who can never see each other; or a Negro prisoner in white trousers sensually swaying his body with his penis hanging out. These are some of the intense worlds that unravel as we pass by, moving from man's inner loneliness to his natural desires. Structurally, our viewpoint is that of the guard. Yet we can also watch the guard, as he himself becomes involved in the reality and the desires confronting him. He becomes part of the involvements and himself fantasizes about the prisoner he is watching. One prisoner is having a day-dream about being with another prisoner, outside in some field, free from prison. The guard, in his own frustration, enters the prisoner's cell, and the tension over making direct physical contact results in his shoving his gun into the prisoner's mouth. This confrontation, apparently the only physical contact between two people, breaks the dream. Another day is marked off on the calendar on the wall.

Un Chant d'Amour is not a coherent narrative. Instead it is a lucid and sensual experience created by a visual portrayal. Not a word is spoken and, in its original form, the film is totally silent. It is merely through film, through the soft blending of tonal qualities, through slow and close-up movements of face and flesh or through suggestive actions and vantage-points that this poem is related. This is poetry peculiar to film, for no other medium can combine these necessary tonal and light qualities with movements and direct imagery. In this form, with this material, direct narration is no longer important. What is important is that this combination of elements with the personal feelings of the film-maker unravels a visual gesture that is part of man's spirit and subconscious. Subconscious iconography, if you like, but also its own reality. As iconography it provokes and creates its own images, which are also within us. In this way, too, it is poetry, for it provokes a real feeling and not a studied intellectualization. Perhaps the reason why films such as *Un Chant d'Amour* or *Flaming Creatures* cause such distress and even fear and hatred in so many people is that they so instantly become an iconography for our own subconscious, unrestricted by our conditioned power of reason. This is true of most independent subjective films. The viewer can no longer cope with them by judging them by means of a received system of values, since they reach his nervous system before they are grasped by his intellect. This is the basis of the films' magic. When sex and sensuality are portrayed openly, the social discomfort the viewer experiences is dispensed with by quickly taking surface elements and slotting them into the easy pigeonholes of 'filth', 'pornography', 'abnorm-

ality'. Once they are safely tucked away in the pigeonhole they can be dealt
with when needed and peered at once in a while with curiosity.

The often severe controls laid upon film seem to me to be related to an
identification of visual forms of art with magic and mythology. The human
mind will very readily equate a symbol, an iconograph, a representation with
a 'real' experience, one becoming as valid as the other. The visual arts in
general have always been one of man's prime ways of creating symbols, and
film in particular has probably been the strongest image-making force in our
contemporary world. This is clearly because it can set recognizable symbols
in motion and place them in time, thus creating experiences that can
easily be fused with actual physical time and the life about us. This relationship to actual experience is the general process that underlies mythical
thought. According to Cassirer:

> Myth lives entirely by the presence of its object – by the intensity with
> which it seizes and takes possession of consciousness in a specific moment.
> Myth lacks any means of extending the moment beyond itself, of looking
> ahead of it or behind it, of relating it as a particular to the elements of
> reality as a whole. Instead of the dialectical movement of thought, in which
> every given particular is linked with other particulars in a series and thus
> ultimately subordinated to a general *law* and process, we have here a mere
> subjection to the *impression itself and its momentary presence.*[3]

In other words, myth or mythical thought involves taking an object, impression or action out of the context of the general flow and interchange of
all the elements of daily life. With mythical consciousness a part is taken as
a whole. The whole becomes its own experience, and like the name of a
person repeated endlessly it becomes the embodiment and the particular
experience of that person. But also: 'The image like the word is endowed
with real forces. It not only represents the thing for the subjective reflection
of a third party, an observer; it is part of its reality and efficacy. A man's
image like his name is an alter ego: what happens to the image happens to
the man himself.' Film is image; and each film is an object or impression
where everything is crowded together on a single plane to make a single
entity. Films can (and do) become an alter ego of living reality. As Chinese
philosophers might put it, the image houses the soul of what it represents
and is that reality itself. The process of creating imagery seems to demand
that we should isolate an object or event and translate it into word or image.

Our relationship to the symbolic object or experience, with the strong
emotional element it involves, explains the nature of our relationship to
film. When a film dwells on areas of personal inadequacy or social inhibition, the experience is real enough to provoke fears and to make us want
to switch off from that experience. It can also realize unfulfilled experiences
or desires, or can allow us to feel as though we were undergoing new
experiences, though such experiences are mere myth or fantasy. Films that
satisfy the unfulfilled experiences (dreams) of a frustrated group elevate

them, through the iconography of the experience, to an elation that is outside the ordinary realm of their life. It isolates the experience for them so that they can feel it as something complete in itself. So, like a drug, they want it.

It is easier for the average person to cope with the more hallucinatory and simple experiences. When experiences brought by film are associated with the more abstract and complex portions of the human system, they as it were become the reincarnation of these complexities.. They can embody the poetics of the self, but on the other hand they can also embody fears, prejudices and superstitions. If the film experience seems real, and yet totally new, it will appear to present a situation of disorder and unrest, and as such be totally alien to the existing system. In either case it can either be rejected or be absorbed into each individual system. When absorbed (or accepted) it becomes a positive extension of experience. This way films testify to the abstractions and conceptions that are necessary for an expanding system of values.

I am not speaking here specifically of *Un Chant d'Amour* or *Flaming Creatures*. All films function as a total experience. Their effect on us is in the realm of mythical consciousness. *Un Chant d'Amour* or *Flaming Creatures* present such a real experience, created by the interplay between the film-maker and his abstract emotional situation, that it soon comes to represent a confrontation between the viewer and his emotional situation. When a film such as *Un Chant d'Amour* is shown a background of fear and personal distortion about sex is created. So sharp is this experience for some that they react with violence, trying to get the film banned. *Un Chant d'Amour* presents the feeling of homosexuals in such strong and natural terms that, western Christian morality being what it is, it is counted as an evil and unnatural film. Yet the situation in *Un Chant d'Amour* is so natural (as is the transvestite relationship in *Flaming Creatures*) that one can think of it as unnatural only if one is blinded by conditioning.

In cases where the film experience is basically accepted as real, yet is in conflict with existing values, confusion or discomfort clearly arise, sometimes leading to verbal 'vomiting' in an attempt to reject the experience. This is very true of *Flaming Creatures* and *L'Âge d'Or*, as well as of my own film *Times For*, about which the critics could do no more than utter confused paradoxical adjectives.

Faced with this strong physical reaction, critics try to link such films with pornographic films or 'blue movies', which represent in their general attitude a low form of sexual experience. An attempt to equate poetically erotic films with mere pornography is obviously a simple way of dealing with them, but it also reveals a feeling of embarrassment stemming from an inability to live with deeper, more personal sexual relationships. (Incidentally the view that pornography itself is 'low' is debatable; I personally would not rate it any 'lower' than Donald Duck.)

This rejection of the experiences presented in the personal film does not only affect all conceptual, environmental and social values. Snow's *Wave-*

length, Brakhage's *Art of Vision* or Costard's *Besonders Wertvoll* (Extremely Good) do the same things in their own ways as *Un Chant d'Amour* or *Flaming Creatures.* Too many people reject the experiences presented in these films because they are too close to reality.

Very different from films presenting experiences of a provocative nature are those that are soft, gentle and still very personal. Yet these too tend to be rejected by critics and many members of the public. The reason this time is that they are embarrassed by the sentiment, the romance, the gently drifting colours and sensations. Perhaps they have been taught that such freedom of spirit or simple joy in seeing and feeling is a weakness, that it lowers the human condition. Examples here are Massimo Bacigalupo's quartet *Fiore d'Eringio,* a series of films that fuses simple daily occurrences and people into a translucent experience like a pleasant memory; or Antonio De Bernardi's *Le Cronache del Sogno e del Sentimento* (Chronicles of Dream and Feeling) or *Le Opere e i Giorni* (The Life and the Days), where the faces of the children in the school in which he teaches, or among their families, create by the expressions and their natural attitude a feeling that we are meeting 'real' people. These straightforward visual experiences, of which there are many more examples (including Barbara Meter's *Windows* and the films of Brakhage, Harry Smith and so on), have often produced a feeling of discomfort because of their direct and honest sensitivity.

Here, where no sexual, social or political elements intervene, the difficulty experienced by many viewers is as sharp as with the other more overtly provocative films. The point is that we live in a society in which the majority of people are conditioned to a narrow range of experiences, particularly to experiences that are based on the mythology of ideas, not on the mythology of feelings.

The 'soft' film sensitivity, which is tied up with what is popularly known as the 'art of vision', is difficult to classify. The essential point (and I must emphasize this) is that the best of such films, however different one from the other, are independent, individual creations. Some 'soft' films see everyday life as Brakhage sees it; others see it with the eyes of a Jonas Mekas. Brakhage tends to use amorphous, fluid imagery, while Mekas uses a series of remembered events in the form of a diary. It is not enough to say that all independent films represent personal insights; as their forms are physically different, so they are capable of offering their own independent experiences. Thus I choose to call some films 'soft' because the imagery, being full of sentiment or romance, creates for me a feeling of softness; or because a similar feeling is evoked by a concentration on simple everyday things. Apart from the film-makers already mentioned, those who seem to me to fall into this category include Alfredo Leonardi, Bargellini, Pia Epremian (and many others from Italy), Dore O from Germany and Etienne O'Leary from France.

> 'Jack Smith just finished a great movie *Flaming Creatures,* which is so beautiful that I feel ashamed even to sit through the current Hollywood and European movies. I saw it privately, and there is little hope that Smith's movie will ever reach the movie theatre screens. But I tell you, that it is a luxurious outpouring of imagination, of imagery, of poetry, of moving artistry – comparable only to the work of the greatest, like Von Sternberg.'
>
> Jonas Mekas, 1963

Let us take Mekas's *Diaries, Notes and Sketches* (also known as *Walden* – the first edition was started in about 1961 and completed in December 1969) as one point of reference, having already used Brakhage as another. Mekas, well known as the leader of the New American Cinema and for his earlier 'hard' films, presented in his *Diaries* a simple, straightforward and natural approach to film. So simple is this approach that there is no need to analyse it, for, as the title suggests, the film is an accumulation of a well-formed 'home-movie', if you like. And like a home-movie it can be watched without effort, and enjoyed as a series of glimpses at life and the things around us. It is a notebook in which the eye of the camera records its impressions, so the notes are presented in film terms, with short and long bursts of image, 'normal' speed, high speed, still or jumpy – as the situation and the mood of the film-maker dictated.

Diaries runs for 3½ hours and contains something like 160 entries. Jonas says on the soundtrack: 'I make home movies because I live', and so the film moves from Central Park covered in snow to Barbara Rubin planting flower seeds on a window sill; to Tony Conrad and Beverly Grant at their Second Avenue home; to a pretty girl running in the grass; to a wedding; to breakfast in Marseilles; to breakfast at Barbara and David Stone's; to flowers; to glimpses of April in the park; to notes on the circus; to September and the Hare Krishna people; to the New York skyline; to the Larry Rivers show; to a coal delivery; to the Velvet Underground; to a winter scene; to police violence in Times Square; to a meeting of the Film-makers' Co-operative; to a cup of coffee; to Christmas Eve; to a visit to the Brakhages; to some children; to John and Yoko; to grass. What can be more pleasant than to while away a few hours watching other people living? Just think how many people are intrigued by looking at someone else's notes, personal letters and diaries, by reading his biography. I know Jonas and some of the people and places in the film, so for me parts of it are shared memories. I've been in Beverly's and Tony's Second Avenue apartment and I've been in Central Park too, yet others who have never known these things have also retained a strong impression of *Diaries*. I have never had breakfast in Marseilles but the film makes me wish I had. There, looking down on a lighthouse, boats move, disappear suddenly and appear as suddenly, or appear slowly; sunlight on blue water, cloud, changing in a flash to sunlight and then to dusk. The air seems warm and the colours are brilliant. Then there are also the notes on the circus, and after all a circus belongs to everybody. The feeling of the circus is brilliantly caught – the movements are quick and things are happening all the time and everywhere. Shot in single frames, or in short bursts of film, the images and events dart about in movements and colours. Jug band music plays on and the excitement and whirling gaiety of the Big Top is remarkably held.

Another important point here is that although I know Jonas Mekas, I did not know him until I saw *Diaries*. The realistic element in such films stems from their totally personal nature. They consist solely of the vision of the person who makes them. The selection is his and his alone. Yet although the film could be by anyone else, because his vision is honest it is the vision of all of us. By watching *Diaries* I learnt that Jonas likes children, that he has a melancholic feeling for weddings, loves parks and has a strong attachment to the romance of spring and the joy of winter, that he has a soft spot for a sweet girl. Behind the bravado front of leading the underground movement, behind that confrontation with the police and establishment is a very shy and gentle person hoping for a simple summer life. (On the track of *Diaries* Jonas says: 'I am searching for nothing.')

Taylor Mead also made a diary. He called it *European Diaries* (1965/66) and it is a single-frame summary of his travels lasting an hour. It is sort of 'around the world in single frame'. It is very different from Mekas's diary. It is a diary of sight, and it is chock full of things seen, whizzing past in an exhilarating tour. One thing is replaced by another so quickly that all you receive is an impression. In a way, this Grand Tour is an impressionistic film – a fusion of a thousand images and colours. Each frame is an entity in itself. In a flash of recognition we might spot that church, or that street in Italy, but they sink in so rapidly that any picture postcard studying is impossible. Instead, without our realizing it all these sights accumulate in the brain, fragments of a total experience.

Just recently I saw a film called *Windows* by Barbara Meter being made. It is a soft film depicting one aspect of the life about us – of life as it is lived behind those windows in those streets round us: people in their living-room or kitchen, eating or watching television or moving about, filmed in strange speeded-up action in which human beings seem more like ants. Movement appears futile at times, because each person is contained in his own tight, supposedly secure box. But this film is not so much a direct comment on life as a portrayal of a single piece of our environment. It is nice to think that such films are being made. The ability to transpose the life about us into an individual expression is one of the few things that makes life (our life) possible – both for the doer and for the seer. What else can we have if we do not possess this ability to see and to react independently of preconceptions and dogmas? What else is freedom?

Just as we can feel awe as we watch a craftsman cutting a diamond, so we can marvel at the intricate work involved in a film of this kind. The concentration on a single facet of life has produced an individual entity. It doesn't have to be a window. It can be anything, anywhere. The Dutch film-maker Joris Ivens's film *Rain* (1929) is a study of rain in a city. The American Ron Finne's *How Old is the Water?* (1968) blends images made almost entirely round one small waterfall. Markopoulos's *Ming Green* (1966) is a still life by a window, evolving in beautifully muted tones and colours, like some great painting. Another simple example of this kind of seeing can be found in a 3-minute film called *Passaggio Misto* (Varied Landscape), made by Lucia Patella. It is just that – a landscape poem. The film easily fades in and out from a tree in a landscape to an eye, from the eye to the tree, tree to eye – slowly in and out in a soft, diffused light. Intermittent movements blur as when you are travelling in a train or a car – a memory passing.

If we can appreciate such painters as Vermeer or Caravaggio, then there is no reason why we cannot appreciate this kind of film. If we can stare, almost hypnotically, at some great painting and relax as we absorb the mood it creates, it is logical that a film should affect us the same way. Yet some people feel embarrassed when confronted with such simple images and feelings. It is quite likely that these people have never relaxed enough to enjoy and take in creations of this kind. One last point here: an apparently simple film like this is not always born as simply as the experience that it produces. The idea underlying it must often be moulded and transmitted through a whole series of references and cross-references before the maker finds the tone that will allow him to convey an experience. At other times it will come instantly. To think that all such films are made without effort is a preconception that bedevils many audiences.

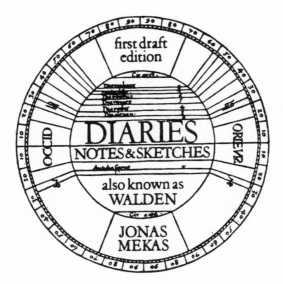

I should like now to come back to Alfredo Leonardi and his film *Libro di Santi di Roma Eterna* (Book of Saints of Eternal Rome, 1968) which, as I have said, gives you the feeling of being in a meadow on a warm summer's day. It creates a sense of space and a sense of freedom. The images are interwoven, as in one's memory. It is like walking round a field – moving from place to place and seeing various things. At some you stop, others you pass by, though you may return to them. You watch, and after a while you are no longer watching, merely drifting. Some movements are retained and repeated, some are never registered, others are just glimpses. You soon realize that images like the superimposition of gliders provoke sensations closely related to reality. To put it another way, the abstract reality that the film creates in us becomes the sensation of actually being in that field, drifting and staring at things. If we 'really' were in a field, lying on the grass, warm and relaxed, looking up into the sky, then things (like birds or gliders) would fuse and blend themselves and overlap in random ways just as they do in this film.

The main quality of Leonardi's films is that they create the feeling of thought. They drift from image to image without any coherent pattern, overlapping, imposing and superimposing images related and unrelated. It is not surprising perhaps that Leonardi has grouped three of his films under the general heading 'Seeing is also a way of thinking'. The individual titles are *Esercizio di Meditazione* (Exercise in Meditation), *Puo la Forza d'un Sorriso* and *Le N Ragazze più belle di Piazza Navona* (The N Most Beautiful Girls of the Piazza Navona) (all 1968). *Piazza Navona* has stuck in my memory more than the others. Like *Libro di Santi* it presents a soft, drifting world in which we sit in a square watching things happen. This is certainly thinking by seeing. In talking about his first long film, *Amore, Amore,* Leonardi remarked that it is hard to say what the exact content of his film is. (In fact this also applies in many ways to his other films.) There is no total plot; it is a sort of subjective experimental novel in which people and actions are presented in analogically opposite situations. The analogies and oppositions are mainly dictated by rhythm, by breaking the chain of cause and effect, interrupting direct visual associations. This is not a deliberate attempt at being esoteric, and the associations are generally intelligible. It is a sort of new *cinéma vérité*, in which people perform ordinary actions. But the link between these actions has a new emphasis (and they are also supplemented by heterogeneous material). The result is a constant fluctuation between the dimensions of everyday life and artistic creation and the realm of images, ideas and passions in which all of us in the modern world participate.

Leonardi puts these ideas into practice in another earlier film, *Organum Multiplum* (1967). Here the images and ideas all concern his children, his wife and events that occur round a theatre (the Living Theater). Parts of it are related to an earlier film about the Living Theater, *Living and Glorious* (1965). By 1970 Leonardi had gone further into the more direct and yet looser concept of the diary film with his *Occhio Privato sul Nuovo*

Mondo (Private Eye on the New World). This lasts 70 minutes and was made as a result of a year's visit to America with a grant from the Ford Foundation to prepare a book on the New American Cinema.

One interesting point that I have noted when watching many independent Italian films – even many of the harder political films – is that Italian film-makers seem to work in a softer, more drifting, stylized and often symbolic manner than their counterparts in other countries. Sometimes we find an almost operatic stylization (without the stage and costumes), a use of poses and pantomime gestures. They tend to break up any narrative or linear structure. Whatever theme they choose, their films create a pronounced sense of seeing. Pia Epremian represents poetics and gesture; Baruchello poetics and symbolism; Guido Lombardi poetics and political tones; De Bernardi poetic fantasy and people; Leonardi poetics and people and thinking, and so on. It is difficult and dangerous to label artists and their work in this way but it will serve in the general sense to describe tendencies.

Massimo Bacigalupo has been making films since 1965, beginning with *Liban* and continuing with *Quasi una Tangente* (1966), *Ariel Loquitur* (1967), a dyptych consisting of *60 Metri per il 31 Marzo* (200 Feet for March 31st) and *V* (1968), and his larger film cycle *Eryngium* (*Fiore d'Eringio*) consisting of *The Last Summer, Nel Bosco: Una Conversazione* (In the Wood: A Conversation), *Migrazione* and *Envoi* (Coda), all made between 1969 and 1970, and altogether lasting about 125 minutes.

Bacigalupo's films are strongly visual and extremely rich in their sense of: 'I see what I see and what I see, I love, and I see it because I love it'. Though they sometimes have political and, even more, literary overtones, they still reach out to us in the experience of seeing. Perhaps the best way to explain these films and to give you an idea of what I mean is to quote you most of a letter he once wrote to me:

Rapallo, 22/11/70

Dear Steve,

It is so beautiful out here today that I thought I would write to you about it. I've had mainly stormy weather recently – in the last two weeks – the earth needed it badly. Then everything began swimming, and up there on the hill the wind blows the house into kind of a vacuum. This brought the stars out at night at times. Then, today, in the morning, it was good to find out upon waking that all is blue (and the reflections on the leaves of the olive trees are very bright and are 50% of the show). The windows are open and it is mild. . . . After coming back to Italy I still went over to Yugoslavia to show the films to people who were, most of the time, sincerely interested. . . . The young scene over there is very open, and they are naturally after anything western. (There are lots of 'avant-garde' in the other arts, but I would say it is more external and having a very well done varnish than a feeling for it.) Zagreb is a typically middle-Europe town with Hapsburg cafés and theatres. Split a magnificent place that Goethe may have discovered when he first came to Italy. The whole town is contained within the walls of Diocletian's palace; you walk among all the picturesque ruins and houses. Since returning, my main job has been writing some stuff for a book that we are bringing out with Feltrinelli in Rome (the same publisher that published my trsl of 'Metaphors on Vision') on the Co-op. Each of us is writing what he likes over his stuff – love, bombs, etc. Mine naturally takes the form of a long monologue, opening with childhood memories of films I wanted to make when in 5th Grade but was never allowed to, until the moon closing 'Coda' – something like Beckett's 'Malone'. So I've found out a lot more about my film but cannot decide whether they add anything. As I told you, one only says a few words and feels very badly about all that goes unsaid. But if you keep up the tension towards communication, looking at other people's faces, painful as it often is, it is like a glow to fill all our life at least, being the only thing we know. I wanted to tell you more about my films so that you'll write beautiful things in your book! I have no criteria for relevance; it is just the power of a few things to fill up space and time.

Did I tell you that 'Eryngium' (being the title of my cycle of films) [*Fiore d'Eringio* 1969/70] is a flower that appears in a self-portrait of 22-year-old Dürer, hanging at the Louvre? Apparently he made it to promise faithfulness to the girl he had just married. That's what the Eryngium is supposed to mean. It is a sort of faithfulness for me as well, towards other people, things, that you go on looking, towards myself. . . . 'The Last Summer', the film [in the cycle] is about Nepal. I went there last summer – 69 – and did the film on returning. I mean, I found out a few things over there, about being reconciled; that the Himalayas in the morning haze are very similar to the hills in Rapallo that I, at times, forget to look at, the hills, more as I see them in memory (partly from childhood) than actually. (There is 'really' something Chinese about this landscape. Pound has a whole canto in which he appears to talk of some far east place, but it is, instead, just around the corner.) So 'The Last Summer' is about nearness in distance (it is in colour): I describe carefully the garden in which I (and others) have grown, showing its more pleasant and more sinister aspects; the big people that move around the child (all the people in this film are my relatives), and things that one can never understand (night) and dawn thereafter, a sequence with my brother walking around his horse, in a clear morning, towards autumn.

The second film, 'Nel Bosco: Una Conversazione', opens with two superimposed shots of landscape from renaissance paintings (unrecognizable); after that it is only a painful succession of words. There are two voices speaking (the film is silent 16mm), one black over white, the other white letters over black (negative). There is a love conversation; we listen to the sounds (whispered) of the words in our mind, not really knowing what the lovers are up to, if we are not in love as well – I mean if the mere words I have given don't suddenly begin to move on a whole immense landscape if we don't lend ourselves. There are memories of Solomon's Song, of peasants celebrating May Day in the country, whispering to each other in the evening. . . .

Of 'Migrazione' you know: it is (I have decided) a long and loving reflection over the child-mother Demeter/Kore, being the little girl and the various incarnations of women in the film – Amalia, as told by Kafka in 'The Castle'; Heaulmière (the prostitute from Villon, of whom the girl sings in the long music sequence); the girl in Solomon's Songs (which is what Stockhausen's piece is about) etc. On one side in the film you have the continuum (of which the Migration is a metaphor) of perception and life; on the other hand the moments in which the travellers stop in the evening and tell each other a story. The story seems to be a mere interruption in the flux (the early marked sequences) but tends to become, later, the pattern (metaphor) of the whole continuum, which can become significant, that is alive, only through the story-telling process, this being, at the end, the film itself. The film is naturally crammed with references (mainly literary, that being my handicap) . . . but they are just very many signs (or inscriptions) you find when travelling and you don't have to read them if you don't want to. As in life, there is a possibility that if you read one message, this will lead to another one, and so on until you have reached a full vision of the whole process. . . .

'Coda' is built around the idea of self-portraiture; it serves as a tragic (but then suddenly luminous) conclusion to the whole affair. The main reference is to Stroheim's 'Foolish Wives', where he gives a self-portrait certainly lacking every dignity. Other points are Dante, Caravaggio (the head of Goliath in his David and Goliath is himself), Pia Epremian (whose film 'Medea' is so near to my work and Tonino's – De Bernardi – is quoted), with a final emergence of the flower, real, and the cities in which I have passed, or all have passed, the hills, Jerusalem, Rome (the subtitle reads: 'A Requiem for Soldiers lost in Ocean Transport', a title of a poem of Melville's). Heraclitus said once: *'Remember those also who have forgotten which way the road goes*!!!!!
Caro Steve, I must run. . . .

Ciao

MASSIMO

> Since self-knowledge is getting to know the individual facts, theories help very little in this respect. For the more a theory lays claim to universal validity, the less capable it is of doing justice to the individual facts.
>
> From *The Undiscovered Self* by C. G. Jung

Stan Brakhage stands out as one of the strongest and most influential makers of the subjectively personal film. His influence can be seen in the work of many of the film-makers I have already referred to, including *Mare's Tail*. Even more than that, Brakhage has become the symbol of the subjective

K

film-maker both because of his films and because of his personal attitude.
His personality follows the idealistic image of the poet and over the years
he has withdrawn from the complexities and pollution of the cities and
commercialized civilization, moving to the mountains of Colorado. There
he devoted himself to the art of film, evolving a type of film that is the
essence of film seeing. His coherent and uncompromising approach to film-
making as a 'pure' art form, combined with the fact that his films are
excellent by any standards and with his 'old man of the mountain' image,
has made him a much-revered figure, as well as an influential one.

Over the years he has turned his camera on himself, his life, his moods.
His films have become a dossier on a man's life. They increase in maturity
as the man matures, and they become richer as they are increasingly interwoven with the development of the man's life. The process of watching
makes us feel that we are listening to a man talking of his existence. For
me, the beautiful portrait evoked is even more haunting because I feel
that Brakhage is playing Virgil with Dante, searching by means of poetry
for a beauty seen only in dreams, yet always saying, 'Life's but a walking
shadow. . . .' His films are great works of film vision and he has established
one of the most important forms and attitudes for film.

Brakhage's films involve putting on to film the process of the poet's mind.
It is a process in which an image, like a word, represents a single intimate
reference, but in its relationship with other images it is transformed into a
universal abstraction. Such abstractions establish a totality of feeling, like
the accumulated verbal abstractions in a poem. Though each word is still
its own distinct symbol, only in combination with others does it pertain
to its full meaning. It is the same with an image, and with a personally
subjective film, and most particularly with a Brakhage film. The choice of
image arises out of an indefinable cross-reference system growing inside the
film-maker. Brakhage's vastness (and vagueness) can be reduced or concentrated to single images. That tree, that moon, that dog, that girl or that
house represent his personal store of references, yet they also represent our
own store of references as viewers. The reasons why the film-maker has
chosen the image, or has chosen to make that particular film, are obviously
interesting; but a knowledge of them is not essential to us. We can still see
and experience the film. (Many personal abstractions are in fact felt to be
beyond many people's own references, which is why they claim that having
an idea of the maker's intentions and reasons gives them a better understanding of that work and allows them to relate to it. No doubt this is true,
since this can reduce the viewer's confusion on being confronted with
something new. But too much explanation gradually reduces the work itself
to mere acquired knowledge and prevents it from creating a genuine experience.) With Brakhage the choices evolve out of his situation, a situation
he has himself chosen; the film has become his dialogue with that world.
He starts to see with the camera, and what he sees creates a store of references for his next film.

The very large amount that has been written by and about Brakhage often creates the impression that he fulfils a generalized ideal of the classical poet. Though his work has a feeling of amorphousness, there is an ordered and intellectual tone behind it. So it is not only the object or event on which Brakhage turns his camera that counts, but also how he puts his films together; in other words, as well as personal imagery and symbolism we have a formal organization of the material. Editing is essential, perhaps more essential than the camera work. Sometimes Brakhage is more consciously 'structural' than so-called 'structural' film-makers such as Michael Snow. The 'structuralists' first establish a structure or framework for their film, retaining their freedom of choice within that framework. Brakhage, on the other hand, starts with an accumulation of images which he then proceeds to structure – the framework is created only when the film is finished. This is really a case of semantics, since basically all films have a structure by virtue of the fact that they exist. The really essential point about Brakhage's films is that their images are composed into a whole by a formal and conscious procedure (even the fact of allowing an element of chance becomes a conscious process). Brakhage is also the most formal of all the translucent and 'soft' film-makers. That formality is his art, and is what makes his films so different physically. Every image and every frame (even the splicing marks) are tightly woven into a mosaic of poetry. P. Adams Sitney, who has had a good deal of contact with Brakhage and his films, has said that Brakhage considers that 'films should not be mere object studies; they should have the formal wholeness and intellectual depth required of any other work of art'. So well-knit and ultimately so rich are Brakhage's films that there is no need for sound. The density of images is such that sound would pollute sight. The silence seems to purify the vision, as it does in the work of certain other independent film-makers. Brakhage's poetry is really the pure experience of vision.

In his earliest films, from *Interim* (1952) to *Flesh of Morning* (1956), Brakhage adopted a more narrative style, using psychological symbolism representing personal feelings as his main vehicle. Interesting as these early films are, they remain somewhat immature psychodramas. It was not until his *Anticipation of the Night* (1958) that the form began to evolve. It was at this point that he got married, and his wife, Jane, gave a new direction to his life and to his work. The marriage clearly gave some tangibility to Brakhage's life, drawing him away from the isolation and the sense of being lost that is apparent in his earlier films. It gave him the perspective and position he needed, and through this he was able to begin his dialogue;

he was no longer isolated with the world watching him, but became secure enough to watch the world through himself. The situations he found himself in, or the things around him, became the immediate stimuli for his films. An argument with his wife was transformed into the film *Wedlock House: An Intercourse* (1959). Here the anger and tensions were immediately removed as they were recorded with the camera. The camera became the means by which the dialogue took place: she films him, he films her. The films began to live. The birth of his first child became *Window Water Baby Moving* (1959); the death of his dog Sirius was transformed into the film *Sirius Remembered* (1959). Not only did these intimate events become stimuli, they were part of his life. They were not merely acts in passing that could be simply recorded; they involved him so closely that the filming of them became total acts. All the subtleties and ramifications of each act are reflected in each film. By building in this intensity Brakhage wove the film into an independent tapestry of transformation. The family dog in *Sirius Remembered* is not a dead and decaying animal. The emotion that Brakhage felt becomes the reason for the movements in the film, and through this Sirius is reborn, as if there were a form of 'sympathetic magic'.

In the finite world of Brakhage, moods, feelings, events, even objects become things he must come to terms with and reflect on through film. His fear that his wife might die while he was in Europe became his film *The Dead* (1960), in which his reflections on her death were transformed into the death of Europe and the living people there, who seemed dead. Brakhage explains, 'The graveyard could stand for all my view of Europe, for all concern with past art, for involvement with symbols. "The Dead" became my first work in which things that might very easily be taken as symbols were so photographed as to destroy all their symbolic potential.'[4] Each situation that Brakhage is in produces a personal response almost to the point of obsession. Film is his only method of dealing with it. *Cat's Cradle* arose through his conception or misconception of marriage/sex relations. In this situation he found the cat on heat emerging as a way to create a structure for the film. Brakhage said about this, 'I didn't have enough film to waste trying to create symbolic structures. I had to move right into the shape/form of what was developing straight off that cat. That cat became a source of hyper-forms and a touchstone visually and formally of everything else that happens in the film.'

Brakhage's self-scrutiny is continually revealed again in another birth film, *Thigh Line Lyre Triangular* (1961), which differs materially from the earlier birth film by the addition of hand painting, and in *Films by Stan Brakhage,* an avant-garde home-movie (1961). He says about this latter film:

I had a camera with which I could make multiple superimpositions spontaneously. It had been lent to me for a week. I was given a couple of rolls of color film which had been through an intensive fire. The chance that the film would not record any image at all left me free to experiment and to try to create the sense of the daily world in which we live, and what it meant to me. I wanted to record our home, and yet deal with it as being that area from which the films by Stan Brakhage arise, and to try to make one arise at the same time.

Later, in 1966, Brakhage began an autobiographical film, *Scenes from Under Childhood,* continuing his exploration inwards.

In the realization of his finite feelings, Brakhage is infinitely involved with film movement, with colour, with tone – with every filmic detail that helps to create a fuller vision – superimposition, fusion and overlaying of image, colour, tone and movement; painting on film; the addition of new abstractions to the existing density of abstraction; editing; increased juxtaposition of image; abstraction and movement. Film is not merely subject-matter, but the interrelation of all the techniques and styles used by the media, and this interrelation creates the richness of what we see. A simple example of this relationship can be found in *Mothlight* (1963). A simple description, it is made up of moths' wings fixed to the film and printed on to colour film stock. No verbal description can explain the effect created by the moving image when it is projected; it becomes a blend of natural form, colour and movement, giving off a light and life of its own. This painstaking work and an involvement with such fertile detail is a feature of the visual sensibility of Brakhage's films (of which *Mothlight* is the simplest in form).

Whatever I say, or Brakhage says, or anybody else says, Brakhage's films are intrinsically a question of seeing, as in *Lovemaking*. Seeing is seeing soft lips pressing flesh; legs, more round than round, moving, thighs and backs flaring out to yellow, to white, to return as hands in hands. The movements are fast and slow; the camera, like the bodies, moves and, like the eyes, the film is blinded by the light, and then turns back to the flesh. Sometimes we are voyeurs. Sometimes we seem to be physically involved, physically making love. This is organic seeing, seeing of a kind that is rarely experienced elsewhere. Even with a static camera, the organic sense is touched, as with Brakhage's *Fire of Waters* (1965), which evolves out of a flash, then comes darkness, rising light and a fade into flash again. A house is caught in this white light, seeming like something from the past, but remembered. (This is one of the few films in which Brakhage has used sound.)

This quality of seeing is found again in other films made by Brakhage, such as *Blue Moses* (1962), *Oh Life, Woe Story, The A test News!* (1963), *Blue White* (1965), *Blood's Tone* (1965), *Vein* (1965) or *Black Vision* (1965). But it reaches its highest point in two major works: *The Art of Vision* (1961/5) and *Songs* (1965). *The Art of Vision* is probably the most intense and most closely interwoven example of film seeing. It represents the fusion of image and movement into hypervision. The experience cannot be described simply, yet somehow it is a simple experience. It is like watching a river go by; it flows and changes; it is surface and it is depth, light and dark, sameness and difference; it is layers of life, of time, of subtlety, yet it is fresh, alive and always new, and it rides with the full confidence that it is there.

The Art of Vision began as a narrative epic called *Dog Star Man* (1959-64), which in its final form is the story of a mountain-climbing woodcutter and his journey through the four seasons. *The Art of Vision* is a fugue of visual counterpoints, composed out of the various layers of film which go to make up the multiple superimpositions of *Dog Star Man*. The structure of the film or the expository narrative is merely an intellectual layout. It explains the complexity of the film; it gives reasons, but it in no way explains the quality of the vision. What one sees is the river, a panorama of moons, suns, trees, man, dog, sex; of cosmos and of micro-organism; a moving accumulation of image into abstraction and abstraction into image, a panorama representing 4½ hours of intense visual experience. *The Art of Vision* has a rather elaborate structure of relationships, and it is these interrelationships that make up the content of the film. The basic action is Brakhage himself portraying a woodsman with an axe, climbing a mountain with a tree, followed by his dog. He plants the tree, then tears it down and chops it up. But the things that are filmed mean far more to Brakhage. He has said, 'I saw the whole forest in relation to the history of architecture, particularly religious architecture, at least in the western world. Sensing structure, architecture, history of the world emerging, I began seeing prismatic happenings through snow falling, etc., and in relation to stained glass windows, for one example.' This explains the specific source of these images, and Brakhage's reasons for using them. Another example is the symbolism of the white tree, of which Brakhage said: 'There are other kinds of white trees (there can be a silver tree), but if it's a white tree, then in the mind it's a dead tree.' The journey up the mountain is another gesture; and perhaps the fight with the dog represents man coping with beast? The man is Brakhage himself – he is his own alter ego. This symbolic complexity (Brakhage has a reason for every fragment) is combined with an attempt to illustrate the dream process. That, he says, was the determining factor behind the editing. There is also hand painting on the film. 'The hand painting was always in direct relationship to the particular kind of "closed eye vision" that comes only in dreams. The commonest type of "closed eye vision" is what we get when we close our eyes in daylight and watch the moving of shapes and forms through the red pattern of the eyelid.' Painting on to the film was the closest approximation Brakhage could find for this. Apart from the natural abstraction of hand painting, everything else in the film is 'hyperconscious'. In essence, *The Art of Vision* is composed of the sum total of Brakhage's own accumulated experience from what he sees and how he lives, to what he has read.

Dog Star Man, from which *The Art of Vision* originated, runs for 70 minutes complete. It consists of a 'prelude' and four other parts, the 'prelude' being made first. Brakhage states, 'I realized that whatever happened within this prelude would determine what was to come; and in that sense I wanted it to be as real from the very beginning as life happening.' All the filmed material in *Prelude* is the same as that for *Dog Star Man* and for *The Art of Vision*. What is different is the way these elements are combined, accumulated, overlaid, and juxtaposed in an expanding and abundant visual relationship, leading to visual abstraction. *Prelude* represents for me one of the richest film experiences I have ever had. All the basic forms, like the sun, and trees, and woman, and colour, and house, and snow, and fire and patterns are our essential references in the process of image retention. And though they are recognizable, almost symbolic images they are fused into a metamorphosis on film. P. Adams Sitney breaks *Prelude* down into four visual themes: (1) the four elements – air, earth, fire and water; (2) the cosmos represented in the stock footage of the sun, moon and stars; (3) Brakhage (man), his wife, flesh, dog, cat, house (everyday life); (4) artificial yet pure filmic devices (representing the 'closed eye vision'), such as painting and scratching on film, distorted image, double-exposure and clear film. Clear film is visual silence.

Prelude is made up of two layers of superimposition. Part one is a single image (A Roll), part two a single superimposition (Rolls A and B); part three is on three levels of superimposition (Rolls A + B + C) and part four on four levels (Rolls A + B + C + D). The four levels represent, according to Brakhage, the four seasons. The physical manifestations of the vital editing that makes up *The Art of Vision* and which includes *Dog Star Man* (bear in mind that every frame in *Dog Star Man* is the same as in *The Art of Vision*) are as follows:

Prelude appears as Roll A, then B, and then A + B (superimposition),
Part One appears as Roll A (from *Dog Star Man*),
Part Two appears as Rolls A + B, Roll A, Roll B, Roll A,
Part Three appears as Roll C, Roll A + B, Roll A + B + C,
Part Four appears as Rolls A + B + C + D (as in *Dog Star Man*),
Roll A + B + C, Roll A + B + D, Roll A + C + D, Roll B + C + D,
Roll A + B, Roll A + D, Roll A + C, Roll B + C, Roll B + D,
Roll C + D, Roll A, Roll B, Roll C and finally Roll D.

Yet whatever all the symbols represent, however many intellectual explanations are produced (and a great variety have been produced, including Brakhage's own *Metaphors on Vision*), and whatever the complexities of the structure (and Brakhage is one of the most precise of film editors, depending on that aspect more than on any other for his final form), *The Art of Vision* is first and foremost the art of vision – independent of the background, because it represents what the eye beholds first, not what the mind conceives as possible. It is the first major epic film poem.

Brakhage's other major work is his *Songs*. The *Songs* belong to the category of 'attitude' films that I have previously mentioned, along with, for example, diary, portrait or notebook films, in that they are simple films based on simple, random ideas, events and objects to do with daily life. That is all they are – twenty-five simple, beautiful little pieces all on 8mm. One person I met sitting outside the cinema after seeing *Songs* and meditating on them slowly turned to me and said, 'It was like watching moving Rembrandts.' The *Songs* are some of the most lyrical film pieces ever made. *Song 1* is a serene portrait of a woman reading; *Song 2* is wind and dust; *Song 3* is water; *Song 4* is children in red, red/brown; *Song 5* is childbirth; *Song 6* is a bug running across the linoleum; *Song 10* is a room; *Song 13* is a train in a train; *Song 15* (a cycle of songs) is called 'The First Branch' and is a cycle of portraits (Robert Kelly, Michael McClure and Robert Creeley, Ed Dorn, Jonas Mekas) interspersed with scenes of Brakhage's family; *Song 19* is girls dancing, and *Song 21* is flowers and abstraction. *Song 23* (another 'branch', called the '23rd Psalm Branch') is the most complex. It is built round Brakhage's reaction to the Vietnam War, using television news reports, Second World War stock footage and children playing at war, all as a statement on the concept of war.

All told, the *Songs* cycle and its characteristic attitude towards film-making represents one of the most important facets of the independent and personal cinema. The attitude is one of freedom, of immediacy, of the need for a more spontaneous and direct relationship between what is seen (or felt) and what is portrayed. This attitude resembles the process of sketching or drawing for a painter or designer – and sketching and drawing are the most essential and physically the most direct way in which the visual artist can think and react into form. It is just this attitude that frees the cinema from its commercial and ivory-tower ethos. Independent and commercial films are both films – it is just that one group (the one in control, the cinema industry) does not like seeing its own myth effaced.

One feature that seems repeatedly to occur in a large number of films is the use of superimposition. This is fundamentally the imposition of one thing on top of another, the two being combined to make something like a double image (double exposure). It is what used to happen when you took snapshots and forgot to wind the film on before you took the next. Seeing Mum as a giant on a mountain or coming out of Dad was just rather a funny mistake, sometimes even fascinating, but in fact this is one of the main possibilities offered by the photographic/film medium. The technique of superimposition has been used throughout the history of film itself. It allowed Méliès to make his magic heads float; and it is also the basis of dissolves (lap dissolve or mix) in more theatrical films. For the independent and poetic film it no longer remained a mere accident or a hidden technique; it became instead a major item in the vocabulary of film, capable of conveying a basic visual sensation that is inherent in the media. Superimposition can create a visual sensation that causes the image (or images) to appear transparent, lucid, fluid. It can allude to the disembodiment of an already suggested concrete form (the photographic representation of solids), being part of the magical association that is already possible with film. It can present opposites at once, can mix colours in movement and give a greater sense of fluidity and drift.

Superimposition indeed has such potential that it has become a substantial aspect of film. It is not necessarily a feature only of the 'softer', more poetic and romantic films; it is often used in films based on a very different approach. As we have seen, it is an essential part of Brakhage's language, but he uses it completely differently from, say, Ron Rice in *Chumlum*. Quite apart from the difference in intention and in the underlying subject, Brakhage makes his superimpositions very consciously, preparing each level on separate rolls, so that they fall where he wants them; the physical superimposition is done in the laboratory. Ron Rice does his in the camera, by running the same piece of film through three times and accepting the random occurrence of the superimposition. Brakhage's results differ from Ron Rice's as much as Ron Rice's differ from Harry Smith's *Late Superimpositions*; and Harry Smith's differ from Alfredo Leonardi's as much as Leonardi's differ from those by Storm de Hirsch; and Storm de Hirsch's differ from those in *Wavelength*. Even *Wavelength*, a purely sculptural and structural film, uses the technique of superimposition to create space transformations in its overall form. The mistake that most people make is that they become so conscious of superimposition as a technique that they become obsessed by it – and this applies to a lot of film-makers as well as to viewers – sometimes to such an extent that any superimposition represents 'another underground film'.

One 'old master', if I might make so bold, in this particular attitude of fluid seeing is Ian Hugo (Hugo Guyler). He told me once that he even taught Brakhage a thing or two (the experience of superimposition). Hugo began making films (in the United States) in 1948, after following a career as a painter and an engraver, in which he was particularly successful as an engraver. He worked with Maya Deren and the early core of the New American cinema. For Hugo, film represented this basic, lucid and blended movement of form and colour. He blended soft superimpositions of landscaped image, which created a series of endless rhythms and mutations. Form remains only in identity; the experience conveyed is formless and drifting. His relationship to water, to lights and to rhythm is the essence of his work. *Ai-Ye* (1950) is based on the rhythm of chanting and drumming (by the musician Ozzie Smith); *Bells of Atlantis* (1952), like *The Gondola Eye* (1963), uses water, as in Venice; *Jazz of Lights* (1954) is an 18-minute rhythmic fusion of two years of lights in Times Square. Hugo developed his superimposition and montage technique by using film that was superimposed during projection; this method mutates and softens the image into even more impressionistic tones. By this method (he called it 'electro-mechanical') he also manages to acquire more subtle control over the degrees of superimposition, a fact that is evident in films such as *Melodic Inversion* (1958), *Venice Etude No. 1* (1962) or *The Gondola Eye*.

Piero Heliczer is probably the most form-freed film-maker of all, making the smallest-gauged, most erratic, most star-bound epic fantasies ever documented. He rushes about all over the place, New York, London, Paris, swinging camera and hat (for cash) and running film shows that are the Heliczer show. He's a British poet (so his passport says), but he's from the New American Cinema too, coming from Italy somewhere along the line, but then he is always in France. . . .

He often achieves great images in his films, like superimposed madness. *Joan of Arc* (1967) is women, battles, prisons, costumes, flags and marching people. The screen opens further out and puts the cinema into everyone's hands. The films also contain the terror of chance superimposition, the risk of destroying an image at the same time as making it. Heliczer's rather more lyrical film *Dirt,* black and white on black and white on colour, is described by Jonas Mekas as one of the four best works on 8mm (the others being by Brakhage, Ken Jacobs and Bob Branaman). *The Autumn Feast,* made with Jeff Keen in southern England, at Brighton, is a return to Victorian pop made contemporary (and marks the beginning of a new 'Brighton School' with Jeff Keen), while *The Soap Opera* with LaMonte Young, Angus Maclise, Jack Smith, uses television material. *Satisfaction,* the *East Village Other* tells us, arouses strong reactions: 'A film [*Satisfaction*] by Piero Heliczer was shown, in the middle of which a Bernard Feeney, of 226 W. 238th Street, suddenly threw over the projector and attacked a nearby person. Other persons were attacked and Feeney was struck once. A girl was cut by a piece of glass. Police officers No. 858 and No. 21350 arrived and asked the assailant for identification.'

Heliczer the writer, writing on film, puts across a point that is an essential feature of all independent films: 'Now everyone in those photos is human, even the false nose, *even the camera is human, for is not the camera you, dear reader, is not the camera now you*?'

Film is the materialization of seeing, the transference of fantasy, dream. Film-makers become alchemists transmuting dreams and images and distilling form from them (forms that dissolve the moment they appear and return to being images of the mind). The film-maker is like a sorcerer, making things appear and disappear.

'I think that, if you don't get put off by the word, you can see that what is happening is what I call Magick. Magick is when you put two and two together and you get five. This doesn't mean like making up something and – Bang! It means ideas and things happening – action. And I think there will emerge an entirely different way of looking at the world.'[5] So said Kenneth Anger, invocator of dramatic dreams and necromantic documents – film-maker. My memories of Anger's films are rather strange – his 'Magick' is like opera and dreams wrapped up in symbolic gesture and rhapsodical exaggeration. These are romantic yet caustic films, made of oppositions and conflicts that are still congeneric, sometimes with flashes of Cocteau, sometimes horribly poetic, perhaps a hint of *The Tales of Hoffman*. It is hard to say. When women appear, they seem mythical, like goddesses in some fairly tale. And the men emerge as a brutal and lost Narcissus. The films create the effect of dreams, bad and broken dreams; of paranoia and a search for a way out. Anger the magician waves his camera wand to fight the demons and we see him flying about in a mist of movement and colour, as in *Invocation of my Demon Brother;* a magician among ritualistic men, making and breaking the dream.

Directly based on symbols, his early film *Fireworks* (1947) creates the effect of a dream drama full of homosexual claustrophobia, with one sailor seen as representing phallic narcissism and the phallic ego. A man (Anger) is carried by the sailor. The man wakes up; is he dreaming? His hand moves – his hand, then a plaster hand. Two fingers are missing, is something missing? Walks about. A gesture of adjusting; trousers touched. Out of door marked 'Gents' and in the streets. Sees muscle-man sailor, flexing and posing like those beach-boy magazines. Watches muscle-man do the flexing tricks. Then a large group of sailors comes at him, beats him up (chains). Phallic sadism. Fingers up his nose. Blood, cruelty, torture. Ego aggression. Chest is cut open. Face bloodstained. Milky, sperm-like fluid squirts and runs down face and then on to chest. A nightmare. Have you ever been caught by a group of men? Men from a world where only men live? (Like sailors, like prisoners.) Men turn phallic to club; the phallus is the ego and it drives them to blind aggression. It turns them in to drive it out. We see this beaten man wake up. Was he dreaming again? He sees another sailor. The sailor unzips his trousers. He sets his penis alight, and it goes up into a firework display. A phallic Roman candle. The man again comes into the room where he may have been dreaming, wearing a Christmas tree headdress, and burns it in the fireplace. Also in the fire are the burning photographs of the sailor carrying him. The film ends as it began, but with the missing fingers on the plaster hand returned.

Though sometimes awkward in its search, *Fireworks* becomes a theme situation underlying Anger's work, and his later films become more splendid and more esoteric. *Inauguration of the Pleasure Dome* (Sacred Mushroom Edition, Spring Equinox, otherwise known as *Lord Shiva's Dream*) was finished in its final form in 1966. Here Anger succeeds in blending the majestic forms of opera more fully. The footnotes read:

> Lord Shiva, the Magician, wakes. A convocation of Theurgists in the guise of figures from mythology bearing gifts: The Scarlet Woman, whore of Heaven, smokes a big fat joint; Astare of the Moon brings the wings of snow; Pan bestows the bunch of Bacchus; Hecate offers the Sacred Mushroom, Yage, Wormwood Brew. The vintage of Hecate is poured; Pan's cup is poisoned by Lord Shiva. The Orgia ensues; a Magick masquerade party at which Pan is the prize. Lady Kali blesses the rites of the Children of the Light as Lord Shiva invokes the Godhead with the formula 'Force and Fire'.
>
> Dedicated to the Few; and to Aleister Crowley; and to The Crowned and Conquering Child.

And so unfolds this masque for screen, like an elegiac pleasure poem. Gesture is exaggeration; awkwardness is turned to symbol. The colours are strong and rich, in degrees of chiaroscuro, rather like the allegories of the Pre-Raphaelites. The movements of Lord Shiva (who is also Osiris, Cagliostro, Nero and Great Beast 666) remind me of the movements of Heurtebise in Cocteau's *Orphée*, but Shiva goes the other way, almost like a puppet, ruled by another force – perhaps an alter ego? Lord Shiva awakes, as does the dreamer (Anger) in *Fireworks*. The process of visualizing the dreamer waking seems to perform an act of magic, which is also bound up with *A Midsummer Night's Dream*; (Anger played a part in the film of the Shakespeare play as a child, and he has called his films 'Puck Productions').

Anger has said; '. . . I suppose my films can be said to have symbolism in them, but I don't see a difference between a symbol and a thing; it's the same.'[6] So in his *Scorpio Rising* (Autumn Equinox, 1963/4) the astrological gods take their form. *Scorpio Rising* is a film in which ritual symbol and action become a witnessed truth; our feared and secretly preferred hidden fires rise from the grave. *Scorpio Rising* creates the mood of Scorpio, in the tenth month, in the autumn, when things begin to die and fall. Scorpio centres on the inner self and is ruled by the underworld (Pluto); Scorpio is associated with death, rebirth, brutality, violence and dictatorial force and restraint. As the summer dies and the reaping is done, the witches and the underworld rise in the sign of Scorpio. *Scorpio Rising* is just that, and Anger's magic works. The images and the action are the totem of the machine; the power phallus; the ego aggression of the boys riding to death. The motorcycle, the power machine; the new god; the toy totem come alive. The motorcycle ride is the ritual ride of death (just as the motorcyclists are the guides to Hell in *Orphée*). The leather boys, the phallic narcissists, prepare for the breakdown, and so the film is this ritual realization for the trip. Boys and boots is part one. The shine and glint of handlebars, steel pistons, ring of cold power, caught on film, spreading across the emulsion. The skull is in the frame, rising above the cycles being rubbed; the phallic god caressed; the dressing of the self; tight jeans and bright chains; the film remaining true in ritual and the passion of the self. The images of the heroes rise, and the icons of the myth perform to bless the boys. Marlon Brando, leather jacket, god of the inner self, rides as 'The Wild One' on the magic television altar, while cyclists prepare themselves with rings and ornaments and get high for the drive. The sound is ritual pop music, 'She Wore Blue Velvet'. And Christ, the superman of myth, comes through, and Hitler rises too, god of violence, and the ritual increases to a greater pitch. The Walpurgis Party; the boys have their last night 'fling'. Homosexual sadism; ripping the clothes off one of the boys, pouring mustard on his ass, and all in ranting war-dance joy, wearing masks of the Sabbath of Mardi Gras. The sound is again pop ritual music – songs of the day, and 'Torture Me'. The leader begins his speech, standing high above them, like Hitler exhorting his men, and the Rebel Rouser pees in his hat and pours out his non-sex fluid as the sign to ride. The Dark Legions ride – Hell's Angels – to the underworld. Erect and driving, they spend their urge in a thrust of death. The red light flashes as the body and the cycle are dragged away.

The sound track of *Scorpio Rising* is made up of pop music – a chant for today. Song after song is played through, each song with its own relevance and reverence for the image and the act. This series of songs puts forward a curiously powerful statement. They are songs full of myth, with a simple repeating rhythm – basic hypnotic, dense. Anger's juxtaposition of ritual sound and ritual image intensifies the mood. His use of existing records in *Scorpio Rising* is one of the best examples of the use of such material in the independent cinema. This is one of the most common sources of sound for many film-makers. The relationship of symbols and gestures is again both apparent and complex. Sex and power, sex and guilt, sex and ritual; fear and power; fear and ritual; icons; dreams of the lost world of childhood, and so on. Anger sees Christ as two thousand years of hang-up based on renunciation, guilt and sacrifice. Machines are also a way of inventing power, a way of going 'way out'. He sees the hand-tended machine as 'some sort of Buck Rogers rocket ship', because he considers that, if man is to change, he will have to become a child all over again.

The same idea is reflected in his short preview film (begun in 1964/5) *Kustom Kar Kommandos*, which portrays the worship involved in polishing a magnificent chrome custom-built car. Filmed like a majestic animal or a magnificent goddess, the steel and chrome are enhanced with plumes caressing the metal glow. A man with a T-shirted torso guards this goddess, filmed in clear colour precision, like a perfect advertisement.

Kenneth Anger's films are very rich. It is not that his dreams and visions are his alone, nor that his symbolism is different from that of other film-makers; the point is that he can take the obvious and present it in a symbolic way. He treats inner dreams and fantasy as the essential living being, in a way that makes others feel afraid. But he also presents his own fear, his inner self; the film becomes an act of voodoo, the transference of the inner self to form; a myth of its own, but existing openly. Anger goes even further with his transcendental methods, bringing out this fearful inner self even further. In *Invocation of my Demon Brother* the ritual men are more calm, and nude, like demi-gods, poised as Buddah bearing the blade of a knife, more contained leaders. Their inner strength is growing; no longer does the skull of death hang over them, it is in their hands, their peace pipe. The musclemen and the motorcycle men pose calmly, and their faces are studied more. Anger himself appears, swirling as the Master of Ceremonies, the magician and now the invocator. The film becomes much looser and the imagery and the ritual become more lucid, blending into processions of people, moving from the stage to the real world. Hidden somewhere in all this is the sperm, waiting like sexuality on the edge. This is the best filmed of Anger's works, and also the most recent. It rides clear with the throbbing sound made by Mick Jagger, yet Anger's formality remains, a strange stiffness as though the demon remains elusive. At the end a sign appears: 'Zap – you're pregnant – that's witchcraft.'

Eaux d'Artifice (1953), an earlier film made in the gardens of the Villa d'Este at Tivoli in Italy, is very different in form. It is full of relaxed inspiration in which the demon does not exist. It flows through splendid baroque water fountains, pouring gargoyles, endless stairs and walks. Through it runs and walks a woman, the only human being there. An apparition from the grand ballroom, moving like Cinderella in the palace garden. *Eaux d'Artifice* is a beautiful display, like a film dream in newly transmuted colours, a sonnet for the eyes. The programme note says: 'Hide and seek in a night-time labyrinth of levels, cascades, balustrades, grottoes and ever gushing, leaping fountains, until the Water Witch and the fountains became one.'

                              silence

                              is
                              a
                              looking . . .
                                        ee cummings

Fairly close to this sensibility, but very much on their own and utterly different in form, are the sensitive films of Gregory Markopoulos. Markopoulos, like Kenneth Anger, began making films in the mid to late 1940s in America. His preoccupation with film has been long, continuous and highly devoted, and he has evolved a form of film expression that comes from deep personal involvement.

His films are derived from personal dreams; from the poems, stories and myths of the Greeks; from the overlapping sensations of his thoughts and desires; from the configuration of the homosexual consciousness. They evolve in a time/space of image – image as symbol and as truth – reaching a strong degree of personal sensitivity in the form Markopoulos gives them. They recreate the tempo of breathing while sleeping, rhythmic and intensely delicate and invaded with a personal element. They use formal and precise gesture to evolve a structure of a trance-like density, uncompromisingly and unashamedly displaying themselves and the nakedness of being. A fragile, hypersensitive atmosphere is created.

Markopoulos's use of driving rhythms, a poetic beat, gives his films an unusual presence. At the same time there is a subtle, yet limitless change in the rhythm, which is often overlaid with verbal synonyms, with symbols and visual metaphors. A pause is followed by a repeat, a swaying back and forth, but each time further out. In many ways the rhythm is like the phrases of a written poem, with the images making the counterpoint and balance and reiterated with the voice. The visual phrases are often accompanied by phrases composed of single frames as alternating image, such as A, B, A, B and so on, fluttering like a butterfly. Markopoulos has said that with *Twice a Man* he utilized a form of editing which contained everything that he had learned over a period of some twenty years; the inherent possibilities of classic editing according to groups of shots in various lengths. To this form he added a new form in which the idea of the classic shot-to-shot was applied to the film itself, i.e. a single film frame to another single film frame, and its 'obvious inexhaustible architectural possibilities'. He realized for the first time 'that sense which is inherent in the lyricism of the independent, silent spaces.' A sensation of a pulsing in-and-out rhythm is created, but though Markopoulos uses such a strong and precise formality his imagery remains an esoteric abstraction of the self. What are the right words to describe this? A deep emotional attitude is endless portrayal, apparently within the confines of formality. This formality is related to the Greek model in which calm and solid outer strength allows the inner depth to be revealed. Yet it is not just in the architectural form, but in the mythological form that Markopoulos seeks his realizations. The human conflict, stylized by mythology, becomes associated with his own feelings and the two combined are made into a film.

Markopoulos's *Twice a Man* is based on the Hippolytus myth. It is the story of the mother, Phaedra, and her tortured love for her son, Hippolytus, and his for her. In remorse for this, Hippolytus is carried by horses to be drowned in the sea. He is reborn in heaven when the physician Aescalapius grants him immortality. Markopoulos develops this complex story of dual love methodically and with contemporary references. It is his own conflict as much as that of Hippolytus (who is called Paul in this film). The hetero/ homosexual conflict, and the drawing in of the son by the mother, is a vital element in the film's architecture. The conflict of duality is emphasized by the alternating, single frame in and out, occurring when the two forces present themselves simultaneously. The visual 'phrases' pass by and then come back: the mother as a young lover; as an old woman; then Paul being mourned; the girl he sees and avoids; the other man, the physician; the physician's hand on Paul; the mother trying to draw his love back home; Paul's death and rebirth giving him to the physician – a measured unfolding of inner complexities.

Markopoulos's films all have a narrative basis, and a passion of conflict emerging into firmly structured illumination. The basic conflict always remains, and is reconfirmed with each film, but each time it becomes more resolute and more controlled. It starts with *Psyche* (1947), the first part of Markopoulos's trilogy *Du Sang de la Volupté et de la Mort*. As the title suggests, it explores the mentality of the self. An attempt at realizing the self is begun in film – an abundantly rich process in which the self becomes forms beyond experience. The trilogy is completed with *Lysis* and *Charmides* (both 1948), both of which are based on a dialogue of Plato. Once again Markopoulos is seeking lucid answers through the metaphor of myth.

As with so many independent film-makers, the effect created by Markopoulos's films is difficult to put into words. With *Himself as Herself* (1967), for instance, description seems a mere cliché. The film is built on cutting – quick-cutting, changing to slow and delicate cutting. Images are intercut to overlap, as the conflict of dual self takes shape. The erotic clinging to the fur, a flash of a hand, the figure at the fireplace, a movement up and down presented in a rhythmic image of masked players. But the precise memory of each stands out less, for me, than the feeling I experienced of delicate tension, as though different lines were meeting only at fixed points, and then separating once again. Similarly in his earlier film *Swain* (1950) a duo-inner growth is formed, like two lines converging, passing and then spreading out again. There is a total absence of sound at the beginning, with the image of the moon, but the film ends with sound over a blank screen. It traverses the light of the night, through earth's being and earth's forms and earth's death, out to the open light.

Markopoulos finds in Prometheus the symbol of conflict. *The Illiac Passion* (1967) shows an increase in personal complexity yet has a stronger visual fluency than many of his other films. It does not portray self-involvement (though this may have given rise to the film), but a sanctity found in movement, image, colour and time. *The Illiac Passion* begins with the alternate presence of the personalities – the characters, as it were. The alternating images are sometimes obliterated, sometimes disappear and then return unexpectedly to refer to another image in the film. The moments turn into single or clustered single frames as film phrases. The build up of alternating images on the screen was done, said Markopoulos, 'so that a summation results in the figure of the protagonist'. I can still see the figures slipping by and rising again, as though no one could touch them, and the space between each one is the chain, or the wall of nothing that is there; like time, the wall becomes invisible but never breaks down. We are, each of us, our own jailers. The words on the soundtrack are uttered again like a monotone echo: 'Unapproached solitude . . . high, high, hanging rocks . . . reproach.'

The rhythm in Markopolous's films comes from his sensitivity and he chooses his colours with great care. They are chosen as for a painting, as if he were a Giorgione, or a Riberg, or a Carracci, or a Tiepolo. The lighting, the focus, the symbol, the gesture, even the slightness of movement are the delicate differences that constitute and make possible the film's full potential. He poses his figures or objects in a manner reminiscent of the painting of the sixteenth and seventeenth centuries. His phrases suggest that period's formal gestures, its lighting and its colours. All are treated with the same attention to detail. In the hands of anyone else some of his subtle images could seem absurd. To take the classic symbol of sex and homosexuality (an egg, a motorcycle) and yet to avoid cliché demands the greatest sensitivity for the form and the medium. All his films, from *Psyche* to *Serenity, The Illiac Passion, The Divine Damnation* and *Bliss*, have this sensitivity. Only Robert Beavers, who stars in *Eros, O Basileus* (1966), has succeeded in capturing the atmosphere of Markopoulos's world, as in his own *Winged Dialogue*. The imagery is more fluid and more diffused, even softer, in *The Everyday Use of the Eyes of Death* (1968). Beavers is like an Impressionist painter using the forms created by the Cubists, while Markopoulos is like the seventeenth-century masters in his classical lucidity. Yet beneath his formality there is a passion, and he recreates it with as much seriousness as imagination. His *Ming Green* (1966), for instance, metamorphosizes still life into moving life, while in *Gammelion* he transforms a castle in Italy called Il Castello de Roccasinibalda. Armed with only two rolls of colour film and his Bolex, Markopoulos shot only short film phrases as he traversed the ancient castle, spacing out each phrase with darkness, then darkness fading into image and fading out to darkness again. The camera travels for an hour through a mood of muted poignancy with the richness and strength of classical antiquity; it travels through rooms and halls, along the road round the castle; sweeping over the façade and through shimmering gold and red-brown colours. The phrases become like massive columns breaking through the space as in some great church or castle. The architectural sense, the structuring of light, dark, image, scale, distance, movement, are so strong that the film becomes a monument in itself.

It is important to note that Markopoulos uses and develops his sound with the same precision as he does his images. He does not merely use spoken words, but also music, even opera. Phrases are used as poems, becoming auditory counterpoints positioned so that they either blend with the atmosphere or punctuate it.

These studies, in many ways conceived like paintings (rather than as music or sculpture or dance or theatre), illustrate another approach found in the independent personal film – the idea of making portraits. We judge and respond to a man's nature and his character from the features of his face and the form of his body, from the things he surrounds himself with and his actions or his pose. The portrait becomes the artist's or film-maker's interpretation of these clues. In film, the portrait becomes a moving modulation of expression, of personality, sometimes a caricature. A film portrait is one of the most direct processes available to the film-maker, in many ways akin to the diary approach, like a snapshot (portraits often appear in diary films).

In 1966 Markopoulos made *Galaxie*, one of the major attempts, and one

L

of the first, at film portraiture. This film is a collection of some thirty portraits, each filmed on a hundred feet of film superimposed to reveal a multiplicity of character. Markopoulos also made a single portrait (15 minutes) of the artist-poet-dancer Mark Turbyfill called *Through a Lens Brightly: Mark Turbyfill* (1966) a film called *Political Portraits* (1969), which portrays Rudolf Nureyev and Giorgio de Chirico.

Brakhage made his *Song 15* as a portrait film, and Warhol made his *13 Most Beautiful Women* and *3 Most Beautiful Men*; Peter Gidal made one called *Heads*, in which I appear, and Birgit and Wilhelm Hein made one simply called *Portraits* (1970), a didactic, structural presentation of stills of Charles Manson, Ronald Biggs and Wilhelm Hein. Klaus Schönherr made a girl in his *Gedanken beim Befühlen einer Mädchenhaut* (Thoughts on feeling a Girl's Skin, 1968) almost a caritcature, while his *Das Porträt der Cordua* (1969) shows the beautiful German dancer Beatrice Cordua. De Bernardi constructs much of his massive film *Le Opere e i Giorni* (1969-70) out of portraits of the children he teaches and his family, and it is one of the most relaxed and watchable films ever made. Even a self-portrait can be seen on film, as with Lutz Mommartz's *Selbstschüsse* (1967), in which he films himself running, walking and being himself.

The individual urge of different people to make films as expressions of themselves is profound, beautiful and necessary. Nevertheless, the results of this activity are often received unfavourably by others. Authority especially has a deep mistrust of things it does not fully understand. All films have the power and the potential of hypnotic-like suggestion and this underlying power is feared. Film's magic is such that it has within it a high potential of suggestibility especially when it is personal and expressive of specific emotional attitudes. It is when inner emotions are challenged that people without the necessary understanding and freedom of appreciation react and reject but they are quick (when the time is right for them) to absorb the new attitudes and forms to be found in the film or work of art. This process has a lot to do with our emotional development.

For artists the continuous creating of these forms and attitudes is a necessary release. The new forms can be witnessed, or experienced by others as the symbol or realization of inner feelings and as such can be productive and useful. Social order, however, appears to thrive on existing and more generalized forms and people fear and reject new ideas that strike at their inner emotional attitudes. Because film is such a direct form of expression it thus has the power to move the masses; therefore it comes in for the maximum amount of criticism.

It is always curious to me how, through the generations, new forms of representation are always decried when they first appear but later they become the common form of expression. Yet rejection on a massive scale continues, as though we shall never learn this lesson. The names and shapes of the forms change, but the nature and the necessity of their creation does not. Each time they become the affirmation and re-affirmation of the emotional flow; that is the self, and every new form allows that affirmation to be experienced. The rejection of those forms and the rejection of those experiences soon becomes a rejection of the self.

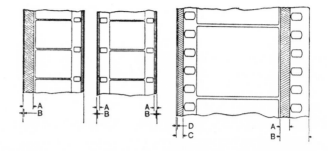

There is a poet called Robert Lax and a film-maker who has made films based on his poems: Emil Antonucci. The poems are simple, hypnotic and penetrating; they have the unstrained and natural rhythm of a human pulse. Antonucci's films represent a collection of various Lax poems. Each film is like a visual collection of poetry: each poem has its own visual and auditory position in the film, just as each poem has its own page in a book. A precise image or series of images is presented for each poem, which is read over the visual material on the sound track. The poem 'The First Goodbye' (from *New Poems* – film and book) is read over images of the face of a dark-haired girl, presented in a continuing series of fadeouts:

> the first goodbye
> the second goodbye
> the third goodbye
> the fourth goodbye
> the fifth goodbye
> the sixth goodbye
> the seventh goodbye
> the eighth goodbye
> the ninth goodbye
> the tenth goodbye
> the eleventh goodbye
> the twelfth goodbye
> the hundred and twenty-first goodbye
> the hundred and forty-fourth goodbye
> the hundred and eighty-ninth goodbye
> goodbye
> goodbye
> goodbye

The images, like the poem, drive forward, suddenly speeding up on the last three goodbyes. The fadeout functions as though your eyes were slowly closing; in the next image they suddenly open, only to return to the slow closing motion. Each of the images shows the girl's face in a different position.

Each of Antonucci's poem pieces is a gem of precise and personal imagery – an imagery that never interprets the words, but involves our visual senses so that our ears can hear. An important point here is that the images are so rich that they can be viewed with equal strength on their own, silently. The images are like magnificent photographs, transposed into a particular time, and therefore a movement, as with the poem 'What does it matter?', which offers an image of a crumpled pillow presented in a rich chiaroscuro light. Another fixed image is that of a cup presented in porcelain tones for the poem 'Is', which reads:

is
is
is
is
is
is
is

is
is
is
is
is
is
is

is
is
is
is
is
is
is

is
is
is
is
is
is
is

The imagery in 'Telepistemology' revolves round a rhythmic and almost cyclic view of a girl leaning on a table. The views dissolve into each other. Each view is different, though the subject is the same – sometimes close, sometimes further away, always from a slightly different angle from the one before. The poem's images sometimes develop into action, as in 'Man with Big General Notions', where we see a man miming the building of a house. This is an instance of a more direct interpretation of the poem, an illustration of the verbal by the visual.

Taken together, Antonucci's films reveal an approach to film that is directly linked to a pure, almost classical way of seeing. This strips the image of any obvious struggle for technique (though it is only by mastering a technique that one is able not to make the technique obvious). This stripping of the obvious and conscious is important because it gives depth and independent life to the image. This particular kind of independence, which is a feature of the best work produced in the other visual arts, such as drawing and painting (and sometimes photography), has not often been allowed in the cinema. Not, at least, until recently, or only in very personal film activities. Even here this purity of isolated and independent imagery has been limited or used only to create associations. Warhol's earlier films, such as *13 Most Beautiful Women*, are an example of an approach that is being increasingly used by many other film-makers, though each gives it his particular direction and emphasis. Another example here is Carlos Paex-Villaro's and Gerard Levy-Clerc's *Une Pulsation* (1969), made in Uruguay and France, where the images are isolated 'takes' or actions assembled like stanzas to create a feature-length film.

Brakhage's *Songs*, as we have seen, are a collection of short visual poems, independent lyrics. Another outstanding example of visual poetry is the American film-maker Bruce Baillie's *Castro Street* (1966), which makes use of imagery assembled like the lines of a printed poem. The lines are fluid, visual renderings of the sights and activities in an industrial street in Richmond, California – an oil refinery, a railway switchyard, a timber company. Baillie combines colour and black-and-white film stock in a rhythm produced by superimposition and diffusion. The mood is soft and dreamy, skilfully conveying the life of the landscape. By shooting the film through reflectors and by localizing actions and images, by altering the shape of the frame (with 'matter' placed over the lens), he has transformed industrial forms and activities into a personal interpretation of a particular environment. It is a beautiful film, very dependent on visual subtlety for its emotional effect. Carl Sandburg's words help to conjure up something of the mood it creates:

> The steelmill sky is alive. The fire breaks
> white and zigzag shot on a gun-metal gloaming . . .
>
> . . . a spectrum and a prism held in a moving monolith—

Yet they miss much of Baillie's personal tone. Even the soundtrack of this 10-minute film is a chamber piece constructed from the sounds of Castro

Street itself. The sound blending is soft and of a kind seldom achieved by others, except perhaps by Vertov in his first sound film.

Not many independent film-makers have focused their gaze on the man-made landscape in such a positive sense. Another is Ulrich Herzog, a German film-maker whose *Film Z Teil 1* is a very sensitive and poetic work centred on a council-type housing block. It sounds funny (and many people had a good laugh when the film was screened), but I found it a rich and positive statement about an increasingly common aspect of our environment. Images of the housing block seen by night, by day, moving past, far away, through a distorted lens, in close-up, through a hole, and so on, reveal a positive relationship between man and his own artefacts. Herzog's attitude can also be related to earlier films such as Ruttmann's *Berlin, the Symphony of a Great City* or Léger's *Ballet Mécanique*. Yet Baillie's work has a greater consciousness of the actual material he is using to develop his subjective visual interpretation.

Film can be described or explained only in terms of light and optics: visual effects. But if we are too aware of the effect (what it is, or how it is done) we are drawn away from the overall statement for the sake of a detail. An ultra-physical and ultra-rational description can be misleading. For instance, such a description as 'Baillie's talent most often lies in the separate image, usually with bizarre technical effects (i.e. overexposed film, colour filters, reflected images)', leaves the viewer seeking, remembering and questioning the methods employed to make a visual statement. This is certainly not to deny the importance of technique. Any image on film creates a 'visual effect'. But to stress, say, Baillie's 'bizarre technical effects' is misleading, for it is the statement, not the effect, that makes the film. Although film-makers may explore or 'experiment' with effects created by particular kinds of image, the experiment is over when the film is complete.

Baillie does not stick to one genre of visual expression but uses visual language for a particular purpose. His poetic black-and-white film *Mass* (1963/64) exposes the paradox of life within the American environment: the violence, the materialism, the destruction of the landscape by industry. The soft imagery is created by a multiple film language of superimposition and smooth, slow passes (sideways camera movement) flowing into or superimposed on to other slow passes. *Mass* is dedicated to the Sioux Indians of Dakota, where Baillie was born, and reveals his personal preoccupation with them. One of the programme notes states that he dedicates it to a religious people who were destroyed by the civilization which evolved the Christian mass. The film becomes the Christian paradox as exemplified by the mass, a celebration of life, with an imagery that illustrates its powers of destruction. It contains an almost Cocteau-esque death. The rider on a motorbike (a recurrent image in American films from *Scorpio Rising* to *Easy Rider*) escorts a hearse through the new American man-made wastelands, while the sound track develops into a Gregorian chant.

Some of Baillie's films, such as *To Parsifal* (1963), *Quixote* (1965), *All My*

Life (1966), *Still Life* (1966), plus earlier works in a more documentary vein such as *The News* or *Mr Hayashi* (1961), are even richer in their use of the resources of film language. All in all, he is one of the most committed, as well as one of the most poetic, of film-makers.

Because many independent film-makers are inspired to make films by a personal urge to express themselves and have never been connected with the cinema industry or conditioned by it, they revitalize film language. Their exploration of the visual language enriches our seeing, just as poetry enriches ordinary verbal language. Cocteau once said: 'I've been completely free only with *Le Sang d'un Poète*, because I didn't know anything about film art. I invented it for myself as I went along, and used it like a draughtsman dipping his fingers for the first time in Indian ink and smudging a sheet of paper with it.' The same applies to most personal/independent/experimental film-makers, though some do conceive their films in the terms of the cinema industry. This 'naïve' exploration of the medium, unhampered by any preconceptions, has resulted in a widening of the visual experience. One development has been the attempt to use the physical nature of the film process as the subject of the film. Another is the effort to remove any associations from the photographed image, and to have no narrative links between images (though it can be argued that we all interpret even the most abstract images and give them some narrative structure). Yet another development is the attempt to arrive at a purer sense of the space, time and motion involved in the film process: to make the film a more self-contained, phenomenological experience.

One vital development of the visual language and our comprehension of it has come about through films that differentiate between the ability of the film to contain an image and the ability of the film to be an image. There is some overlap here, as with films in which physical qualities (such as grain or blurriness) merge with the recorded image. There are innumerable examples of this physical blending, particularly in the work of Bruce Baillie or Jack Smith.

> But this isn't seeing! – But this is seeing! – it must be possible to give both remarks a conceptual justification.
>
> Ludwig Wittgenstein

But more important to the development of the language is the work of certain film-makers who have concentrated on evolving a *film which is of its own image* by breaking down any inherent symbolism or associative values of the recorded image. The aim is to create a visual language that in no way refers to anything outside the film itself. The attempt to make the film

an immediate object of perception and a self-sufficient experience represents a repudiation of the dictates of the photographic tradition. This
tradition transposes forms and actions from outside the film (i.e. from life)
on to the film, and by allusion constructs relationships among these forms so
that they recall life. This representational tradition distracts from the clarity
of the total film experience. If symbolism cannot be eliminated, it must be
'direct' symbolism, arising as directly as possible from the sensation/percep-
tion. This purist approach demands, in effect, that visual statements should
be directly accessible to the senses and the mind without being dependent
upon representational symbols or narrative sequence. Obviously, few films
can achieve the ideal in this pure form. P. Adams Sitney has labelled this
general approach 'Structuralism', and defined Structural films as those which
minimalize content as 'subsidiary to the outline' – as opposed to films that
develop out of 'form', by which he means the interrelationship (usually
created by editing) of the photographed material.

There is a continuous overlap between these two basic approaches of form
and structure when we apply them to individual films. Such terms and categories serve here merely as a means of presenting certain basic attitudes and
they are by no means definitive. We must also recognize the semantic
ambiguity in a term such as 'visual experience', which can be applied to
many types of film, whether they are narrative, poetic or structural. If
used in relation to 'structural' or 'minimal' films, it relates to a formal experience provoked by a concrete object. Here, in principle, the object states
itself directly through its own presence and individual properties with the
minimum amount of allusion to external content. The confrontation between
the viewer and the object becomes the action of the film. In this way there
is no allusion to anything else except that event or action. The so-called
'structural' films, on the whole, make their physical presence felt, since this
is their content. They often use images (representational or abstract) to
support the structure. In other words the structure is considered as primary,
and all other things must refer to that structure (even if the structure was
originally suggested by an image or a narrative theme).

The term 'structural' is misleading in that it can be interpreted in many
different ways. Films that are not called 'structural' still have structure, so
they should not be taken too literally. I should prefer a term such as 'physical',
because many of these films are based on their physical construction (conceptual and actual); on their physical presence and on the external effects
and changes created by the immediate relationship between them and the
viewer; and on the use of the physical properties of the medium. This combined with the physical characteristics of perception and the reaction of
the viewer's nervous system, and also the physical presence and use of sound
in conjunction with film are the basic material of these 'physical', 'structural'
or 'minimal' films. There is no allusion or poetic suggestion to anything
beyond what is witnessed; no attempt to achieve an external narrative as
such; no suggestion of creating another time or another meaning.

A dot (on a piece of paper, for example) or a line are active. A dot is active because it is present in the environment. A line is movement: it goes from one point to another, it is active. The line is an object because it is contained between two points. The presence of a line is the presence of an object in movement. Movement occurs in time because time is the experience or sensation of duration. Duration is distinguished by a beginning, a middle and an end. The nature of duration also contains the idea of past, present and future, by which an experience or an event can be circumscribed. A beginning, a middle and an end present a contained form, something you can locate. (The basis of a myth is an event that has a beginning, middle and end, and as such is removed from the continuous, never ending flow of life – in this sense myth is also an object.)

The line between the two points (or dots) can be straight, curved, curly, thin or thick, textured, coiled or a Japanese brush letter; each presents its own set of circumstances and projects its own conditions. All these concepts apply as much to film as they do to painting or sculpture or dance. A film is itself a line, an object, a form involving duration. An image can be a texture, and a texture can be an image. A scratch can be as much of an image as a photograph of a face. A dotted line can be a repetition, or a straight line can be a continuous shot; two lines criss-crossing each other can be superimposition, or a self-circumscribing line can be an overlapping repetition with subtle changes. A film can be seen as an accumulation of textures, patterns, colour and lines, occurring within a framework of time, space and light and experienced within particular environments. Even within a so-called narrative film certain aspects of the way the subjective mode is treated involve basic alteration of the material: light colour, or diffused colour, or dark colour are all able to establish an underlying mood for the narrative. The length or brevity of a shot gives a completely different meaning to what we witness. The point really is that whereas all these methods are the essential properties that establish subjective communication, there is no reason why they should not be expressive in themselves. If a line drawn in pencil seems softer than a line drawn in ink, so a diffused film image seems softer than a precise image. Similarly, each texture or colour (and their relationship to each other) sets up its own system capable of creating its own expression.

Wavelength is a classic example of 'structural' forms in film, yet it by no means encompasses all possible forms. Another example is *Rohfilm* (Raw Film, 1968), made by Birgit and Wilhelm Hein in Cologne. When I first saw *Rohfilm* I felt as though I was undergoing a visual (and auditory) bombardment. The film is a grinding collection of images, patterns and textures made from all the physical ('raw') aspects of film. Some of the images are created photographically (rephotographed photographs), others are just scratches on the film stock. As an unprojected strip of film it looks like a strange collage 16 millimetres wide and over 200 metres long. All kinds of film pieces – images, parts of images, sprocket holes, film perforations – have been assembled and printed on to the film, sometimes within frame shapes, at other times without any regard for the frame shape. When this film is projected no one particular image can be retained. The eye and the body receive only the physical experience of the film combined with a grinding soundtrack (made by Christian Michelis). Hardly any part of it is seen long enough to be retained in the conscious memory, either for recall or for association. In other words any form of narrative has been eliminated, and the structure of the film exists only by its accumulated physical presence over a period of limited duration. The whole film can never be seen as anything other than an experience or a sensation, and can only be described as such. The Heins' concern for the physical qualities of film is such that they proposed to have new copies of *Rohfilm* made from old prints that had been worn out and gathered more scratches and dirt. These new prints would replace the older prints, thus keeping alive the active and changing nature of the form.

In this category, George Landow, a New York film-maker, made his *Film in Which there Appear Sprocket Holes, Edge Lettering, Dirt Particles, Etc.,* a self-explanatory title. This film was made in 1965, before *Rohfilm*, and began with a frame image from a commercial test film of a girl staring straight out taking up half the frame space, while the other half of the frame was a colour spectrum guide (normally used for testing the film's colour balance). This overall image was reprinted out of register, so to speak, so that only half of the original frame (or almost half) was visible in the new, reprinted frame. The remaining half of the new frame was printed with sprocket holes and edge lettering. Landow looped this film and got the film laboratory to print the loop over and over again. He also told the lab not to clean the film but to allow dirt and dust to accumulate and to print that along with the rest. The result is a film in which there appears a static girl's face (except that she blinks with sprocket holes in the middle half, which joggle as the film runs) and edge lettering (which wiggles) while direct particles accumulate. Landow has said:

This film is experienced as a composition of images, letters and other elements which is more or less constant. Although it is never exactly the same from frame to frame, the changes are so subtle compared to the changes that normally take place within a film that people tend to see no change (aside from the blinking eye). In other words, it is on a completely different level of expectation. Ideally it would fit a situation where the spectator is ambulatory.[7]

Like many other independent film-makers, Landow began as a painter. 'As a painter,' he writes, 'I was interested in creating images. Whether the material be paint or film is more or less immaterial. What is important is *creating* those images.'[8] He saw the film's texture as a dynamic visual element. An image can remain, though the film grain (which is the actual physical construction of the photographed image on the film surface) can go through many changes ('You can actually see the pigment of the film beginning to slip off, in certain places, and you can see areas of pure light coming through'). His *Bardo Follies* (1967) is also built out of looped film of a woman (Southern Belle type) who waves her hand with each repeat of the loop. Then the same image doubles (in two circles within the same frame). The images in the circles then begin to appear as if they were burning. The screen fills with the burning frame (in slow motion), which disintegrates into a soft focus. Another frame burns. This 'melting' of the film changes to coloured bubbles on the screen (as though the film were being boiled). Then the screen goes white. Landow's films exemplify the use of film as its own image (film as pigment) while adhering to the 'structural' sense of repetition involving simple or subtle permutations. The result is an overall, simple film with a minimum of ambiguity. *Fleming Faloon* (1963) has more complex imagery, though it maintains a 'flat' image look. In his later films, such as *Institutional Quality*, a stronger narrative sense becomes noticeable. Though *Bardo Follies*, like *Rohfilm*, uses film material as a basic image source while attempting to break down the narrative form, there is an important difference between the two. *Bardo Follies* uses just a few subtle images, dissolving slowly and repetitively. *Rohfilm*, on the other hand, floods the senses with rapid impulses, with the result that nothing really remains retainable. It is subtle only in that it depends on the accumulation of sensations while being aggressive. *Bardo Follies* starts more or less solidly and softly breaks itself down.

The first appearance in the Heins' films of the idea of the accumulation of images was in the silent *S & W* (1967). In this film each frame is a different image (a style that had been employed by Robert Breer since the 1950s in films such as *Image by Images I* [1954] or *Fist Fight* [1964], of which he said 'Every frame is a painting'). Landow's early film *Fleming Faloon* uses a multiplicity of images in one frame, not a different frame for every image. Unlike the Heins, he uses the loop principle, in which the front of a film piece is attached to the end to achieve a continuous but repeated action.

KRIWET: TEXTFILM

The particular feeling created by seeing refilmed film is that it displays a richness and source of imagery that is possible only in the realm of film or photography. Any artist soon discovers that it is through the particular nature and characteristics of his materials and tools that he can achieve his expression. His materials thus become a physically expressive part of his work and working methods. Watercolour creates a different effect from oil paint; stone differs from wood, wood from plastic. Whether we like it or not we all respond to the qualities or properties of materials (most of us can *feel* the difference between wood and steel just by *looking*). In many cases, the material also dictates much of the form. Film, as a material, is no different in this from other materials and can therefore offer a vast range of impressions. (It also has 'magical' properties because it *seems* inexplicably to emerge out of nothing.) It is through these physical and material qualities, combined with the individual conceptual processes, that we can achieve particular relationships that allow us to see, to feel and to experience afresh.

In *Reproduction* (1969) by Birgit and Wilhelm Hein old photography becomes a material; when rephotographed on to moving film it establishes a new contact with a once static form. The film appears in and out of focus. But this effect does not seem to be created so much by the camera lens as by the movement of a fixed image in front of the camera. The images are made up of old slides and snapshots from the Heins' family album. The process of refilming (the camera lens has a short focal length which causes the rapid effect of moving in and out of focus) presents a visual situation that grossly exaggerates the image. It is rather like staring at a static image for a long time in that thoughts intrude and one's degree of concentration changes. In film this change no longer has anything to do with the content of the image. Instead the nuances and the rhythm of the change become the meaning. The change from a recognizable (figurative) image to a blur represents the experience. The film produces a total feeling of amorphousness in that we become caught up in the process of fluid change. The image is always in motion, and it is through our physical relationship to rhythm that we become engrossed in it, and not because we 'know' anything about the original picture.

The structure of the Heins' film *Grün* (Green, 1968) is composed of obscured and passing glimpses. None is fully remembered, and each glimpse is engulfed by the next. The images are destroyed before they can be fully retained by the brain. The texture of the images in *Grün* is more fluid and less flat than in *Rohfilm* and they last longer.

Work in Progress (1970) is a cumulatively 'structural' film since its strength is increased by the successive addition of smaller 'structural' units. The first image is a beach – a blurred snapshot of two people sitting on the beach, as though the camera moved when it was taken. This image stays, becomes exaggerated by its permanence. It penetrates and it grows. It is no longer photographic but graphic. It develops into a strobing and flicker of the original image. It varies in degree and pattern. This intensive presentation of an image lasts for something like twenty minutes, with a soundtrack consisting of a high-pitched, continuous tone. We seem to be enveloped by the image. After this beach scene 'photograph' image the film cuts to a straight, long continuous take of a view down a shopping street. The camera is fixed and only the people walk about. The mood is relaxed. The film cuts to the words *'Der Raub'* ('Rape') and then goes into a black image built up into numbers. After the final blacking out the film becomes a repeat (sometimes seemingly looped) of a male nude moving and running back and forth across the camera plane, towards and away from the camera. The gestures are staccato, as though the frames are changing speed, and sometimes freeze for seconds at odd times – almost like a flick-back. The movements of the figures create the same impression as Muybridge's early series of photographs of the figure in action.

This film represents a 'structural' category that is exceptionally pronounced in its physical and textural qualities. The Heins maintain a formal tension, a 'didactic tension' almost. The film is strong and penetrating, offering not an experience that drifts and floats about, but one that is very much directed. This direction, which is not smooth but pointed, like a jagged line, is a feature that many critics and viewers do not like.

Smoother and more purely structural in that they are more noticeably concerned with structure are the films made by the English film-maker Peter Gidal. His film *Takes* (1970) (not to be confused with another film of the same title made by the Heins), is structured on the cinematographic process of 'takes' – the taking and retaking of the same action until the right 'take' is achieved.

Takes is a eurhythmic film whose movements are highly homogeneous. Its primary image is a filmed image, the action consisting of a camera panning round a room, passing a girl standing by a bed who takes off her bra and walks out of the frame. This happens while the camera maintains its sideways movement. This action is then repeated, but as a refilmed, slightly out of focus series of images. The sideways movements, though repeats, differ in length. It is rather as if one were to take a sentence or a phrase and repeat it, but each time taking out a word or two from the beginning or end and then putting them back again. The film is not only refilmed out of focus, but the shape of the original film frame appears within the new frame. What we see is a film within a film. This exaggerates the grain of the film and increases the feeling that we are really looking at something through something. But most of all the whole film occurs in a circumscribing action, a slow world rotating onto itself but each turn slightly different and with renewed intensity.

Gidal believes in using objects, transposed on to film, as catalysts for perceptual reactions, for emotional involvement. To do this he tries to establish a position by means of what he calls 'precise vision'. In order to achieve this visual precision he uses the camera for an intense scrutiny of objects (people become objects). In this sense the film creates a very formal structural impression because it is almost always dictating a specific position or movement. It establishes a space that puts you in the position of looking at a piece of sculpture. It is related to the sculptural approach attained in masterly fashion in Michael Snow's *Wavelength*, in which you become part of the sculptural space instead of merely looking at it. In many ways Gidal's *Takes* (1970) can be related more specifically to Michael Snow's *Standard Time* (1968). In the latter the camera moves almost always on a horizontal level, mostly from left to right. The movements are not specifically circular, but horizontal sweeps going in the same direction. The return to the beginning of a sweep is never seen, only the sweep itself. Each sweep exposes something new within the scene, but since the camera never comes to a halt it is never entirely clear what this is, or whether it was in fact there before. A bed is empty, then there is a woman on the bed, then the bed is empty; there is a cat, another time a turtle; or else a doorway is first empty, then frames a nude woman. The varying speed of the sweeps creates a feeling of excitement, of discovery.

In his *Rooms* (1967) Gidal explores a room as a total object, with the camera travelling round the room in one direction. Through an in and out of focus zoom lens he moves into and out of objects – books, doorknob, posters – until he arrives at a figure smoking a hookah. The camera stops while we watch him inhale, relax and inhale again. This whole action is repeated a second time, exactly as it appeared the first time. (Gidal calls it 'double take'.) This use of repetition heightens our perception of the image in that it eliminates everything external to the film. At the same time the in and out of focus zoom increases the visual experience by allowing us to see an object by means of the contrast between blur and sharpness. In Gidal's *Hall* (1969) a similar situation is created, except that here the object is a hall entranceway. Instead of a sideways camera movement our relationship to the object is achieved by a visual movement into and out of various focal planes. With these films the feeling develops as a meditative search, is therefore more psychological experience than physical experience.

This meditative mood becomes more of a macro-scrutiny in the films of Ernie Gehr. In *Wait* and *Moments* he adopts the same approach as Gidal in *Hall* and Snow in *Wavelength*. He also uses altered film exposures, creating light changes, along with staccato zoom actions, and he also has a sculptural sense of confined and selected space. The experience that we undergo when we actually see the films is of course very different. They may be almost alike, but each produces a totally different experience, worlds apart from each other. The description 'tall, dark man' may fit many people, but individual expressions, gestures and personalities distinguish one from the other. Similarly, Michael Snow's films are encompassing and overwhelming, Gidal's establish a paced but objective meditation, while Gehr's offer a melancholy analysis with an exaggerated sense of time. I can remember feeling while watching a Gehr film a strange sadness, like watching the slow agony of waiting for someone. I soon felt as if I too was waiting. Movements and actions seemed to be slower than slow motion, but fragmented actions were repeated and became familiar, as they do when one waits in one spot for a long time. I remember a couple walking between the grey, cloistered columns of some old building, their walk becoming a romantically sad and claustrophobically endless love affair. A subjective response, born naturally from my experience of the film.

Gidal's film *Neck* (1969) (both a 10-minute and a half-hour version exist) is not so formally constructed (though it is structural). It looks at an object (a girl's neck) from a fixed point of view. The neck merely twists from left to right, otherwise everything else seems frozen. At least it seems frozen until you keep watching. After a while your vision fragments and explores the image. The film grain becomes a sandstorm for a while, or else merges with the image of flesh, producing a feeling of sensuality. The experience becomes a personal exploration of new territory.

One of the most euphoric films I have seen is Gidal's *Clouds* (1969), which looks at the sky over London. Grey and formless, the cloud shapes hardly discernible, it creates a strange and euphoric sensation because the image is really a grey light giving a sense of space through a void. It is related to Kasimir Malevich's paintings in which he made the jump from negative to positive by placing a black square on a white background, thereby recognizing the void. Every once in a while in *Clouds* a jet aeroplane appears: sometimes jumping along the lower edge of the frame; sometimes jumping up into the centre; sometimes resting on the frame edge; but always flying by. The aeroplane's appearances punctuate the space, giving the grey void a strong presence (like a dot in a white space). Space exists here on a two-dimensional plane and time exists in a continuum of light. The aeroplane's appearances along and within portions of the frame constantly state its area. The feeling is of a drifting daydream, the intensive and mesmerizing soundtrack helping to create the mood. The aeroplane is like a kid's bit of joy.

Clouds has an intensive soundtrack, which is used to force the viewer into one image. Like Michael Snow or the Heins, Gidal uses sound in a very pointed and direct way, to enclose the physical space and thus enforce a relationship between it and the image. It also produces a physical response that works in accordance with the imagery. In this way the overall presence of the object (the film) is increased and the totality of Gidal's experience is guaranteed without any other external points of reference.

Yet sound can also be used in what seems to be a diametrically opposite way – the creation of silence. In Gidal's *Bedroom* (1971), for example, only one single sound, a pip, occurs somewhere near the middle of the film, accentuating the silence that accompanies the rest of the film. *Bedroom* is a yellow/reddish colour film made in one 30-minute take. It consists of a floating, circular, in-and-out search round a bedroom; a freely moving line; a look for look's sake. Gidal claims that *Bedroom* is 'the most inclusive of my most involved [film] preoccupation: zooming, panning, focusing to constantly redefine reality and the process of seeing/filming. . . .' He further explains that 'the films are conceptualized before shooting, to a very detailed degree. They are also shot with a large degree of openness to momentary impulse and chance-happening. It's a matter of my response (partially spontaneous, *each time again*) to the camera (machine) . . . and film and lens and light and space and my hands and my eyes. . . . The films may be reconceptualized after shooting, sometimes they are, sometimes they're not.'[9]

'Pigment' sensitivity combined with intensity created by repetition and a contrast between textures is a keynote of many of the films of Malcolm Le Grice. By 'pigment' sensitivity I mean the building up (or destruction) of an image through film (photographic) material. Tones and textures seem to be laid on, diffused or shaped, shifted and reapplied, manipulated almost in a constructional way, yet also very definitely in a painterly way. By intensity created by repetition I mean that images (whether representational or textural) reappear, often in different positions, or doubled, or first negative then positive; or at the side, at the bottom; for a short time or for a long time. By contrasts I mean a literal juxtaposition of light and dark, of crowded frame and empty frame, of fast movement and slow movement, of representational image and no image. In *Castle 1* we have a contrast between a real (three-dimensional, physical) light bulb and one on the screen, and of course, the space in between.

Talla and *Yes, No, Maybe, Maybe Not* probably best express these features of Le Grice's work. *Yes, No, Maybe, Maybe Not* uses only two basic images: waves crashing against a breakwater and the ominously 1930s-looking Battersea power station. These images are contrasts, the waves being horizontally rhythmic while the power station is vertically solid and heavy (with its filthy smoke rising up). The ironic title expresses the film's basic rhythm – as far as words can do so. The waves are repeated, the power station is repeated – in negative, superimposed, in positive. At times one image in negative appears over the same image in positive, giving a feeling of solarization or bas-relief. The whole film is made up of rhythmic use of contrasts, like a simple and obsessive tune.

Talla is a particularly intriguing film. It drifts about, searching and wandering visually from one indecisive position to another. For me it represents an abstract vision of the mood and environment of Britain, for with its grey, flat and oblique drifting it contains the whole feeling of the country. In its physical presence its structure involves moving into and out of one point through a textural void to another point. It moves in waves of slowness, from wet streets to grey ones, to grey rocks, to an ambiguous figure, to more misty greyness and then to a dark lost factory. It attempts to dislocate the narrative in that none of the points is any more important than the voids. They fall into textural relationships, creating a patterns of gestures. Motion itself is as expressive as anything else and as such allows emotional involvement. A similar movement, though in a higher key, is used in Le Grice's *Blind-White Duration*. The image is more light: a white screen with near-white imagery, made up of twenty shots or reference points.

Le Grice increases the texture and the use of overlaid imagery in his later film *Berlin Horse*, in which the overlays become repetitions that accumulate and combine. In metaphorical terms it represents a switch from the grey drift of his earlier films to a denser wandering in a forest. The textural richness is heavier, the mood more sombre. He made the film by refilming on 16mm off a film made on 8mm near Berlin, printing it with negative and positive superimpositions on both black and white and colour. Le Grice's film-making aesthetic is based very much on the technology of the film process, though the results seldom have a 'technological' or 'mechanical' feeling. (His technical involvement has also led him to work on computer films.) The techniques he uses are not so much those of the camera, but rather involve laboratory processes. It is by exploiting and exploring the potential of the laboratory chemical and optical process (developing and printing methods), and combining this with such 'structural' forms such as repetitions and loops, or superimposition and multi-media, that Le Grice develops his imagery.

Well it's not really fiction, nor is it a documentary, so we can't find a place for it, and there is no other department for it.

BBC on a proposal for a subjective film

This laboratory area of film-making has been explored relatively little by film-makers, mainly because the laboratories themselves have been 'out of bounds', because processing equipment is expensive or inaccessible, and because film has traditionally laid the emphasis on the camera, on photographic potential and on editing. Few film-makers have ever been involved in processing, developing or printing their own films, though most have been confined to small quantities of film. They have also experimented with some of this potential to achieve new imagery. Hans Richter says that he had the use of a film printer while making his early films. More recently, many other film-makers, including Le Grice, have become involved in this aspect, other examples being Frans Zwartjes in Holland, Klaus Schönherr in Switzerland and myself. (Incidentally in the 'thirties my father was developing his own 8mm films – which for processing purposes is 16mm.) Other film-makers, such as Landow, have given specific instructions to some co-operative laboratories about making certain alterations to their films. Though most laboratories can do many things with film, most commercial labs are rather conservative (sometimes even reactionary) and as commercial businesses they naturally aim for a technical 'norm', as well as for a quick turnover. Most labs are therefore reluctant to experiment and most independent film-

M

makers have no contact with laboratory technicians at all and have never even seen the laboratory process in operation.

However much of this laboratory process has been obscured, it is still one of the most essential aspects of the film and the photographic process, and in it lies a whole world of potential. Still photographers have constantly explored the laboratory aspect of their work, and have found whole new forms of photographic expression and richness. For creative photographers like Billie Brandt or Man Ray their involvement in the laboratory aspect has become the essential factor in their work and the few film-makers who have sought to explore this aspect have come up with some exciting results.

The process is a simple one, particularly for black and white film (for colour, the chemistry, temperature and timings are more critical and more complex). There are two major pieces of equipment: a printer and a processor (developing machine). The processor develops the exposed film, the chemical process being similar to that used for processing still films. The difference is that a film-developing unit has to cope with long and continuous lengths of film, many of which have to be washed and dried as well as developed. Film developing units can range from small home tank units taking 50-foot to 100-foot lengths, working like a normal still film developing tank to continuous developing units taking thousands of feet of film and washing and drying as well. With continuous developing units the film must move continuously and consistently to achieve a consistent image. (The small tank developer holds the film on a spiral, as with the tanks for still film, so the film does not need continuous movement.) With continuous developing, the film must travel through the chemicals, the same amount of time being spent in each chemical bath.

The printer, the other piece of equipment, transfers the image from one piece of film (i.e. from a negative) to another, unexposed piece of film (to make a positive). In other words, negative film is transferred to raw stock to make a positive image. The raw stock is then put through a developer to make a finished print. (For reversal film, which is positive, it is transferred to a reversal raw stock, to make a positive image.) Printers transfer the image either by contact with the raw stock (contact printer) or optically by projecting on to the raw stock (optical printer). Optical printers can also blow up 8mm film to 16mm or 16mm to 35mm, and some can reduce as well. In either case light is used to expose each frame to the raw stock, as both lengths of film are simultaneously passed through the machine. Optical soundtracks are transferred separately through a special secondary printer. It is in the printer that grading or exposure ratios are determined, and that special effects such as fades, superimpositions or freezes are made.

This basic process offers an infinite number of possibilities. Film-makers like Le Grice, who use continuous developers, use the printer more for exploration while keeping the developing more consistent, while those who use the smaller developing units, as Zwartjes does, explore more with the developing and less with the printing.

Le Grice built his processor out of a Meccano set (erector set), worked out how long it would take for lengths of film to pass through the chemicals, drove the whole lot with a toy motor and dried the film with his wife's hair-dryer. He converted a normal 16mm projector into a printer. In 1970 his involvement had led him to establish a processing lab via the London Film-makers' Co-operative (and incidentally with the help of an unusual bene-factor). A proper, reconditioned printer and a standard commercial printer became available. Most of Le Grice's films were, at some point, processed by himself, which explains much of the 'pigment' feeling they have. His richest film in this context is *Little Dog for Roger*, which is usually shown on two screens. Describing the film, he said:

> *Little Dog for Roger* is made from some fragments of a 9.5mm home-movie that my father shot of my mother, myself and a dog we had. This vaguely nostalgic material has provided an opportunity for me to play with the medium as celluloid and various kinds of printing and processing devices. The qualities of film, the sprockets, the individual frames, the deterioration of records like memories, all play an important part in the meaning of this film.[10]

Little Dog for Roger is an excellent example of film expanding and speaking in a language of its own. It combines recorded image, repetition, film mater-ial, sound and the sensation of versatile movement. It is in some ways like the work of George Landow and in some ways like that of the Heins but it also becomes (whether Malcolm likes it or not) a film romance. In this way it is rather different from the purer 'structural' or 'minimal' aspect found in his other films (though it is quite close to the Heins' *Reproduction*). The movements of the film are not passive and controlled, but fluid, rhythmic, diversified. Sprocket holes joggle and edge lettering races by like a machine counter; everything swims by while swaying sideways, sometimes stopping, then floating to another side, or repeating itself to the same side. All the while a dog, a boy and a woman encased in a frame move or stay still, somehow repeating this cycle that goes nowhere except back on to itself – as a conscious memory. This effect is enhanced when the film is given a two-screen projection.

Le Grice returned to a more 'structural' or almost kinetic film with his later *Spot the Micro-dot or How to Screw the CIA, Part I*. It is full of visual sensations, exploiting the ability of the brain to retain or forget an image. A dot (sometimes coloured, sometimes textured) appears on the screen, perhaps for a fraction of a second (one frame = 1/24 second); some-times for a few frames longer; sometimes in different areas of the screen. The rest of the time the screen is black. The sudden and fractional flash of the dot and the subsequent return to black gives an 'after-image': the brain registers the dot flash and, because it is suddenly dark, retains it; but since the brain cannot remain still, it also fragments or analyses the dot. (Frag-mentation has also been used in Britain, particularly by Dr Chris Evans at the National Physical Laboratory.) The film uses this 'persistence of vision', as it is normally called, as the basis for its form, and by the nature of its physical characteristic creates a definite visual experience.

There is a never-ending richness in physical and structural films, because each alteration even to a finite aspect sets off a whole range of new film experiences. And each method or process mentioned can be combined with different attitudes and in different contexts. But it is important when discussing physical and structural films not to confuse content with technique. It is easy to describe a film with reference to its physical attributes of the media (film grain, refilmed film, specially printed film, painting on film), in such a way as to leave the impression that such films are merely experiments. Many people respond this way and see the films.as a mere gimmick, even if an interesting one. The greater emphasis on the actual medium and its material is experienced by those used to traditional methods as a physical change. If it dazzles or interests them they become impressed by the superficial effect. If they are bored or upset, they merely write the film off as a bad experiment or a superficial experiment lacking in content.

Refilmed film is one particular extension of film language. It can speak of the film as its own material; it can speak in a structural manner, or a physical manner; and it can also maintain narrative. Like a pigment, it can be applied endlessly. And it can take a film itself as its subject: film can become its own drama, developing its own character. It follows that film is as 'real' as a tree, a car, a landscape or a soap box. So why not film a film? Even more than that, the film engenders various actions and attitudes that are peculiar to itself. Thus some film-makers see the perforations or a scratch on a film as intrinsic to the material and therefore part of its expression, while others see refilmed film as an intensification of film itself.

Watching a film is an action: a basic relationship is set up. Watching a film is a real situation, just like watching people talking across the street. Their actions and gestures can be scrutinized and emphasized. Their hands, their head movements, their postures can be caught on film and help to convey an impression of these people and their situation. The same is true of film. The film is an illusion created by many single photographs passing at a speed such that our perception fuses the single pictures into a continuous array of movement. If this perceptible film speed at which actions seem 'normal' is changed, our perception of the action begins to change as well. A man running, filmed and projected at the standard norm of 24 frames per second, gives the illusion of a man running 'normally.' If the film is slowed up (in projection) the running slows up. But even more the running action becomes staccato and flickering, and if it is slowed up enough one begins to see the movement as a series of single pictures, of frozen moments. We no longer have an illusion of running but photographed split seconds of the action of running. If the film is stopped at any point the man becomes a picture of a figure, perhaps with his legs stretched out, suspended in a slight blur, giving the illusion of a man 'unnaturally' off the ground, though of course he is behaving quite naturally, as this is part of the process of running and of the process of photography. If one films the film of the man running while this speed change occurs, one then has a film about this change in perception – from the illusion of 'normal' running to the suspended action and the frozen movement of a gesture. But because it is refilm, the frozen gesture is alive in time, as it is held as an image on a film having duration. The frozen action can be released two frames and then held again. The perception is changed, the image is changed, the movement is connected to an 'idea' of non-movement, and so on. A whole realm of possibilities is opened up. Conversely, everything can be speeded up, or the amount of time given to 'normal' movement in relation to fast or slow or frozen movement can be altered again, thus setting up new sensibilities. While all this is happening one is also discovering other things, such as the nature of film illusion or even the textural quality of film material, which is as important as the nature of the stone used by a sculptor.

In my film *Dirty*, the refilming of some film of two girls enabled their actions to be emphasized to convey the tension and beauty of such a simple and emphatic gesture as a hand reaching out: frozen, then moving slowly, then freezing, then moving again, and all the while creating tension and space before the contact. For this film the refilming was done on a small projector and this enabled me to capture the pulsing (cycles) of the projector light, which gave off a throbbing rhythm throughout, and increased the mood of sensuality. Those of Gehr's films that make use of refilmed film put great emphasis on the duration and repetition of an action, almost to the point of seeming endless.

One of the most exciting and most expressive films that talks as reperceived film is Ken Jacobs's *Tom, Tom, The Piper's Son* (1969), made from an old film of the same name. The programme notes state that the original film was made in 1905, photographed and possibly directed by G. W. 'Billy' Bitzen for the American Mutoscope and Biograph company. Jacobs's notes explain: 'It [the film] had been lost, no one knew it was lost, and then found, discovered, and we've carried the process of discovery further.' He continues:

I've cut into the film's monumental homogeneity (8 statically photographed sets woven through with human commotioning) with some sense of trespass, cropped and given a Griffith emphasis to parts originally submerged in the whole – but (this is a didactic film) it was necessary to do so in order to begin to show much was there. Inescapably, of course, I've also made a new film, where all I wished to do was merely make a gesture.

What happens in *Tom, Tom* is that one first sees the original film (that is a filmed version of the original film, which itself was made from rolls of paper contact prints by Kemp R. Niven deposited with the Library of Congress in Washington). It is a simple situation film based on a nursery rhyme ('Tom, Tom, the piper's son, stole a pig and away he run'). There is the street scene, the pig among the crowd; Tom grabbing the pig, running away, the crowd chasing him. Jacobs then went back to the film, and started to look at it again from the beginning, at the gestures, the movements. Parts of it are frozen: Tom is caught sliding off a house roof and is suddenly transformed in a freeze into an amorphous blob. Movements and mood are changed and reordered by a change in tune and in emphasis. The original film dissolves and a new one emerges. Once narrative, the film is now the drama of an action, the vision of a form. The situation becomes secondary, and the primary element is the development and discovery of particular images, the relationship between them, the nature of the image itself: the film now looks deeper, as if seen with a microscope, drawing out of the hidden areas a new vantage-point and formulating a new aesthetic. The closer observation shows the basic organic composition which is the film's essential beauty.

So in *Tom, Tom, The Piper's Son* a multiplicity of expressions occurs: the film in its dramatic narrative form (as in the beginning); the film as variations of motion (in terms of analysis and in terms of possibilities); a complexity of many pictures created from a continuity; the intensification of a single image; the alteration of accustomed associative movement; and subsequently, also through association, readjustment to various time sensations. There is also the emphasis, by these variations, on the structure of the film, and of the original film, and at the same time an acute awareness of the physical nuances of processes and materials.

In the case of *Tom, Tom* this kind of expression is arrived at by a refilmed situation, but it can easily be related to the other physical possibilities of film, as, for example, through the printer in Le Grice's *Little Dog for Roger*, or even with such physical possibilities as superimposition on the grain in the film. Thus each method or material aspect of the film can give a direction and a basis for a film expression and through each method a physiological statement is developed. So the use of a wide-angle lens creates a broad distortion, and then this distortion can be altered again because a different make or type of camera is used. Or else the same technique can be used in different ways. For example, the slow and subtle zoom in *Wavelength* gives a steady sculptural depth to the film, while the rapid and continuous short-burst zooms in the films of Peter Schönherr create a quick tempo and an optical density, yet both film-makers are using the same physical aspect of the medium to make their statement. Obviously, this argument can continue endlessly, and we would be in danger of obscuring the films with an overdose of technique. The point I want to make here is that certain physical aspects of the medium can not only suggest a direction, but also generate feelings by their very nature.

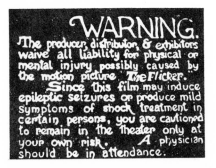

Light is an integral part of film, and one feels a bit ridiculous in saying it – after all, film would not exist without light. Yet it was only when I saw Tony Conrad's *The Flicker* (1966) that I became fully aware of the phenomenon of light, the hypnosis of film. In terms of its form *The Flicker* approaches the pure physical presence of film, because it represents the isolation of light through projected film. This isolation becomes exaggeration. As the alternation of light and dark (one making the other more positive) is one of the basic principles of film, in this case it becomes the form of the film as well. It is also a physical presence because of the sheer confrontation with alternating light, which automatically produces a physical sensation in the viewer. In describing the technique he used for *The Flicker* Conrad said:

> The range of perception of flicker or stroboscopic light is below a frequency of about 70 flashes per second (40 fps), above which the light is seen as continuous. Normal sound projection is at 24 fps. Below about 4 fps, the only real effect is of a light switching on and off. But in the range from 6 to 18 fps, more or less, strange things occur. *The Flicker* moves gradually from 24 fps to 4 fps and then back out of the flicker range.[11]

It is rather hard to find the right term for *The Flicker*, as it sounds too like a scientific film when broken down to its basic structure. It is a non-image film in that there are no photographic images, though the interplay of light and dark does produce an after-image. The after-image is light on dark, or dark on light. The result of all this is hallucinatory and creates hypnotic sensations, so that anything from colour (the film is in fact in black and white) to an illusion of representational imagery, to a trance or even sleep can occur, depending on the viewer. In basic terms, the film illustrates the visibility of harmonic relationships. Conrad considered: 'There is a way to apply harmonic structure to light, and that is to modulate its [light] intensity with time.' The overall physical result of the film is some forty-seven different patterns based on the standard projection frequency of twenty-four frames per second. The film patterns (based on the differing ratio of clear [white] space [time] to black) are structured so as to move into a density of pattern and then out again. In other words we have a strobe pattern that starts thin, then thickens in the density of strobing and finally thins out again.

Conrad studied mathematics and has been considerably involved with music and sound. He worked on the soundtracks of *Flaming Creatures* and *Chumlum* and also collaborated with the modern sound composer LaMonte Young. He was concerned with harmonic relationships, and most particularly with polyrhythms (a slow form of harmony). He continues this in *The Flicker,* with its *visual* harmonic relationships. Conrad also became very interested in what he calls 'static' form – though by 'static' he in fact means repetition. He also speaks of 'static atmosphere' (as opposed to factual elements) and contrasts this with atmosphere in motion. The creation of this static atmosphere involved eliminating any representational imagery and putting this non-imagery in the form of light into a pulse-modulated repetition. The result is a pure and intense film involving the viewer in hallucinatory stimuli. This particular involvement is unavoidably noticeable round the flicker frequencies of 8 to 16 cycles in the range of what are known as 'alpha-rhythms'.

Thanks to Conrad's involvement with music, the soundtrack of *The Flicker* presents, in combination with the film, a stronger and ever-denser environment for the visual situation. The track is structured in a similar way to the image pattern, and consists of a motor-like sound. According to Conrad: 'The soundtrack consists primarily of homemade electronic music composed indissolubly of tones (pitches) bordering on the lower range of audibility and of very rapid rhythms, rhythms whose speed is comparable in frequency to the tones.' The sound gives a strange space to the strobing and the whole environment becomes a revelation of luminous time. It is important to note the use of sound with film, because few independent film-makers manage to achieve such a vital integration between the visual and the auditory elements.

Conrad married Beverly Grant, who was (and still is) one of the vital 'stars' in the early days of the New American Cinema movement in New York. So many independent film-makers speak not only through film, but through the people whom they film. These people also become the vehicle for many of their expressions and statements. It can sometimes be hard to find such people when one is trying to develop such individual film expression (and is even harder to find people to do it without payment). Beverly has appeared in films made by Ron Rice (*Chumlum*), Jack Smith (*Flaming Creatures, Normal Love*), Gregory Markopoulos (*The Illiac Passion*), Jonas Mekas (*Diaries*) and Andy Warhol (*13 Most Beautiful Women*). She has also helped me a good deal and has appeared in two of my own films (*Chinese Checkers, Naissant*).

(A number of other people have worked with many independent film-makers and have helped to make their films possible. Examples are Taylor Mead, Viva, Mario Montez, Frankie Francine, Vivian, or Zelda Nelson, Joel Markham, Joan Adler. Some have been fellow film-makers or artists, friends, wives, girl-friends, but apart from the few 'superstars' they have never really received proper credit for their efforts, so this little digression is my own little tribute to them.)

In 1970 Conrad, working with Beverly (who was not acting), made the short film *Straight and Narrow*, which is described as:

> . . . a study in subjective color and visual rhythm. Although it is printed on Black and White film, the hypnotic pacing of the images will cause most viewers to experience a programmed gamut of hallucinatory color effects, through the intermediary of rhythm. The maximal impact is drawn from the simplest of universal human images: straight horizontal and vertical lines.

Also in 1970, Tony and Beverly made a major work called *Coming Attractions*. This film, which lasts seventy-eight minutes, became a fusion of fantasy and of optics, using much of the superstar, transvestite situation and character to create a structure that includes strobing, solarizing and superimposition. In 1971 they expanded their non-objective feelings into a multiscreen production (intended for four screens) called *Four Square*, which represents a further development of Conrad's earlier experiments with *The Flicker* and *Straight and Narrow*, except that in this case it includes colour as well.

> We talk of cinema killing theatre, and in that phrase we refer to the theatre as it was when the cinema was born, a theatre of box office, foyer, tip-up seats, foot lights, scene changes, intervals, music, as though the theatre was by definition these and little more.
>
> From *The Empty Space* by Peter Brook

Light as an absolute part of film becomes, as with Conrad, the effective material for the films of Paul Sharits. Sharits's early statement of intent runs:

I wish to abandon imitation and illusion and enter directly into the higher drama of: celluloid, two-dimensional strips, individual rectangular frames, the nature of sprockets and emulsion, projector operation, the three-dimensional light beam, environmental illumination, the two-dimensional reflective screen surface, the retinal screen, optic nerve and individual psychophysical subjectivities of consciousness. In this cinema drama, light is energy rather than a tool for the representation of non-filmic objects, light, as energy, is released to create its own objects, shapes, and textures. Given the fact of retinal inertia and the flickering shutter mechanism of film projection, one may generate virtual forms, create actual motion (rather than illustrate it), build actual color-space (rather than picture it), and be involved in actual time (immediate presence).[12]

Probably the most straightforward example of his own statement occurs in his colour film $N: O: T: H: I: N: G$ (1968). Here the structure and the feeling develop out of a flickering colour evolution. The frames waver past in light-generated flutters. Colours often fuse in passing, presenting strangely soft blends, and there is often a strange sensation of the colour edge, or the vibration caused by two colours. Although a flicker principle is involved, the term 'flutter' might better describe the film. Throughout the film Sharits inserts an occasional figurative frame (in the case of $N: O: T: H: I: N: G$, this is an image of a face flanked by two half-coloured light-bulbs). These insertions present a punctuation, at times jarring with the more fluttering and softer flow in the rest of the film. This frame insertion makes me think that Sharits's essential concern is with the characteristics of the single frame – that one-twenty-fourth of a second of frozen time. When projected the pure coloured frame makes a direct statement about light, but the figurative frame insertions become a complex of image, of contrasts, a frame-by-frame thought process that results in an accumulated linear structure.

This aspect is even more clearly presented in Sharits's 5-minute colour film *Piece Mandala/End War* (1966), where the single but accumulated frame is the basic structure. In *Piece Mandala* the figurative image is a copulating couple, spaced out with blank coloured frames (the figurative images are black and white). The accumulated sensation creates a movement close to that of a 'flick book', except that the colour spaces punctuate the time and the light, causing a loss of hardness, and going back into flutter. The punctuation is the colour frame just as in $N: O: T: H: I: N: G$ it was the figurative image. Sharits evolves his films basically within this arena, extending his idea into two screens with *Razor Blades* (1965-8). Sharits once wrote:

'Razor Blades' begins as a mandala [a repetitive theme in his films], the mandala is visually sliced open (as if one had passed through the center of the mandala, 'through a looking glass' into a realm of pure imagination – consciousness dissected) and as the film's 'theme' gradually expands it becomes less and less 'centred', less and less rational. After the midway point in the film, the themes – images become more coherent again, begin to 're-center'; at the end of the film the mandala is reformed and the overall sense of the film is that a large cycle has occurred. Since 'Razor Blades' ends as it began, an infinite loop is suggested – metric time is destroyed. Apart from the beginning and ending footage, which is linear, the film is made up of 14 loops which, staggered, play against ('slice' back and forth, interpenetrate) each other. Each loop, in itself, is made so that one can chart variations in one's own consciousness of speed, rhythm and image recognition; when these loops are projected side by side, so that both images are seen as one larger image, because of their differences in cycle length, this variability of consciousness is geometrically increased; since there are constantly different pairs of images on the screen, the repetitive characteristic of loops is transcended.[13]

This passage helps to clarify Sharits's intentions. The structure of his films represents a very conscious and positive statement that can be likened to the formed and shaped thinking found in the Bauhaus, or perhaps more loosely that of an architect, but using frames as forms and textures, and light and time as space. Other examples of this are found in Sharits's *Ray Gun Virus* (1966), *Word Movie/Fluxfilm 29* (1966), and *T.O.U.C.H.I.N.G.* (1968), which he claims as his final mandalic work.

Sharits once prefaced a catalogue entry with a quote from Artaud: 'All writing is pigshit. People who leave the obscene and try to define whatever it is that goes on in their heads are pigs.' To define $N:O:T:H:I:N:G$ by setting down its structures, its plan – will not give you the sensation it arouses – which is its real meaning. The basic mood of Sharits's films, or Conrad's *The Flicker*, is hallucinatory. Its structure is amorphous, whereas verbal description makes it seem formal and hard. Too many people cannot accept the feeling of abstraction, of obscurity generated by even the most precisely structured film. Their criterion for understanding is that it must be capable of definition. Yet they cannot accept that a subjective response is in itself a 'definition'. I remember that once during a lecture held after a screening to a film society of some of the films mentioned here the audience claimed to like Michael Snow's *One Second in Montreal* because they understood the mathematical structure of the film and yet had previously considered Snow's *Wavelength* a 'torture' and *Tom, Tom, The Piper's Son* useless because they 'understood', after the first few minutes, Jacobs's intention, and once they understood that there was 'no point' in watching the film.

Appreciation in the broadest sense as far as film is concerned is very important today. The viewer, having been conditioned to accept the story as being the main conscious experience, has difficulty appreciating film on the intuitive and unconscious level. With the advent of sound film the verbal story has become more dominant than the visual narrative. We experience a 'minimal' sensation in that long, long shot of the empty street in the basic cowboy film – just before the gunfight – we accept this tension because it is resolved by the eventual gunfight. Our sensation is resolved for us but my view is that the tension can be and very often is a valid statement in itself and this tension is a thing we have to live with and resolve for ourselves. The sensation without the familiar narrative resolution can provide an active situation for the viewer where he is a part of the whole, and is very much alive in it; no longer escaping but growing.

I have recently seen two early Russian films, Dovzhenko's *Earth* and Pudovkin's *Mother,* and I begin to wonder how much we have lost in the way of seeing and feeling because the need for a profit and quick political propaganda have weaned generations on the simple escapist films ('let the workers rest – they will work better tomorrow'). As a result, most cinemagoers hear the patter of pipe dreams and register sensation solely by dictionary definition. In the two Russian films the lack of sound means that if a point or statement is to be made it somehow has to be rendered visually; the statement has to be felt rather than grasped intellectually. Contemporary independent films have not really departed from this essential form of film statement, but the problem is that cinemagoers have departed from this essential form of experience because now we think we know beauty merely by understanding the 'word' beauty. Excessive reliance on verbal definitions has been a corrupting factor in the pursuit of knowledge and understanding. According to John Stuart Mill:

> They [the Greeks] had great difficulty in distinguishing between things which their language confounded, or in putting mentally together things which it distinguished; and could hardly combine the objects in Nature, into any classes but those which were made for them by the popular phrases of their own country; or at least could not help fancying those classes to be natural, and all others arbitrary and artificial. Accordingly, scientific investigation among the Greek Schools of Speculation and their followers in the Middle Ages, was little more than a mere sifting and analysing of the notions attached to common language. They thought that by determining the meaning of words they could become acquainted with facts.[14]

This idea has been clarified by Alfred North Whitehead: 'Language is thoroughly indeterminate, by reason of fact that every occurrence presupposes some systematic type of environment.' He continued:

Verbal expressions which, where taken by themselves with the current meaning of their words, are ill-defined and ambiguous. These are not premises to be immediately reasoned from apart from elucidation by further discussion; they are endeavours to state general principles which will be exemplified in the subsequent description of the facts of experience. This subsequent elaboration should elucidate the meanings to be assigned to the words and phrases employed. Such meanings are incapable of accurate apprehension apart from a correspondingly accurate apprehension of the metaphysical background which the universe provides for them. But NO language can be anything but elliptical, requiring a leap of the imagination to understand its meaning in its relevance to immediate experience . . . the development of culture cannot be understood without remembering that no verbal statement is the adequate expression of a proposition.[15]

I do not know if one can say that there is a concern for the frame without being too misleading. It sounds almost too precious, even though the basic nature of film is a series of still frames projected one after the other to create the illusion of motion. Even the most 'minimal' of films is composed of single frames; and even if it seems like one picture, it is really made up of flashes of many pictures, with the viewer in darkness 20 per cent of the time. Many film-makers find that their constructive concern with the film comes from manipulating this aspect of film. Yet it would be wrong to put too much emphasis on the frame, for although the maker is concerned with the single frame as a frozen image, with groups of frames as movements, with the frame as a composition in light, as a rectangular shape and so on, he is ultimately concerned with the *whole* film as a total statement and experience. In traditional terminology we might refer here to editing or montage, though the amount of editing varies greatly. A film can be edited to achieve an overall consistent flow so that the visual statement seems unedited or continuous, as in Michael Snow's I——I, or my film *Alone*, or to break and contrast elements as Vertov does.

'For me,' said Peter Kubelka, 'film is the projection of still frames.'

> My economy is one single frame and every part of the screen. So I feel that every frame that is projected too much makes the whole thing less articulate. So I always work in frames. Even the African film *Unsere Afrikareise,* which doesn't seem to be like that, because it's very natural, is worked frame by frame. I have twenty-four communication possibilities per second, and I don't want to waste one. This is the economy. And the same is with the sound. Because one of the major fields where cinema works is when sound and image meet. So, the meeting of every frame with the sound is very important.[16]

Kubelka epitomizes the category of film-maker who concentrates on precision in using the frame and on cutting. As we have seen, his film *Arnulf Rainer* (1958/60) has some links with *The Flicker,* in that they are both non-image films, or rather the image is merely a pattern of light and dark. But *The Flicker* is more didactic and physically enclosing; *Arnulf Rainer* seems far more rhythmic and has a strange pulsating fluidity. The light wavers in it, sometimes in a staccato pulsing, sometimes like an eye blinking when the light suddenly goes on. As with a piece of music the rhythmic sensation results from a breaking down of the frames into beats, the basic rhythm involving twenty-four beats per second. *Arnulf Rainer* can almost be described as co-ordinated abstraction creating harmonious physical activity. One has light, and a white screen; darkness and a black screen; sound, an undetermined pitch and silence.

Kubelka is meticulous to the point where every frame is like a jewel. He works and memorizes each frame and each sound, until each one represents a precise concentration of articulation. The amount of time he spends scrutinizing his material and his frames is considerable (about eight frames a day for fifteen years). Films such as *Adebar* (1956/7) and *Schwechater* (1957/8) are both meticulous and metric, and are excellent examples of the highly concentrated frame image. *Adebar* is a few still moments of people dancing. Negative, positive, black and white. Hand outstretched, body in frozen movement, silhouettes, hair streaked out, held and then recycled, reflashed. Charted movements, plotted in some simple mysterious beat, continuing for ninety seconds with the sound moving in the same simple back-and-forth gesture, then held for a moment, then repeated. There is no beginning, no end, no increase or decrease – but there is the constant feeling of concentrated life. *Schwechater,* another short film (90 seconds), began life as a commercial for the beer company Schwechater. It too is both rhythmic and meticulous. The concentrated images still relate to the beer commercial – a group of people, a hand reaching for a glass, a pretty face. Negative colour, positive colour, hand coming from the left and then from the right; a face, a hand, a glass, a smile, a group; repeat, return – strict and unmistakable. Again the same clarity; the same absorption. It ends with the word 'Schwechater' before the necessary repeat and recycle.

Unsere Afrikareise (Our Trip to Africa, 1961/6) is Kubelka's major attempt to date at bringing together this precise framing with a juxtaposition of concentrated meaning in picture and sound. Every gesture, every picture when juxtaposed with the next gesture or picture and with the sound helps to build up a statement about the white man's rape of the black man's world. From *Unsere Afrikareise* I remember its never tiresome pace; the rhythm of a woman's sway; the lion putting its heart into life, and man putting his bullet into it; the drums; the lion lifted as trophy; the green, green grass; the slow lazy whites moving up the blue river; the rifle crack; the hysterical white woman's laughter; and, of course, the moon, the clarity of the colour, the greatest attention to the smallest detail, and the natural presence of film. Throughout this and other films Kubelka's involvement with film is an essential part of his statement. Personally, too, he represents a major link in the development of the independent cinema, as he is associated with both the New European Cinema and the New American Cinema. As we have seen, he is one of the directors of the Austrian Film Museum (Österreichisches Filmmuseum) in Vienna, and of the Anthology Cinema in New York; he has also been one of the most active members of the New York Film-makers' Co-operative.

I have recently seen Werner Nekes's *Spacecut* (1971), which makes the frame a very strong culminating structure. Not that a single-frame make-up is particularly unusual (Mekas's *Diaries*, for example, is essentially based on the frame), but Nekes has managed to use it to build up a structure. Every frame is different, yet the almost half-hour assembly of images results in a picture of one place being filmed. *Spacecut* has two sections, the second being the frame composite, whereas the first consists of long takes. Within the swirling, fleeting frames the eye receives picture after picture like an enormous, exciting puzzle. Strangely enough, it receives it only by absorption – of the sky, trees, valley, rocks, shadows. The automatic retention of these flashes gives you a sense of being in this bowl of land made by the gold-diggers in 1871. You might think that this use of single frames would hurt the eye, but in fact it does not. Rather the experience is one of total relaxation. You do not try to register each frame, you simply sit there with your eyes open to receive the information, but making no effort.

One cannot maintain in this type of discussion such a limiting aspect for the frame, or the single frame, though some independent film-makers approach their editing or filming with this in mind. Nor can one exclusively maintain the principle of editing as an isolated activity, because content and/or statement is so much more the point. The process of editing, which generally involves a statement by contrast, whether literal or abstract, is one of the essential processes in the commercial cinema. The non-editing principle has come to fruitful life with Warhol and the minimal and structural film-makers. It is important to remember here that most of the cameras accessible to independent film-makers take loads of 100ft/30.5m, 200ft, 400ft/120m, 1,200ft/365.8m, which means that the longest single take with a motorized 16mm cine camera is 32 minutes. Most independent film-makers normally use cameras taking from 100ft (2 min, 47 sec at 24 fps) to 400ft (approximately 10 minutes at 24 fps), and many allow for even shorter takes, for example in the region of 17ft or 20 to 30 seconds.

For many film-makers editing is a natural process if they want to make a longer statement. To attach one continuous sequence (one full length of film as held and shot by the camera, either continuous or single frame or superimposed) to another cannot really be called 'editing', (which would be the case of a 2-hour Warhol movie). True editing involves cutting one sequence or image with another. The classical example of this is the montage technique developed by the Russian film-makers and originated by Abel Gance.

One technique that is produced by a primary concern with editing, with juxtaposition and contrasts, is collage or assemblage. (I refer here to a collage approach, not to an actual collage within the frame, which is often used in animated or semi-animated films.) This technique is based on 'found' material, generally on existing film material such as newsreels, old films or old advertising films reassembled to create a single film entity by a process of juxtaposition. Collage is by no means limited to 'found' material but the employment of a variety of material, and images perhaps made for other applications re-assembled and resolved in a new and single film unit.

Probably the funniest film that I have seen that uses 'found' material is Grifi's and Baruchello's *La Verifica Incerta* (The Uncertain Inspection). The film is based on the Hollywood cliché, for what the makers have done is to take from numerous Hollywood-style films all the similar film gestures from each section. The films from which the material was selected range from cowboy films to ancient Egypt and medieval knights, to gangster and romance films. The structure of *La Verifica Incerta* follows that of the traditional entertainment film, showing, however, that no matter what period was presented the cliché repeated itself, and the narrative remained the same even if the Egyptians were attacking the cowboys and ultimately being chased by the gangsters. The result, including the titles, with MGM taking over from 20th-Century Fox, with Cinemascope rising over Columbia, mirrors the death of Hollywood.

Bruce Conner is a good example of the film-maker who adopts this collage approach. His *A Movie* (1958) is a collage of everything that goes to make up films. It sounds like a satire, though in fact it is a condensed dramatization of film build-up and image association. It begins with academy leader (standard film leader, not normally shown, consisting of numbers appearing at every foot mark in diminishing order – 12, 11, 10, 9, 8 . . .) followed by the title (*A Movie*), a credit (Bruce Conner) and some dramatic music (Respigi). After a series of false beginnings of film hopes intercut and rising, the film launches into images of the movies. Some you know (moments of greatness, newsreels portraying real-life dramas) and some you don't know (chases with cowboys, motorcycles from old films, roses, animals, crescendos of exciting film moments, push button, torpedoes, crash, gush, a bridge bends, a Hindenburg sinks in flames). So the film's dramatic structure, always accompanied by the full orchestrated sound drama, grows from found pieces into an independent existence.

Conner lays particular emphasis on film movement and rhythm in his next film, *Cosmic Ray* (1961), which uses a quick cutting and collage technique to build up to a climax. A girl stripper is constantly juxtaposed with images such as cannons, fireworks and toppling phallic symbols or a superimposed lighthouse until the final climactic release is achieved. The structure is obvious and the harmony smooth. In *Report* (1964/5) Conner makes a poignant, even a stinging comment on the assassination of President Kennedy. The intermixing of existing newsreel material relating to the assassination with other television material, particularly advertising commercials and horror films, offers a severe comment on the blinding cruelty of the television medium. *Report* is not solely a juxtaposition of these particular image sequences. What Conner has done is to select a few sequences from the television report on Kennedy's death and to repeat them again and again to build up to a feeling of intensity through repetition. The two sequences that I remember most clearly are the moments just before the assassination and when the police were carrying the alleged assassination weapon. The sequences are not repeated in full, but individual sections are repeated at intervals through the film. This build-up creates great tension and the use of commercial and entertainment material introduces a note of questioning. How much did media bombardment make the Kennedy assassination another horror movie? How much truth is there in a newsreel? Did Kennedy die? Did he even exist? Was it just another way of selling something? Did television blind us to the truth of Kennedy's death, allow us to forget it, allow the villains to ride off into the sun? The re-use of existing film material thus gives a totally new meaning to what has become familiar.

Conner has also made, from his own material, *Vivian* (1964), in a delighted, high-speed style (creating an almost single-frame feeling, though it is not completely single frame) often referred to as 'pixillated'. Other Conner films are *For Mushrooms* (1960/66) and *Breakaway* (1966/67).

SHELBY KENNEDY

The use of found material is not, of course, exclusive to Conner. Anthony Scott (Scottie) has literally fished film out of the dustbin, assembling it regardless of content, into *The Longest Most Meaningless Movie.* Other film-makers have taken whole films and virtually remade them by refilming them, looping, reprinting and restructuring. As we have seen, Ken Jacobs's *Tom, Tom, The Piper's Son* began with a complete old film and Werner Nekes and Malcolm Le Grice have followed much the same principle. The use of 'found' material gives spontaneity and scope and, as with other expressive movements, it allies the film to its own environment; one other aspect of the 'found' film should be mentioned here – the use of existing film material as quotation, just as writers quote from the work of other writers. The underlying aims are virtually the same: emphasis, confirmation, amplification or introduction. This technique is widely used by independent film-makers and is also fairly common in commercial films.

The pacing in some of Bruce Conner's films, plus the mention of popular and comic-book imagery, conjures up the images of Jeff Keen, who is working away over in Brighton, home of some of the first films ever made. Jeff clicks and plugs away making films that race through the head, with images that gather in strength as they accumulate. What makes the memory so strong is not just the rapid pacing, or the style, but images: human Mickey Mouses, red lips that open like a willing vagina; dolls melting and plastic movements – a surrealist world of left-over England; the island of pieces; someone else's flat; and enough cheap bits to make the factories in Hong Kong leap with delight. The frame edges get dark, just like rooms with little yellow lightbulbs hanging dull and dust covered. In *Marvo Movies, Meatdaze, Wail and Like The Time Is Now* the images rush by at great speed, cut and superimposed.

This is the moment to discuss the constantly recurring term 'high-speed' in relation to film. It refers to movement that seems faster than we are accustomed to experiencing it. I must emphasize the word 'seems', because the sensation is not necessarily caused by an actual speeding-up. One way to give the illusion of speeded-up movement is to film at a lower than normal number of frames per second (eighteen) and then project at normal pro-jection speed (twenty-four frames per second), thereby apparently speed-ing up the movement. This high-speed technique has been used through-out film history to create comic effects both in the commercial cinema and in the independent cinema. Simple humorous films, such as Ron Finne's *Demonstration Movie* (1968), on the process of using a folding chair, or Yogi Kuri's *Chair* or my own film *Asleep* (1961), which films the feet of someone sleeping, all use this technique. But the high-speed technique can also be used to make a sensitive and personal statement from which humour is totally absent. A good example here is Barbara Meter's *Windows* (later called *From the Exterior*). In this film the stylization of the images conveys an impression of the timeless element in man's existence. Other examples in which statement overrides technique can be seen in *Flaming Creatures* (Smith), *Invocation of my Demon Brother* (Anger), *Mare's Tail* (Larcher), *Quick Billie* (Baillie), and the films of Ben Van Meter, Piero Heliczer, Hy Hirsch, Robert Nelson, Ron Rice and Stan VanDerBeek.

The speeded-up sensation is often caused by short bursts of normal movements which then cut or jump to another movement or sequence of equally short duration. The extreme case of this latter technique is the single frame, where there is in fact no filmed movement but merely a rapid projection of single images, one after the other, twenty-four per second. The use of single frame, and the combination of the single frame with short bursts of film, has already been referred to in connection with many films such as Mekas's *Diaries,* Robert Breer's *Fist Fight* or Nekes's *Spacecut;* again it is only one technique among many for making a personal statement. The single frame can also be used simply to show change, as in *I Change, I am the Same* (1969) by Shelby Kennedy, in which different figures and different sexes, flash by, producing a sort of mental overlapping. The point is reached when there is a sense of fusion into oneness. All these various aspects of the technique can be developed to the point of straight animation, which is the single frame-by-frame filming of many still pictures (graphic or otherwise) in sequences that give the sensation of motion and gesture.

The idea of editing, cutting, juxtaposition, montage, call it what you will, is to create tension, 'edge', contrast. Tension and contrast are primary elements in the plastic and graphic arts (balance and scale; line and solid) as well as in music and dance. Tension is an active state that has neither beginning nor end. There is always a dynamic sense of continuance, of something happening and about to happen, as opposed to the sense of being diffused, softened and spread out. The tensile properties of film are inherent, and edited or montaged or juxtaposed tension is a facet of its language.

One particularly rich exponent of both tension and gesture is the Viennese film-maker Kurt Kren. His films are large-scale, though they are usually short. They are expressive and elaborate, with a wide range of content and comment that is always full of freshness, energy and honesty of expression. Kren's involvement is constant and it is rare to see films of such total sensitivity. Though his films are by no means didactic, his work reaffirms the possibility that individual values and poetry can always be expressed in film. He loves making films and has made a very large number despite the difficulties of having no money, no job and no home. His visual source material is drawn from anything from shitting to 'actions', to an old photograph, to people sitting by a window, to trees and cutout faces. Thanks to his own honesty, his total belief in his film, he allows others to see something that they would never look at otherwise, or would never see.

Kren's first film dates from 1957 and is called *1/57 – Versuch mit Synthetischem Ton* (Experiment with Synthetic Sound). It is only two minutes long.

(Kren generally labels his films according to the order in which they are made and the year; many have no verbal title.) This first film is made up of three interrelated landscape settings with the primary emphasis on a hand-made optical soundtrack. In *2/60 – 48 Köpfe aus dem Szondi-Test* (48 Heads from the Szondi Test) – the Szondi Test being the *experimentelle Triebdiagnostik* or the 'experimental diagnostic of the implied sexual driving force' – Kren's rhythmic montage of faces builds up subtle and varied rhythms. Some of the faces appear for only one frame, some for two, some for a few more. There is no coherent pattern. Raymond Durgnat's description gives a good idea of the sensation created by this film: '. . . a montage of photo-portraits so tensely cut and neatly assembled that each face had scarcely appeared before it flicked into another one. The effect was of utter pulverisation of humanity in some Marienbadian dossier: in this con-centrationary universe, no one's his own self, everyone's everything and nothing.'

3/60 Bäume im Herbst (Trees in Autumn) is a more concisely assembled 5-minute film of silhouetted, slightly moving trees. But since the trees are filmed only in bursts of frames, the movements and patterns are more impressionistic than anything else. *4/61 – Mauern-Positiv-Negativ und Weg* (Walls, Positive and Negative) runs for six minutes. The walls are hardly walls, but become an abstract patch of texture which strobes and flashes like a textured flicker. In *5/62 – Fenstergucker, Abfall, etc.* a 5-minute film (known in English as 'Lookers from the Window'), Kren's editing creates a highly sophisticated series of relationships. The images are of people, ordinary people, hanging out and looking out of their windows, interrelated with short sequences of blurred camera movements. The shots of the people are also seen in short bursts, though the length of both the images and the blurs is not determined by any obvious rhythmic pattern. Nevertheless, an unusual rhythm is attained between the direct image and the blur. It is rather like looking at pictures in a book while at the same time remember-ing and recording the movements involved in turning the pages.

With the making of his sixth film, *6/64 – Mama und Papa*, Kren intro-duced subject-matter that was considered at that time to be highly revolu-tionary or even explosive. He began filming 'actions' and 'happenings' staged by Otto Muehl and Günter Brus, and by the Vienna Institute for Direct Art. Now 'happenings', 'events' and 'actions' had been put on film often enough before; what was radical was the content of the Vienna 'actions', which involved a high degree of sexual assault and often seemed to reach a state of psychosis. Kren's *materialaktionen* are more positive and purer than those of others because he has never lost his feeling for film and film gesture. The temptation to film 'actions' did become for many a way of making films that were more like newsreel documentaries. But Kren has allowed his personality to come across in the films he made by offering his own interpretation of the 'actions'. It was at this time that Kren became in-volved with DIAS (Destruction in Art Symposium), as well as with the Vienna Institute for Direct Art.

There is a particularly large amount of documentation about the activities of the Vienna Group, perhaps because all the film and related activities revolved round a small central group, and Vienna is a small city. Both Kren and Kubelka came from Vienna and both used the pure and esoteric attitude of film tension to be found there. The importance of this was that in such a closely knit situation the extreme actions being created in the city had their effect on films, and on the attitudes that people felt towards looking at and experiencing film material, as well, of course, as on film comment.

The 'actions' created by Otto Muehl and Günter Brus (and by Hermann Nitsch in Germany) took the form of violent assault and destruction, frequently with a sexual and shocking content. They include public killing of animals and pouring their blood into vaginas; excretion and eating shit; tying and twisting penises; masturbation in public and so on. Almost all the 'actions' involved the human body and all were directed at blasting the sacred and the pure through violent and flagellant methods, often to the point of self-negation. This is particularly true of Günter Brus, whose 'actions' gradually became more and more self-destructive, to the point where he would cut himself open and tear his own flesh with hooks.

Some of Muehl's directions read as follows:

Pour out 5 litres of milk into your chamber, all garbage cans, all fags collected in a month, 3 litres of salad oil, 5 kg of wheat flour, cast 50 eggs on it, then wallow with Cora 5 minutes like a steam-roller across the chamber; then get up, tie some boards to Alexandra's body, throw all Austrian newspapers over her, shovel up the filth around her with your hands and clap it on the papers, lift up Alexandra and let her fall down. It will be a sight like after bombing. Hang Doris upside down and let her piss into the air, piss into the cunt once, Libi did menstruate then, therefore we took a colour film.

The subject material for Kren's film *6/64 – Mama und Papa* is described by Muehl as:

Material action XI 4. 8. 64: Mama lies naked on the table, she's covered with a plastic sheet. Papa in a dark suit stands at the table and takes from his pants pocket a long thread and begins to tie Mama down to the table. Papa pumps up with an air pump some balloons that are under the plastic sheet. Papa slams a balloon filled with tomato sauce against the wall. Papa chops up a balloon filled with feathers. Papa places a balloon filled with tomato sauce on a chair and by sitting on it with all his weight causes it to burst. Papa unties Mama and rolls her over on her stomach. Papa sticks an artificial rose between the cheeks of her arse. Papa bites through a tomato over the rose and cracks open an egg. Papa strews flower pot dirt and sand. Papa lets ten pounds of flour dribble down over Mama and the rose. Papa pours blue paint, sour milk and tomato sauce on Mama. Papa sprays the groceries, and sand, off Mama's arse with a siphon of sodawater. Papa rolls Mama over on her back. Papa lies down next to Mama, takes a soda siphon, places it between his legs, sprays it towards the ceiling and does the same with a bottle of beer that he has previously shaken up vigorously . . . Papa sticks a big tomato between Mama's teeth, lays himself on top of Mama and bites through the tomato. Papa puts a balloon filled with tomato sauce on Mama's belly, and then keeps falling on the balloon until it bursts. Mama sits up and Papa, from a distance of three yards, throws lumps of dough at her, sprays her with tomato sauce and raspberry juice. Papa stuffs lettuce, tomatoes, spinach, tissue paper and confetti between Mama's thighs. A naked man places himself at the table, is drenched with cooking oil by Papa, is dusted with flour and bound round with plastic tubing. Paper roses are inserted between the turns of the plastic tubing and the man. Papa hands over to the man a blown-up balloon. While the man produces noises on the balloon by rubbing and squeezing it, a man's head covered with a plastic bag appears through a hole in the table between Mama's thighs. The naked man bursts the balloon. Papa, with a lighted candle, explodes a balloon filled with feathers, and throws black powdered paint in the air. Papa unwraps the plastic bag from the man's head and then works over the bald head with eggs, noodles, sauces and talcum powder. Papa sticks plastic bluebottle flies on the bald head and sticks false teeth in his mouth and covers the face with strips of gummed paper. Mama kneels over the bald head and gives him her breast to suck. Papa springs on the table, crawls over Mama from the back, sticks a balloon filled with sour milk between himself and Mama and makes it burst while holding Mama as tight as he can. Mama turns and shows her arse to the public. Mama hands a baby bottle to the bald head under her arse. Papa works with skin cream and feathers on Mama's arse. The bald head blows up a balloon filled with liquid paint under Mama's arse and punctures it. The bald head disappears under the table. A bottomless chest is set on the table. Mama lies down in the chest and disappears through a split in the table. Papa fills the chest with balloons, climbs in the chest and by jumping up and down, pinching and tossing and biting the balloons bursts them and disappears into the chest.

Whatever your interpretation of this sequence of events, Kren produced a 4-minute colour film, using his own particular version of the technique of close-cropped montage to turn events into pure gesture. The change in the duration of each gesture and the subsequent juxtapositions produced ritualistic textures and psycho-erotic overtones. The colour plus the bursts of complex images creates a baroque dream. Most of the forms and shapes filmed usually fill the frame giving a vast array of textures and movement impressions.

Kren's next film was *7/64 – Leda und der Schwan* (Leda and the Swan), also based on a Muehl *materialaktion*. The almost convulsive use of juxtaposition reappears here, but the captured gesture assumes a more erotic sensitivity, though the 'action' itself was primarily a gradual destruction of the erotic. *8/64 – ANA* is Kren's first film of an 'action' by Günter Brus. This 3-minute film was far more akin to the American-style 'happening' in that the content was not particularly extreme. It was built up from items such as broken bicycle parts, a nude model, pieces of furniture and these elements were then obscured or transformed by having a layer of paint thrown on to them. Kren films short sequences from many different angles, using high-contrast black and white film to create an effect not unlike that of a painting by Robert Kline. In *9/64 – O Tannenbaum* (O Christmas Tree) Kren offers a more visually descriptive development of a Muehl 'action'. The images have been chosen to follow a more dramatic sequence, probably because the 'action' itself contained a wide range of images and materials. This extreme comment on the Christmas ritual again lasts for three minutes.

Kren's *10/65 – Selbstverstummelung* (Self-mutilation) is developed from a Günter Brus 'action'. What the film emphasizes is the surrealistic drama of symbolic self-destruction that Kren drew out of Brus's 'action', pacing out each gesture so that one gets a tense, iconoclastic revelation of a man covered in white plaster lying surrounded by razor blades and a range of instruments looking as if they have been taken from an operating theatre. The blades, scissors and scalpels are gradually inserted into him in a ritualistic self-operation. *11/65 – Bild Helga Philipp* is an optical abstraction of an optical abstraction: Kren has simply intercut filmed movements and sections from an Op painting by Helga Philipp. The result is motion opticals. Kren's last film to include any direct reference to Otto Muehl is *12/66 – Cosinus Alpha*, a 10-minute film that completes a cycle of elaborate sensual montages of flesh and materials.

A large number of films have been made in and around 'happenings', 'actions' and 'events'. Approaches vary widely. It soon becomes quite impossible to judge the value of the actual 'happening', for once it is on film, it is the film that is scrutinized. Yet there is no clear criterion for deciding what is a 'happening' and what is not. It is only because a 'happening' artist calls a particular act of his a 'happening' that the film of that act is also called a 'happening'. The word can be applied equally to public demonstrations, strikes or what are called 'home-movies'. Similarly, Jonas Mekas's *The Brig*, which films the Living Theater's performance of the play of the same name, could be called a 'happening film', although in fact the performance was put on specially for the film. Lenny Lipton's *We Shall March Again* was filmed during a demonstration, though Lipton later pieced it together to make certain political points. Again many of these films could be labelled 'documentary' – which only goes to show how dangerous it is to start pinning on labels.

Besides Kurt Kren's 'happening' films a large number have been made by other independent film-makers. Marie Menken, for instance, made one on Andy Warhol called simply *Andy Warhol*. Raymond Saroff has made a whole series of films based on 'happenings' created by Claes Oldenburg. Other examples are Jud Yalkut's *P + A – 1(K)* (1965/6), which portrays the composer Nam June Paik; Vernon Zimmerman's *Scarface and Aphrodite* (1963), again based on an Oldenburg happening; Rudy Burckhardt's films of situations created by Red Grooms. One of the strongest and most indi-

vidual films made of a Muehl 'action' is *Body-building* (1965/6). The work
of Ernst Schmidt, another Austrian, this film involves much longer and
more dramatic camera activity and has a very direct structure. It gives a
grandiose feeling to the action it films, like an enormous primitive ritual.

In *13/67 – Sinus Beta* Kren's attitude seems to change. This film is a compila-
tion of many different situations, including Muehl and Brus at the Destruction in Art Symposium in London, plus elements from the Szondi tests
and related to Venice. His *14/67 – Kurdu* is incomplete and will always
remain so, because it is intended to be a self-perpetuating, ever-changing
film. It is made up of units of film pieces, each piece being sent to Kren by
other film-makers. Pieces are constantly being added, for as earlier pieces
wear out or are damaged they are replaced with totally new pieces. The
process can continue indefinitely. From this point Kren's films become much
more diverse and reveal a number of different approaches. His *15/67 – TV*
is directly related to the thinking of the 'structuralists', in that his editing
methods involve the natural process of repeats. In *15/67 – TV* Kren takes five
different sequence shots of people by a window that resembles a café window
by a pier. These five sequences are repeated in a slow rhythm twenty-one
times in four minutes. (The graphic structure would be 105 sequence lengths
with black frames between every five.) Of his *16/67 – 20 September* – which
has been subtitled *Eating, drinking, pissing and shitting film* – Kren said in
a letter that 'it had to be done'. It is a simple back and forth film, utilizing
the basic montage progression to show someone first eating then shitting
then drinking then pissing. One action follows the other so the structure
is rigidly progressive, no one process being complete until the end of the
film. It is neither disgusting nor horrible; it is a simple statement of fact, as
basic as the functions involved.

Kren continues with the same concise and direct attitude, though his
subject-matter is continually changing. *17/68 – Grün-Rot* was simply stated
to be an almost abstract film about a perverted bottle. *18/68 – Venezia
Kaputt*, which is only 1 metre long, has painting on film, while *19/68 –
White-Black* is an 'expanded movie' that was shown in America in May
1968. It was followed by *20/68 – Schatzi* (the word *Schatzi* is the Austrian
equivalent of 'my precious', 'my lovely,' 'my sweet'). The film is made up of
a single photograph of a German military officer standing in front of some
dead bodies. The image slowly reveals itself, seeming to come out of white-
ness. Sometimes it seems to be solarized, at other times it is like a cloud
lifting. Watching it is rather like developing a photograph. It is Kren's most
linear and minimal film. *21/68 – Danke* (Thanks) is based on an 'expanded
movie' idea and considers the possibility of using railway-carriage windows
as movie screens as the train rides along a road. The important climax would
be at a railway level crossing, as the train crossed the road. *22/69 – Happy
End* shows the intercutting of intercourse. A cunt is intercut between parts
of a traditional entertainment film (which was reshot off the cinema screen)
and becomes like copulation between movies – necking in the back row. It

does, of course, have a happy end. *23/69 – Underground Explosion* is a montage document about pop festivals in Germany and Switzerland. *Campagnereiter Club* (no number, made in 1969) is Kren's only other film return to a *materialaktion*, taking place round a pond in the woods, with people riding people. In *27/70 – Western* Kren comes back to a single close scrutiny of montage tension through the groping-like exploration of a single poster. The film becomes, in the purest sense, an accumulation of pieces that become whole only through the process of seeing.

It keeps occurring to me that there is a very noticeable split when we are watching a film between explicit content (narrative content stated in detail) and implicit content (implied through the form or structure or action of the film). In the second case, feeling, as we have seen, is all important. This means that the audience has to become sufficiently involved in the experience of watching in order to receive the content.

Watching a performance of the ballet *Daphnis and Chloë* recently, I felt that the choreographer had developed the narrative to such a pitch, including specifying the details of the stage sets and costumes, that the individual ability of the dancers to use their bodies and movements as vehicles of expression was totally inhibited. The alleged point of the narrative (i.e. conflict) was not expressed, or rather it could not be felt because the materials of expression were not used. For example, the tension of the body's movement in moments of conflict should allow the audience to feel the tension. This idea can be applied to film or to any other expressive art. Yet when I was on the jury for the Mannheim International Film Festival I found that most of the other judges gave the prizes to films that had explicit subjects that they considered politically and socially important at that time, and rejected films that either used film as its own statement, or introduced more abstract, more emotional and more universally expressive means of communication. This is not to say that the content of the films was not important or interesting, and it is not to say either that many films did not use film to express content. The danger of being too intellectual is that one loses the ability to feel. For instance, if a political statement is to mean anything to someone who is not committed to the same views it is important that he should feel it enough to become involved.

During a film festival the constant bombardment of film after film over a long period creates an extreme situation in which there is a tendency to sum up and anticipate the whole film on the basis of the first few minutes. Though the situation is less extreme, the same is true of most ordinary viewers watching a film, because they are too attached to literal narrative and generalized interpretation. Familiarity anticipates certain results, a projection of what is familiar. Narrative is stylized to form a general statement, and all other things become subordinate to the narrative. Once a statement is assumed to be known, the experience is no longer considered necessary. Traditional film-making has had a bias towards literal narrative (with sound films – a verbal narrative), enhanced and sustained by technique.

Statements are made in the form of condensed generalities, of summaries and specific points from which a conclusion can be reached by a process of logical thought. Film styles have in themselves become symbols, and familiarity with such styles enforces the general statement. This has been such a regular procedure that cinemagoers now expect it, consider it the 'norm'. Traditional narrative film-making (which is derived from the theatre) is based on reaching a conclusion or an end-result and all the preceding elements are clues leading to this conclusion or making it possible. If the film-maker uses common symbols and generalizations there is less risk of his being 'misunderstood'. But the idea of a greater common understanding for film is also of course the result of the commercial attitude that considers it necessary to appeal to the largest number of people to guarantee a sufficient financial return. 'Entertainment' films are derived from this attitude, since something that is easily digestible and simple to understand for the greatest possible number of people is deemed to be 'entertainment'. In this process of summation and literal narrative, abstraction is reduced for the sake of common knowledge. To realize even a literal narrative through greater abstraction would mean that a great physical involvement (time) plus a greater subjective (personal) involvement would be allowed. However, the intellectual risk of not being completely understood occurs because of the indeterminable amounts of change and alteration that would become possible in accordance with the individual viewer's subjectivity and degree of involvement. There is also the risk that the viewer would have to work too hard and not enjoy and understand the film because of this. So more stylized, literal and familiar attitudes have been the dominant force in the film bias.

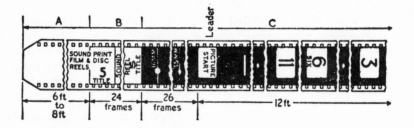

At the same Mannheim Film Festival a film was shown that after a few minutes aroused such mumbled comments as: 'It's another one of those underground films', or 'it's one of those anarchistic type of films'. A quick check at the programmes showed that this film would go on for two hours. Since most people's attitudes had already classified the film and worked out what it was or wasn't about there was no point in watching it any longer. But I did stay to watch it (remembering Jacques Ledoux saying: 'Every film should be seen at least once'). The film was *Summer in the City* (1970) by the Munich film-maker Wim Wenders and was made up of a random series of memories; I had the sensation as I watched it of being caught up in someone else's time. In his programme note Wenders explained that the film is the aftermath of a crime story. A man who has been released from prison no longer wants to have anything more to do with the story of the crime. He runs away from it. He goes from Munich to Berlin, and from Berlin to Amsterdam. That is all the plot there is. But something else happens – your sense of time is transformed into another time. I did not realize this until the film was over, because it was very hard to work out where I was. The film, through the extension of the gesture between the action, makes what in normal narrative film is nothingness, into something positive. These moments in life, although not summations of adventure, are the pauses which make adventure.

Summer in the City represents waiting and the drive after the arrival, the news-stand and the newspaper; shop lights; snow coming down; the petrol station seen from the stranger's window; arriving at a friend's flat to wait. Each detail is a segment viewed in units of 'actual time'. Waiting becomes important because the action of pausing and wandering also contains tension and anticipation. We have a very active sensation of being caught up in a span of time. We see the man leave prison; we see him get a lift; and we see what he sees. We see him turn the television off, and see and hear him having a conversation with a girl-friend. Finally, in the last flat in Berlin, he plays a record of some orchestral work, followed by the dramatic finality of the aeroplane wing as the music goes on with him to Amsterdam. The last shot is no longer one of waiting, but one of action. The structure is precise, though without key moments. The meaning of the film is not the narrative but the time in between. If you leave before the end you can never know what it is about.

Wenders, whose earlier films are *Some Player Shoots Again*, *Silver City* and *Alabama – 2000 Light Years*, considers that when a cut in a film occurs, the beauty of the shot is broken. To him it is vital to allow the beauty (and the meaning) of a shot to be fully realized and enjoyed. The cut ruins intensity. His view resembles that of 'minimal' film-makers, who consider that the traditional narrative cinema uses cuts for the sake of the plot and keeps the images at a distance by breaking them in accordance with the plot, not in accordance with the inherent quality of the image. Wenders reduces the cut in order to allow a long shot, which he considers will give the viewers the opportunity to put themselves into and stay with the film.

Wenders thinks that those who make cuts for the sake of the narrative are trying to dictate to the audience instead of allowing them to develop their own involvement. (Love is manifested by a feeling of not being able to stop and Wenders therefore relates cutting to coitus interruptus.)

Summer in the City is not of course entirely free of cuts, in so far as it is made up of a series of visual units of a given duration placed one beside the other. Each unit has the freedom and purity of total film experience. It is not itself cut; it merely begins and ends and is then put with others to form a sequence. In a sense, what Wenders is doing is taking what would be stylized gestures in a traditional narrative and allowing each to be a full statement. His approach is not unlike that of Warhol, or the firm and theoretically based purity of Jean-Marie Straub's camerawork. But unlike either of them, Wenders uses contemporary narrative elements and lets the more random action in between determine the length of each unit of time.

Wenders followed *Summer in the City* with *Die Angst des Tormanns beim Elfeter* ('The Goalkeeper's Fear of the Penalty'), based on a novel by Peter Handke. In this film Wenders keeps his sensitive and extended drift of time, though the direct narrative brings the film into the critics' idea of being more 'acceptable' for the average audience.

In a film that includes cutting, the idea of using a continuous shot is to achieve intense subjective involvement in the audience by concentrating on a single object or direction. The continuous shot is allegedly 'purer' because it is unbroken, deals in 'real' time and involves less manipulation. Even though the traditional narrative film can generally be considered to have a single objective, this objective is basically relative, whereas the singularity of direction and intent that I am referring to here is absolute. Films of this kind that involve editing change the time sensation by deleting any reference to 'real' time. This means that a certain freedom is lost. Editing can maintain the feeling of continuity and directness in an abstract sense of time, or without a specific reference to time. What we might call 'timelessness' can occur with or without editing, since a timeless sensation depends on viewer involvement. The edited film can be considered as more direct in that its sequence can be arranged in a definitive order, but the continuous shot can be considered as didactic if the camera chooses to be absolutely static regardless of the action being filmed. One further point to be borne in mind here is that some methods of editing can introduce the continuous physical sensation produced by the continuous shot. Though the edited film does interrupt the single image, it can make images seem uninterrupted. The difference is that the edited film is far more dependent for its effect on the significance of the images and actions than the continuous shot, which depends on the way the camera is handled.

The easiest example of the edited film that concentrates on a single image is a development of the loop. Lutz Mommartz's *Eisenbahn* (Railway) uses a fixed camera looking at and out of a railway carriage. The landscape outside passes by, the soundtrack is of the train rolling along. The first sensation it produces is of riding in a train and looking out of the window. The camera focuses first on the window, with the landscape rushing blurrily by. After a while we begin to concentrate on the landscape, and gradually realize that it is always the same piece of landscape passing by. Whereas it seemed at first to be a monotonous general train background it now becomes specific and with the introduction of two different cuts near the end (a pole passing the window) the repetition becomes apparent. Interestingly, although this film is made out of a loop only 5 metres long, it runs for 16 minutes, and for at least the first half we believe that it is a continuous shot of a train ride. The actual details of the movement (what is passing) are not at first our primary consideration. So the film creates a singular feeling of objective continuity, even though it is really a repeated cutting together of the same image (with two additions).

Without the use of the loop, this feeling of continuity is often achieved by our relationship to the subject-matter. In Mommartz's *Wege zum Nachbarn* (Paths to the Neighbours, 1968) a girl writhes up and down presumably on top of a man, though he is never seen. The movements of her face and body change as intercourse progresses. The action is continuous, though the shots are not. Our basic involvement is with what the content implies. Similarly, my own film *Alone* (1964) (and also *Naissant* [1964/7], though there the implication is different) shows a girl lying on a bed and gradually becoming involved with herself. The camera (and therefore the viewer) concentrates solely on her; there is no wandering away from her, though the distance between her and the camera does change. Her preoccupation with her thoughts and with her body gradually becomes the viewer's preoccupation since little else is happening. Her increasing involvement with herself continues, evolves towards masturbatory gesture, which is suddenly frozen. Raymond Durgnat has noted his impressions:

> I have seen *Alone* three times. After the first time, I was left with a vague impression that it was one long take of a lonely girl in bed, half-heartedly trying not to masturbate, and then despite herself, indulging. . . . At the third view, I began to count the cuts (33) as if to assure myself that they were there. I nearly began counting the one softly repeated chord. . . . Everything is vaporized, except this rendezvous of a physiology with its own loneliness. The girl's fantasies are painfully absent, yet lucidly so . . . or maybe this girl is so far gone that her finger is only her finger and no dreams live. The primitivism of the act is matched by the camera, invariably full-face to her bedstead, and by the editing, pitted by shadows that now block out her eyes, now mass under her cheekbones, now caress the long, lean legs whose posture evokes the compositions of Pabst (another master of erotic energy wasted in squalor). Perhaps squalor is the wrong word – there is an eerie solemnity to the nothingness, like the rite of a priestess.[17]

In film the spectrum of content is very broad. It ranges from the narrative plot through associative imagery and abstract imagery to the point where the film or the camera itself become the content. The content can be a single frame, or it can be time. It can even be the environment in which the film occurs. Light and structure alone can be the content, or time itself. The space in which film lives is vast and nebulous.

The spectrum of film is not easily or clearly definable. People, on the whole, seem to have little time to expand, and if they feel that something does not concern them directly they do not make the effort to understand. They tend to stay isolated with their unfelt definitions; words which have little to do with felt images. Language conditions their thinking because it is this that they use to put their thoughts into form.

Definitions become like numbers and are used for convenience. Each film can break every definition and at the same time each film has the potential of every definition. In film one is working in ambivalence where opposites can and do become completely inseparable.

A single image, or a single movement, action or gesture can contain, in condensed form, a multiplicity of reference. Expand this into a combination of many simple images over a fixed period of time and one has not just a film, but a vast potential store of references and associations. Films can inform, by implication or by statement. In this they make use of structure, of verbal narrative and of images, many of which contain gestures or actions. Images are a language; a form of hieroglyphics designed to convey information. Meanings can be conveyed by the interrelationships between feelings, ideas and objects, which can also be related to our own experience. The ability of film language to put across images and emotions in a lifelike form gives it great immediacy. When such images or emotions are put into the context of a whole film, the effect they create is heightened by the concentrated pressure of the frame. In this way each film can become a closed system of association, a self-sustaining entity.

In Peter Emanuel Goldman's *Echoes of Silence* (1965), we watch a strange void in people's lives. Perhaps they are lost; perhaps they are waiting. In many ways it might be said that this state of waiting is our inheritance in society today, whether it is based on fear, or waste, or failure or on none of these. Goldman's film creates this sense of waiting in an almost 'documentary' manner, though it is far from the traditional documentary film. It helps us to understand the loneliness of waiting for nothing, the feeling of being a prisoner yet not in prison: the girl trying to decide whether or not to become a prostitute; the two boys making contact as in the loneliness among Genet prisoners, for another human being does provide a principal identity for the self; the young man standing on the city street, waiting. *Echoes of Silence* is presented in a series of chapters; as in Goldman's shorter films *Night Crawlers* (1964) and *Pestilent City* (1965) the lonely utterances become extensions of fact, bits of life blown into time.

The same type of lonely utterance is extended into the metaphor of the lost child in Klaus Emmerich's *Film für Cheyenne* (Film for Cheyenne, 1971), in which a boy's socially frustrated life is put into a time experience. It begins with a newsreel interview: the real Cheyenne tells of his life; of the social plagues of today; of being unwanted and then, as soon as he does something, of being wanted only for punishment; of a society that can no longer find any time to get involved with a problem unless it has already been solved. The film follows the boy (another boy) after the interview and watches him search for his place in society – and there is no place. As the real Cheyenne suggests at the beginning, he is running away from something that he has no connection with, and yet is hated because he is society's own reflection. The film does not tell us anything; it simply lets us feel, lets us witness a number of units of 'actual' time with the boy. It is this involvement with time that gives it its strength.

A large number of labels are available for films of this 'documentary' type, including of course *'cinéma vérité'*. Not that such terms can be disregarded, but their usage must be taken with a grain of salt and a lot of imagination, but definitely not literally. *Dictionary of the Cinema* by Peter Graham (1964/8), defines *'cinéma vérité'* as a 'term invented by Jean Rouch (and derived from Vertov's "Kino-Pravda") first used to describe his film "Chronique d'un été" (1961) and subsequently applied to any kind of documentary film where emphasis is given to the camera's power as a recording instrument and to its directness of impact through the use of impromptu interviews, hand-held sequences, direct sound recording, etc.'

As with most definitions, this one is far from satisfactory. For instance, Vlado Kristl's *Obrigkeitsfilm* fulfils these conditions but is not classified as *cinéma vérité* or documentary because its situations are considered to be socially unimportant, or contrived. They are in fact natural and anarchistic, without any fictional intention. Conversely, *Shadows* (1959) has been called *cinéma vérité,* even though it represented a fictional situation performed by professional actors. Shirley Clarke calls her film *Portrait of Jason, cinéma vérité,* although the situation was set up in advance and the camera was not hand-held, because the way Jason speaks could be considered natural and impromptu. At the Internationale Filmwoche in Mannheim in 1971 the film that earned most votes was Shimsuke Ogawa's *The Peasants of the Second Fortress,* but it was not allowed to be considered for the *grand prix* because it was labelled a documentary, and the *grand prix* was intended for a first feature-length fiction film. The prize in fact went to *El Camino Hacia la Muerte del Viejo Reales,* made by the Argentinian film-maker Gerardo Vallejo. Though this film seemed to be a documentary in that the characters in the film were played by themselves, not by professionals, it was classified as fictional because they *enacted* scenes to show how they lived and because, for example, the old man pretended to die by showing how he would like to die. One cannot help feeling that the labelling system used at international film festivals is often ludicrous and misleading.

In *The Peasants of the Second Fortress* the images have considerable emotional force when seen in context. The situation is that some Japanese peasants are trying to prevent the authorities from taking over their land to build an airport on it. The film portrays the lengthy battle waged by peasants and students against the police, the emotional content becoming particularly strong when we are confronted with the peasants themselves. An old peasant sitting inside the fortress during a lull in the battle talks to the cameraman about his attitude; he does not make a speech but speaks naturally, saying something, thinking, considering, speaking again and so forth. But it is not his words that are important – it is his face, his expression. It is through his expression that we sense his thoughts, his feelings. It is important to note that the film-maker did not cut out these pauses for contact (as so many people would in order to make abbreviated statements) but allowed the contact to grow as we watch.

The most effective political and socially conscious films allow our relationships to what we see to draw out the feelings latent within us and thus involve us. It is not so much a case of intellectual understanding as of emotional understanding. The majority of independent 'newsreels', 'agit-prop' films, 'cinetracts' use this associative element in film language in the same way that poets use metaphor. What is essential is the way we relate to the image, and to the image in time.

This idea of political involvement brings to mind one of the most forceful films in the context of social or political involvement. Adolf Winkelmann's *Heinrich Viel* (1969) (made with Buttenbender, Grün and Schmidt) is a strongly politically oriented film that exploits 'actual' time to involve the viewer. It is related to the work of the 'minimalists', playing down the camera movement (considered manipulation) while intensifying the viewer's powers of perception. It is only by association that the direct political motive becomes apparent. The images consist of two men working on an assembly line in a car factory. They simply go through their routine of putting various parts on to the engines. Each engine moves along the conveyor belt at a constantly slow speed, the time it takes to pass being just long enough for the two men to complete their various actions. As each engine appears they repeat their cycle, the repetition becoming like a loop, except that it is not a loop. They repeat this mechanical process all day, and throughout the film. The only things that change are the numbers on the engines and, occasionally, the men's facial expressions. The film runs without a break or a cut for thirty-six minutes. The content becomes a representation of a living loop.

The implication is obvious. The political/social process is mirrored in the mechanical and repetitive work of the men in the name of industrial productivity. Watching this film may seem boring, but then one is experiencing the same boredom as the men during their work. If we can find subtle points of interest and change in the operation, then this is probably the only way that the two men manage to avoid becoming mere mechanized vegetables. If a spectator leaves the film because he sees no point in experiencing such repetition yet again, the film has made its point: these mechanical operations and the daily repetition of them imposed on people in order to survive must be very destructive to their sensibilities when the thirty-six minutes of the film time are extended to a seven- or eight-hour day, five days a week, for forty years.

I do not intend here to isolate content that could be described as 'directly political or socially engaging', for it is often only one facet of a film. My own view as to what can constitute a 'political' or 'social' film includes any film that attempts to alter or expand the *values* of the viewer (society), no matter how directly and no matter what its content.

It is interesting to reflect on how much is implied when one watches a film, particularly one that uses recognizable images or actions but has no straight narrative. Interpreting the implications of those images is rather like cloud-reading or Rorschach tests. When seen in context, associative or recognizable images (particularly of other people and their actions) become areas of self-projection. The meaning of such projections refers to or exposes the values of the viewer while the choice of the material and the context reflects the film-maker's values. Individual films can thus provoke confrontation, acceptance and a whole range of accusations and vindications.

As implication is of its very nature imprecise, it is also one of the elements of film most feared by regimes based on oppression. It leaves 'too much to the imagination of the viewer', and this spells danger for those who exercise political control and censorship. Implication can also bring out latent feelings, whether conscious or unconscious, in the individual viewer, which explains why many cinemagoers find films of this kind disturbing, often reacting with an urge to have the film banned or destroyed. Examples that come to mind here are Buñuel's *L'Âge d'Or* and the Buñuel/Dali film *Un Chien Andalou*, in which images and their associations are removed from any familiar context, though they remain recognizable. The relationship between images and events in these two films was no longer familiar, there was no logical progression. One had to abandon any thought of sequence and simply experience them – an idea that aroused considerable contempt and confusion among critics and cinemagoers alike.

The films made by Frans Zwartjes might be considered surreal, but they are also humorous; they might be considered erotic, but they always have a sense of tragedy, loneliness and futility. The subjects are people, the actions are exaggerated, isolated gestures, the images are rich in tone, texture and depth. The characters' faces are strange, still masks suggesting a tragic paralysis. Their movements are extreme and protracted, and yet, even in the outside scenes they always seem to be confined by walls. The images appear in short bursts, with wide angles, a feeling of intensity being created by repeated short bursts of similar but different shots. The humour lies in the fact that the characters seldom make what one thinks of as normal movements, but always move and gesticulate in an exaggerated way that is further emphasized by the use of short bursts with the camera.

o

In Zwartjes's film *Faces* a woman with a stark white face seen against a rich black and white patterned background tries to pour out a drink. Her gestures are staccato, her expression deadpan. The whole film consists of this attempt, until the glass is full. She drinks it and the black liquid spills out of her mouth and over her white face. The whole attempt to drink becomes a panic-stricken struggling, embodying a sense of futility.

In *Birds* (1968) a woman (Zwartjes's wife, Trix) is reclining, again in the stark richness of a black and white setting. She is playing with a toy bird on an elastic band. Her movements are again protracted as she bounces the bird seductively up to her face, to her lips, over her black-clothed body; finally the bird is bounced, in repeated staccato movements, between her legs, while the soundtrack consists of exaggerated bird twitterings. *A Fan* (1968) follows a frustrating, agitated dream. Fan quick, face turn, face turn, face turn, face turn, fan quick, face turn, face turn, in move, in move, out fan quick. Flowers exotic, nervous, decorative, black and white.

Before his cycle of films called *Home, Sweet Home*, Zwartjes made *Anamnesis* (1968). This 18-minute film evokes the futility of human relationships in a mood of stoicism: the woman and the man try to make contact; their bodies are driven by unknown forces and their faces do not seem to know what they are doing. Both in the room where the two (Trix and Lodewijk) start out and during the elongated pursuit outside, they always want to go one way, yet always go the other way, lost and driven through the grass, through the mud and into the water and never making contact yet always together. The constant paradox becomes a statement hard to dismiss. Similarly, in *Seats Two* (1970) two women look at a picture and are in a sort of physical contact, while together they wander into their own neutral worlds. This idea of togetherness/apartness expresses a situation that is constantly recurring in our everyday existence. How often, for example, do you talk to other people or do other people talk to you, when they are really only talking to themselves and have no interest in whether you agree or disagree, hear or don't hear?

The cycle of films by Zwartjes called *Home, Sweet Home* is not yet complete. Among the films in it are *Kitchen, Spare Bedroom, Toilet, Behind Your Walls, Through the Garden* and *A House of Your Own*. The subject-matter is quite simple: people are seen engaged in these universal everyday domestic arrangements. In the 3-minute film *Toilet* (1970) the act of going to the lavatory becomes a whole ritualistic process, a confrontation. The viewer observes his own rituals, his own gestures, experiencing something akin to a revelation. *Spare Bedroom* (1970) has faces looking inwards in sexual introspection, faces that are reminiscent of the early Flemish painters of Zwartjes's own country.

I once made a film called *To Tea* at Zwartjes's house and he made a film of me making a film. Filming in his environment not only gave me a different sense of space, it also gave me an understanding of how he used his space. His is bare, like a white, contained sanctuary, into which he can move (his camera movements tend to be circular) and into which he can put his people. His textures are flattish and very rich looking. The objects are also chosen with great care. The people are fastidiously made up, since each element introduced reveals a facet of conduct and personality. It is through this use of careful and significant details that Zwartjes builds up his involvements, yet his camera, like his people, implies futility. A dream has brought them there, and they proceed as anachronisms. The faces are masks and the gestures with hands and body turn into subconscious sequences. In his colour film *Through the Garden* (1970) the two women will walk together for ever, slowly, shadows of themselves going nowhere. Perhaps we are supposed to fill in the faces. In *Living* (1971) a man and a woman look at and through the empty rooms of a house. They search out the place, their faces take on anamorphic expressions. Their search through the rooms becomes a circular process, always getting closer to the object of the search. The two are concerned about their own selves and seem to be compelled to drift together by the force of the walls. There is a strong sense of enclosed space, to the point where each detail and each movement turns into a world of its own. The mood is strangely mute, as though no one can talk, as though tongues do not exist, because there is never any feeling that anyone needs to talk. The movement is often abrupt, constricted, as if everything is really impossible but is driven to happen by an irresistible force. His people hold back, but the film thrusts forward. The concern moves about as though executing the steps of a folk-dance, very determined, quick and compulsive. The people become puppets into which he inserts himself and through which he makes his statements. These statements become a masque of latent sexuality – telling how we are driven onwards unthinkingly like some unwitting projectile, into an inner space where contact is necessary and inevitable. Zwartjes's films express wanting and feeling while we maintain the masquerade of not wanting or feeling.

Zwartjes is yet another example of the prolific film-maker whose involvement in his work colours his whole style. As with so many non-box-office film-makers, his films could have been made only by himself. The conception, the camera work, the editing, the imagery and the timing are all his and his alone. With his black and white films he even processes them himself, using different chemical methods in order to enrich the visual meaning of his statement. He has thus been able to offer austere contrasts of black and white, the whites seeming to glow and to spill into the blacks. The whites, for example, increase the blank, mask-like expressions of the characters. The environments become a highly graphic chiaroscuro, enveloping the actions in an inky surrealism.

Throughout my many years of contact with the independent cinema, and my subsequent contacts with the commercial cinema outside it, I have constantly found a remarkable belief that in what is currently called the 'underground' film, the primary concern is with sex. This attitude is strongest among those who never see the films but simply hear about them. Naturally the majority of ordinary conservative people stay away from such films and try to 'protect their children' from the awful horrors of sexuality.

The first point to be made here is that directly sexual themes are only a minor aspect of the many different types of theme treated in the independent cinema. Social and political fears and repressions are treated just as often as sexual ones. The problem is that sexuality has long been a controversial topic in our western societies. Yet the appearance of human flesh, human relationships, physical contact between people, parts of the human body, and its functions (and verbal statements about these) are clearly a means of creating communication between people. The human form stripped bare or involved in personal relationships is just another form of personal film expression. After all, the main point of the personal film is that it is totally dependent on the individual who makes it.

The idea that the independent film is primarily concerned with sex is the result of the attempt of the socially 'respectable' media to exploit sexual hang-ups. The media (particularly the press) exploit sex by constantly presenting it, though they diminish themselves by taking advantage of peoples' fears about corruption and yet blaming others for this corruption. Those who show independent films tend to choose only films whose content they consider sexual, in order to attract a larger paying audience. These exhibitors ignore the great majority of independent films, which they feel can never stimulate enough interest to bring in a profit. The most accessible independent films are thought to be those with sexual implications (generally those which have nude images in them). Many well-financed films conceived on a commercial basis play upon this principle, often using such words as 'underground' in their publicity so as to relate the films to the alleged perversions of hidden and secretive artists. The gullible public naturally believes this publicity, and out of this develop narrow and limited expectations.

For me, the important point in all this is that it shows how much stress is placed on content. The same problem arises when cinemagoers and critics are confronted with abstraction. When a film deals objectively with its subject-matter it automatically becomes more acceptable, socially and legally. A 'documentary' about nudism, for example, would be allowed, even though it shows naked men and women together, on the grounds that it is a record of a true situation concerning a particular group of people. It is an emotionally remote and intellectually objective situation. The same applies to films about the pictorial arts: a film about an artist's work is received more readily (and given more financial support) than a film made by the same artist as a piece of self-expression. This objective attitude is safe and means that the maker and the viewer are in a position of non-involvement – a position where no blame can attach to anyone. This is not to say that in certain contexts and at certain times this kind of film cannot arouse intense involvement. The 'documentary' can wield great force by remaining objective, because various types of content can rise to the surface and confront the viewer.

For my film *Trixi*, the manager of Kodak (Britain) refused to process any prints. Only one was processed, which Kodak threatened to destroy; it was released only because both the Edinburgh Festival and the National Film Theatre were to show it. The manager of the laboratory who made the print looked at the film after Kodak's self-righteous censorship. He took up the same position as Kodak, and put forward the argument that, though he agreed that there were no images that could be considered 'obscene', he found that the implications of the film itself were not only obscene but downright disgusting. He ended by saying that he didn't want to see the film in his lab again. The film is printed in a lab on to Kodachrome stock, from an Ektachrome reversal master. Since Kodachrome reversal processing is monopolized by Kodak, it has to go to them to be developed. The film itself, incidentally, confronts the camera, and thus the viewer, with the emotional changes undergone by a girl. This incident made me realize how easily people are provoked when personal feelings are the point of reference.

Sitting here writing, looking through films and film titles and remembering films, I find it very difficult to say that many independent films are explicitly sexual, though sexual images and sexual actions are explicitly shown. Many are erotic, and many more are sensual and sensuous. Some films are devoted to sensuous experiences, but the degree of provocation remains highly personal. In this sense, the extent to which the viewer is provoked depends on his own personal experience. Exploitation of sexual motivation is more often found in the commercial cinema than in the independent cinema. The commercial cinema consciously bases its sexual suggestions on hidden and negative social attitudes, whereas the independent cinema treats sexuality, eroticism and sensuality both personally and as a natural process, as part of the normal process of experience and expression.

Warhol's *Blue Movie* (otherwise entitled *Fuck*) (1969) treats the relationship of Viva and Louis Waldron in such an open and almost unconscious way that there is no longer any suggestion of something hidden. I suppose that in the case of Warhol one cannot even say that he 'treats' this heterosexual relationship, he merely films it. Its imagery is explicit, as in his *Lonesome Cowboys*, but the actions are matter-of-fact and one never gets the feeling that the showing of sexual action is unusual. As a matter of fact, it is typical of the sexual element in the independent cinema that it is never seen as unusual. Rejection of sexual and personal subjects in film is symptomatic of the confined and immature mind. If one says that film should contribute to the senses of the majority of the people then the widest possible subject matter should be used even though it might hitherto have been found unacceptable.

Many so-called 'pornographic' films (or blue movies, or stag films or hard-core films or whatever you like to call them) convey direct and honest emotional experiences. In quite a few 'Danish' films where physical intercourse is shown explicitly, the people who appear are personally involved

FILM IS . . .

in their relationships and are therefore natural. They enjoy their relationships and do not offer a mockery of sexual feeling. Their feelings are real,
and are conveyed to the viewer through the film. Though this is not the
case with all 'pornographic' films, it is very much the case with personal and
independent films.

Thanks to its very personal images, particularly concerning sexual relationships, Andrew Noren's *Kodak Ghost Poems* could be classified as a dirty
film. Being highly intimate in its details it has provoked a great deal of the
sort of reaction that stems from embarrassment. Films such as *Un Chant
d'Amour* and *Flaming Creatures*, with their highly personal connotations,
provoke the same type of reaction. Yet there is honesty in the sexual directness of *Kodak Ghost Poems,* as there is in *A Change of Heart.* (The film-
maker Robert Nelson has said of the latter: 'Noren has attempted a very
difficult reverse – underhand groin grab, and it comes off. . . . I like the
girl's thighs – a cross section of them would make perfect circles; most
are ovals.') Sexuality becomes more erotic in Carolee Schneemann's *Fuses,*
for the film is built round the feelings found in a sexual relationship: holding and touching; twisting and sliding; lost in a world belonging to themselves, forming and floating in light and darkness. The suggestion and the
the combination of sexual provocation and feeling of mystery can create
eroticism, as in Bill Vehr's *Avocada* (1965), or his later *Brothel* (1966), which
stresses erotic fantasy by the use of rich contrasts of flesh, extravagant
textures and colours to make a tapestry of erotic sensations. Barbara Rubin's
Christmas on Earth, on the other hand, conjures up dream-like erotic spirits,
and dares to produce a chaos of sensations in which what might seem explicit
seems to become an imagined possibility. *Christmas on Earth* has been
described as:

> A woman; a man; the black of the pubic hair; the cunt's moon mountains
> and canyons. As the film goes on, image after image, the most private
> territories of the body are laid open for us, now an abstracted landscape;
> the first shock changes into silence, then is transposed into amazement. We
> have seldom seen such down-to-earth beauty, so real as only a terrible
> beauty can be: terrible beauty that man, that woman is, are, that Love is.

Erotic expressions in film are extended to make psychological implications
and suggestions in Carl Linder's *The Devil is Dead* (1964) and *Womancock.*
A more clinical image association becomes the backbone of the films of
Irm and Ed Sommer, such as *Der Deutschen Mutter, Kontakte* and *Striptease
und Emanzipation.* The viewer is first presented with straight imagery, confined by its own frame, then the film becomes a picture-book sex lesson.

The range and ramifications of erotic imagery are considerable. The films
can be as direct and as personal as Peter Gidal's *Secret,* which offers the
repeating freedom of male masturbation, or can continue the erotic symbolism of Roland Lethem's *Les Souffrances d'un Oeuf Meurtri* (1967), in

which the egg and other such symbols suggest personal sexual associations. Symbolism, especially sexual symbolism, on a personal or general level, recurs frequently among some independent film-makers. Some of the most successful exponents of this type of approach being Lethem, Baruchello, Robert Nelson, Carl Linder and Stan VanDerBeek.

an eye
willingly
reeling

One of the earliest films to scrutinize the nude human body is *Geography of the Body* (1943), made by the late Willard Maas. The film flows through ups of the body as over a landscape made up of shapes and tones. The view is often very close and the eye wanders through this familiar terrain of valleys and mountains, while a voice reads a poem. Then the Japanese film-maker Takahiko Iimura made *Ai* (Love, 1962), which shows two bodies making love with microscopic directness. The close scrutiny of the movements and the form of the two bodies becomes an amazing configuration of body gestures, of parts and pieces of human forms enlarged to a scale where they seem to envelop us. Hairs become forests, lips become caves and flesh becomes oceans. We are so close that the movements become ritualistic exaggerations of a sexual love dance, and the sudden movements of legs and arms flung out become a rite leading to a climax. At the same time, there is a stark quality in the film. The black and white are taken to extremes and the whole imagery moves with the body movements, drawing, twitching and touching in the spasms of love.

Iimura's *Love* also restates another possibility, one that has been stated and demonstrated by Brakhage, by many of the independent Italian film-makers such as Lombardi and De Bernardi, and more recently by British film-makers such as Tim Harding, Roger Hammond and Barbara Schwartz. I refer to the continuous potential of 8mm film. *Love*, like other films by Iimura such as *Iro, 6 x 6, De Sade, Dada, Junk, Sakasama* (all 1962) or *Rose Coloured Dance* (1966), were all originally shot (and most still are) on 8mm. The closeness and the feeling of intimacy he achieved in *Love* was due to the flexibility of 8mm film and the ease with which it can be handled; when the film was blown up to 16mm this increased the black and white contrast and also, of course, the scale; he could now add sound (by Yoko Ono) and this, of course, helped to make larger audience projection more available. (Sound can now be used in conjunction with Super-8 films.)

One essential point to be remembered here is that films remaining on 8mm are available for home buyers for personal viewing, since 8mm home-movie equipment is highly accessible, and prints are cheaper than on 16mm. This point was first emphasized by Stan Brakhage. His whole cycle of *Songs*, for instance, is on 8mm and prints have been sold to many individuals to view in their own time, as often as they wish.

Blowing 8mm up to 16mm has great potential for the film-maker. He is left free to think and has infinite opportunities for personal expression. It is rather like using a pencil, for images can be captured in the same way as when one is doing a quick sketch, without the hang-ups and the ponderous business of preplanning and the expense of the commercial process in which the elephantine 35mm Mitchells and crews of seventy or more make every fifteen minutes of working cost over £250. Because of the eternal labelling plague, which classifies 8mm film as 'amateur' or 'home-movie', the would-be 'professional' film-maker will sit and wait, doing nothing but dream of the day when someone gives him some big 35mm Mitchells, the crews and actors and a minimum of £50,000 to start a film. Yet 8mm, and Super-8, is now constantly being used, especially by painters and sculptors (though many more are going into video, or using 8mm and video) either as an extension of their work or for expressing themselves solely on film. Barry Flanagan in England and Tony Morgan in Düsseldorf are two examples here.

One disadvantage of Super-8 is that there is no black and white film available, and even with 8mm, black and white is becoming hard to get. But then between 8mm and the 'professional' 35mm is 16mm, which has the best potential in terms of film stock, equipment, sizes, projection and sound.

Takahiko Iimura's films express a whole range of individual film thoughts and are often very beautiful. *Virgin Conception* (1968) is a dreamy film in which the imagery, though often hazy at the beginning, becomes gradually more obscure as painting on the film takes over, leaving a mystery at the end. *A Dance Party in the Kingdom of Lilliput* (1966) is related more to 'structuralist' films, the images of a naked man being presented as chapters; the sequence is like moving stills, or short statements conveyed by means of gestures. Each sequence is preceded by a title. Just as a concrete poem consists of words grouped together according to sound, and not necessarily according to meaning, so in this film the images are grouped together according to how they look and not necessarily according to what they mean. Perhaps it would be more accurate to call what are generally known as 'structural' films 'concrete'.

Iimura does not have only one approach, as can be seen in *Onan* (1963) and *Flowers* (1968), which are very different from each other and from *Love* or *A Dance Party in the Kingdom of Lilliput* or *Summer Happenings U.S.A.* (1967/8). *Onan*, which is full of rich symbolism, is described by Iimura as a film about a young man who 'lies naked in his bed and burns holes in the breasts and pubic regions of pictures of girls taken from magazines. Excited, he curls upon himself, he is delivered of a strange stone object. Running through the streets in his underwear, he meets a girl and drops the object.' *Onan* is a particularly successful attempt to probe sexual frustration. The sacrificial burning of the pin-up girl pictures symbolizes the relentless smouldering of pent-up frustrations, leading to aggression and destruction. The pin-up pictures become the images of sympathetic magic, enabling him to conquer his unobtainable opposite. The stone object produced by his organism is egg-shaped and the symbol of his ripeness, the result of his picture-poking. When he casts this symbol of ripeness before a woman she promptly rejects it.

Flowers is very different. It is a visually poetic film, a 'soft' personal collage of springtime sights in New York: the flower on the window ledge; the soft panoramas of the city superimposed; the images of an environmental happening all interspersed with warm colours. Parts of the happening, I believe, are the work of the artist Yayoi Kussma, of which the film-maker Jud Yalkut made a complete film called *Self-obliteration* (1967). The images in this film are of nude bodies that seem to be in a cave or hole, making very organic movements; some have varying numbers of large spots on them. The tones are very deep and the interaction of the figures is very sensuous. In *Summer Happenings U.S.A.* the approach is again different. This is a very direct personal view of protests and marches, showing the outsider's attitude to the paradoxes surrounding such events. But for me, one of Iimura's loveliest films is *I Saw the Shadow* (1966). The only images are those of a girl's and a man's shadows. Their movements and interplay reveal very organic and malleable forms that are of the very nature of shadows; they become elongated, stretched, then are suddenly flattened, bent, and then change again and swim about in very poetic and definitely human movements.

Symbolism exists on many levels, but all images in film can broadly be taken as symbols in the same sense that the characters in the Chinese language represent an accumulation of symbols through which one is able to arrive at some meaning by association. Many film-makers, like most other artists, insert highly personal symbols into their work, with the result that no direct or literal interpretation can be made by others intellectually, though they may 'feel' them. But film-makers may also use direct symbols of a kind that are easily recognized by most other people because the social or psychological association they evoke is familiar. Thus certain images or objects are readily identified with another object or action, both action and object being familiar and accessible to the majority of people.

In films the symbol is often substituted directly for the object or action it represents, as with the recurrent use of an egg to represent sexuality. An egg means fertility, ripeness, fullness ready to burst; its external form is smooth and sensuous; it relates to human forms and forms in nature while being whole and complete. The shell holds life inside it, it cracks and organic and fluid matter seep out; the fluid has the consistency of sexual fluid. The yolks are like testicles, and have the tactile feeling of testicles. So the egg becomes a basic repository for sexual and sensuous association. As we have seen, the stone object in Iimura's *Onan* is egg-shaped, but the symbol recurs in a large number of films ranging from Roland Lethem's *Les Souffrances d'un Oeuf Meurtri to W.R.: Mysteries of the Organism* by Dusan Makavejev.

Direct symbolism of this kind is not of course related solely to sexual connections, for a large number of social, political and cultural symbols are used in the independent cinema. A good example here is Robert Nelson's fluid and musical film *Oh Dem Watermelons!* (1965). Nelson is one of the most satirical of independent film-makers and he uses symbols for considerable comic effect. This is very true of *Oh Dem Watermelons!,* though the symbols he uses are basically related to American culture, watermelons being a familiar symbol for the American Negro. The film's theme is the attitude of white men towards the Negro, with watermelons being broken, kicked and generally treated with complete lack of feeling. The symbolism even goes so far as to show a white girl making love to a watermelon. The film starts with a 'follow-the-bouncing-ball' song, 'Darkies is watermelons'. At the end the situation is reversed and the watermelon rebels and chases the people. As with Nelson's *Plastic Haircut* (1963) much of the acting resulted from Nelson's working with Ron Davis and the San Francisco Mime Troupe. This means that the actions and gestures themselves are heavily symbolic, often drawn from traditional mime technique.

An interesting aspect of Nelson's earlier films – *Oh Dem Watermelons!, Plastic Haircut Confessions of a Black Mother Succuba* (1964/5) and *Thick Pucker* (1964/5) – is that Steve Reich worked with him on the soundtracks. By the 'seventies Reich was clearly developing his own very powerful forms of musical expression, primarily with music as a gradual process; this can be related to that of the 'minimal' or 'concrete' films. Reich describes the gradual process not in terms of composition, 'but rather pieces of music that are, literally, processes'. To facilitate closely detailed listening a musical process should happen extremely gradually: 'By "gradual" I mean extremely gradual; a process happening so slowly and gradually that listening to it resembles watching a minute hand on a watch – you can perceive it moving after you stay with it a little while. Performing and listening to a gradual musical process resembles pulling back a swing, releasing it, and observing it gradually come to rest.' Reich's music is thus its own statement, without any hidden or secret meanings. This is ironically very different from Nelson's films, which are full of hidden references to things outside the film. Reich's approach is more closely related to the films of Michael Snow or Landow or Hollis Frampton, and to some extent with those of Wim Wenders or Peter Gidal, or my own film *Moment.* (A literal film reference to Reich's minute hand can be seen in Gottfried Schlemmer's *8h01 – 8h11,* which is ten minutes of watching a clock ticking on for ten minutes.)

In *Confessions of a Black Mother Succuba* Nelson adopts a different approach, using very direct references to Bruce Conner's collage/montage films and creating contrasting effects by the use of juxtaposition. He has said of this film: 'The flip sexuality, the violence, the jump cut, the use of American pop songs on the track, and the academy leader stuck in here and there are all in "Confessions" via "Cosmic Ray". The film follows the whole collage attitude and the constant symbolic build up to make comment.'[18] Nelson's 'flip' or pop montage approach is continued in *Oiley Pelosa the Pumph Man* (1965). This flip or off-hand approach is in many ways a symbolic reference in itself, in that it reflects much of the American West; the 'I don't care' and 'anything goes' attitude.

A good idea of Nelson's casual approach to film-making emerges from his own description of the way *The Great Blondino* (1967, with William Wiley) was made:

> We didn't have any ideas or script. We just had the characters: There was Blondino, a tight-rope walker who wore a funny suit and pushed a wheelbarrow around; the cop who was supposed to look like a cop; and one girl who was just supposed to look like a trollop. The rest we just made up as we went along. Mostly, we just worked out simple visual ideas and took a lot of shots of Wiley's paintings and constructions. The form of the movie was made up at the editing table.[19]

In their strange way his films parody the commercial piped-in culture of America, though not with the same directness as pop painters. At the same time they seem like sophisticated home-movies – playing structural games in *Penny Bright and Jimmy Witherspoon* (1966/7) and stealing from old movies and the truck-off-the-cliff shots in *Hot Leatherette* (1966/7) and the 'I just happened to be there' attitude in *Super Spread* (1966/7). Symbols, it is said, need not have any likeness to what they symbolize because their meaning comes from what the observer puts into them and not what is there. Among other things film is about response to meaning. In each response is rejection and/or acceptance.

Take a film like Vlado Kristl's *Obrigkeitsfilm*. Using symbols in a film can make the audience think differently about things they take for granted, can reveal dishonesty, can even make them accept something that they think do not like. Many people do not like, or think they do not like, anarchy. So, let us undress in front of the camera, and do the things we want to do. Stick your tongue out at the camera man, lift up a girl's skirt; adjust her breasts and then cross the street in traffic, all in a row, just to get to the other side, and come back, but don't forget to argue who should go first and try to figure out if it is anarchy. Make a fire in the woods and then call the fire brigade. Film them and yourself and see what happens. Do you know what is good or bad? Is it just something you do not like (or like) and why do you like (or not like) something anyhow? The camera slips, so adjust it – no – it slips again, and you have to focus. Leap about; pretend you're fucking. Talk to (and watch) a girl in bed and try to understand her instructions on how to get to her place. Who the hell can concentrate, especially when watching her? The instructions lose their sense and so do you, but somehow you arrive at her place anyway, probably because you wanted to get there in the first place and you really knew the way. Besides, you were there already because you were watching her – so you must have been, and so you show yourself and take a picture of both of you – in the dark, of course. *Obrigkeit* – the word really means the power above you or, let us say, the authority of the state, the rulers of the Establishment who provide us with our banal 'goods' and 'bads'.

Obrigkeitsfilm can I suppose be considered consciously anarchistic. Yet the images and actions in the film seem random and the construction is difficult to classify. If the film has any sense of disorder it essentially symbolizes the *idea* of disorder; it is not confused itself. In many ways it seems amorphous in that it flows from one thing to the next, each seemingly having little link with anything except itself. But then this is an essential feature of very many independent films. Whether or not *Obrigkeitsfilm* is bound up with an acceptable idea of order, it does provoke the feeling of freedom if it is watched without preconceived ideas about classifications, mainly because of the random, 'let's do anything' attitude. The feeling of freedom comes from the fact that the film uses recognizable images – people, with whom one can obviously relate – and the fact that these people are apparently doing what they want to do without bothering about why they want to do it. This approach can be seen to a certain extent in some of Warhol's films, and in Kristl's, though with Kristl there is an additional feeling of freedom in the flamboyant use of a comic-book style.

The element of randomness seems to occur only because the imagery or the actions we see in a film bear no immediate relation to any organized and accepted notion of a narrative. Yet within randomness itself a wide range of points of reference can be discovered and a basic acceptance of such randomness will therefore make the apparently random images or actions seem relevant. After all, each film fixes images, notions, thoughts, colours, shapes, structures, time and words and sounds to create an entity of their own. David Brooks's choice of passing landscapes, treetops, and sky in *Winter* (1964/6) or *Letter to D. H. in Paris* (1967) is no less random than Kristl's people crossing the street, it is simply that a tree is a more familiar poetic symbol. For instance, crossing the street against the traffic suggests the idea of breaking through the mechanics of automated rigidity. Both the tree and the act of crossing the street convey the same sense of poetic freedom, of opening out.

The associative properties of moving images are undeniable; we have only to look at the fantasies woven into commercial films. The Kuchar twins took this fantasy theme and put comic-book dreams into the home-movie. Mike and George Kuchar began making their films in 1954, adopting the most direct and happy-go-lucky approach. They seem to be saying: How do you start making a movie when you feel like making a movie? Well if you live in the Bronx a movie is all that dream-weave comic-book stuff down at the local. And what is the world you know? Those movies, comics, bubble-gum, whizzy cars, apartment houses, streets, fire hydrants, crowds of people who work in shops, delicatessens, rag trade, truckdrivers, grandmas, slight girlie mags, hot summers, sneakers, baseball and all the pipe-dream commercial plugging of everything that is not there. So if you think of making a movie those are your points of reference. Those great seductive, enticing, come-and-get-it titles, names and jingles ring out and the movies are boxes that held all the world. So when the Kuchars began to make films they moved Hollywood to an apartment house in the Bronx. At first they used an 8mm camera to make films with titles like *The Wet Destination of the Atlantic Empire* (their very first film, made in 1954 at the age of thirteen), *The Slasher* (1958), *The Thief and the Stripper* (1959), *I was a Teen Age Rumpot* (1960), *A Tub named Desire* (1960), *Pussy on a Hot Tin Roof* (1961), *Born of the Wind* (1961), *The Pervert* (1963) *A Town called Tempest* (1961), *Lust for Ecstasy* (1963), *Anita Needs Me* (1963) or *The Lovers of Eternity* (1964). The titles are not mere titles, but represent an indigenous and electric outburst of dream-culture mimicry.

After working mostly together on these 8mm films (though some were made separately), the Kuchar Brothers began to make their own separate films on 16mm. George developed a more direct form of mimicry, while Mike adopted gentler, more symbolic mimicry. The cast description for George Kuchar's *Corruption of the Damned* (1965) satirically takes the commercial dream into the backyard:

Mary Flanagan, as Cora, a girl with a reputation as long as her hair; Gina Zuckerman, as Aunt Anna, too much woman for even a mob to fondle; Donna Kerness, the top-heavy medium with a built-in set of crystal balls; Francis Leibowitz, a mammoth woman of over-developed mother instincts; Floraine Conners as Connie, big and blonde with a gut full of liquor on an empty head; Mike Kuchar, the vengeful anti-hero with hate in his heart, hair on his chin; Larry Leibowitz, a body too big to be controlled by a peanut; Steve Packard, as Paul, who made love with his body, made waste with his bowels; Michael T. Zuckerman, big business was his line, big bosoms were his curve. And featuring a Large Supporting Cast.

Corruption of the Damned is a sophisticated version of the popular parody. Even the filming technique makes use of Hollywood methods to make a colloquial statement. It has the self-sustaining strength of a Rosenquist or a Lichtenstein painting, with the same use of blow-ups of popular forms. This film is a blow-up and super-dramatization involving the transformation of the pristine movie star into the girl-next-door. George Kuchar's blurb runs as follows:

Overwhelming in Plot, Gargantuan in Theme, trash-ridden in execution, 'Corruption of the Damned' possesses the ultimate in action-drama visuals and starlet stimulation. Big in everything it says, Big in everything it does, this picture bursts from its girdle of traditional Hollywood Pyrotechnics and falls all over the place in a Paroxysm of flabby sensuality and insanity . . . words that aptly describe its maker.

Next – 'A Dazzling Ruby in Kuchar's Jewelry box of cinema gems and gossamer garbage. Financed with unemployment checks and populated by the semi-nude' – comes *Hold me while I'm Naked* (1966). This depicts the sad/funny frustration and loneliness of the Bronx rooftop dreams gone bust. Though a take-off style is used, it is full of truth in form and mood. Though the style is parody, this is probably one of the richest descriptions of the loneliness that really exists in the super-dream environment of the lower-middle class ghettoes of New York. The hero, finding that he cannot finish making his movie, appeals for help. Nobody cares, and everybody pulls away, as if friendship is possible only when you provide fun and entertainment for your fellows. If things go wrong, they leave you. The hero loses his girl-friend and his frustration becomes sexual as well. He tries making his film full of sex but gets none himself. In the end he spins and bangs his head against the sides of a hard bathtub.

Hold me while I'm Naked uses dubbed sound, and throughout sustains the sweaty, lost and trapped dream atmosphere that is found both in the Bronx and in the Hollywood films of the 'fifties. Instead of fancy restaurants we have Mom's kitchen; instead of whisky at the out-of-town bar, Coke in the living-room; instead of rarefied theatrical speeches, raspy Bronx colloquialisms. This 'Be a good boy, sonny, and stay trapped in the sentimental Bronx dreams of lost love' mood is maintained in *Eclipse of the Sun Virgin* (1967) with its picture of life in an apartment house, the fat woman with big tits and crimson lipstick, and the hot breeze through the high curtained window with no place to go, and in later films such as *Colour me Shameless* (1967), and *Unstrap Me* (1968).

Mike Kuchar said of his *Sins of the Fleshapoids* (1965) that it is his 'most dearest dedication to commercial American movies . . .'. This film takes the science-fiction story dream to spin out the commercial dream, the lost world of today being played out in the mocking falseness of the unknown. Where George makes the dream into frustration, Mike makes it sentimental and impotent. Mike likes caricaturing the movie goddess and Debra Paget becomes Donna Kerness, girl from the Bronx, ripe arty girl down the road, star of the future film in the race of the Fleshapoids. The film is played and shot in the soft dreamy style of romantic Hollywood. The images are clear, the costumes are mock-ups and the sentiment true. 'A love story that takes place a million years in the future,' says Mike. Yet the mimicry is not negative, but a positive drama based on the dream of escape; and the maker's love of film is apparent throughout.

Mike Kuchar uses direct symbols more in the form of character, while George prefers the form of drama. In Mike's *Green Desire* (1965) the little big boy is the character – feelings of male youth in the ripeness of sexual innocence; the new man with the fear and uncertainty of the adolescent boy towards woman. In this film there is a shift from the pop dream to the expression of real feeling. The style is fluid, with easy juxtapositions: the dream-like girl on the beach; the boy standing deep in the green; the two silently together; the feeling of summer and the fear of spring urges; the void of the self. In *Madonna* (1966) this theme is extended into the glossy world of the pin-up he-man. The big, buxom, aggressive and ever-so-satisfying female taking the innocence away from the wishing-I-was-that-muscleman boy; the man dreaming he was Tarzan, seen swinging in glory from the trees, is languishly sliding into sensual hope from the ever-so-confident mother-woman taking him, while also seeing himself as the flex-your-muscle-power-pack from the back of *Man* magazine.

The wish-fulfilment urge of the unsure ball-packed man reaches its film release in *The Secret of Wendel Samson* (1966). Red Grooms is the trapped, unfulfilled and haunted man in this film of which Mike Kuchar has declared:

Wendel Samson is a Universe in himself, but perhaps even more complex. The cosmic bubble is governed by the forces of electrical magnetic inertia. He is governed by a need. Unstable. A hunger to understand the impossible. Himself maybe. A quest to find the equation to happiness in a cosmic structure where happiness is not a physical property. He is a star in the cluster of stars. A solar speck in the speckled nebula of souls. A silent phantom radiating in the heavens of shining phantoms. Floating on the islands within islands, in a bubble, fifty million light years curved.

This kind of film expression is very dependent on a stylized visual grammar in which both gesture and attitude become symbolic. It takes characteristics and exaggerates them, making things seem more familiar than they really are. At the same time it makes the wishes and dreams of ordinary people seem possible by fulfilling them on a larger-than-life scale. This is the most obvious feature of the Marx Brothers' films, in that Harpo or Groucho will do or say things that we all wish we could do or say but dare not in the context of our daily lives.

Caricature film-making has recently become popular with many German film-makers, who specialize in exaggerating the clichés of the communications media. The Kuchars based their caricature on the social clichés that were an essential feature of the media, using them to make a personal statement about their lives. On the other hand, German film-makers have in a sense kept the subjective element out of their work. If any comment is made it is implied by an objective concern with clichés, the implication being that it is at this level that society now functions, at the level of the lowest common denominator, the world of clichés and banality. The success of Rainer Fassbinder's films has been enormous. His films such as *Warnung vor einer Heiligen Nutte* (Warning of a Holy Whore), *Katzelmacher, Götter Der Pest* (Gods of the Plague), or *The American Soldier* are rather like animated comics, full of clichés from films, TV and magazines. The story is merely an excuse for parodying such clichés. For example in *Warnung vor einer Heiligen Nutte* all the gangster, girl-beating, playboy, flamboyant scenes appear in a film of a film being made. Even camera angles, tracking shots and the traditional language of film are blown up to seem like clichés. In its way this is the answer to the entertainment film in that it uses elements that are considered entertaining without pretending to have a rational structure or a circumscribed narrative. The films take all that is superficially exciting – the symbols of excitement – without actually being exciting (though they are very watchable) while the soundtrack comments on social or political events. Developing from this, Fassbinder has taken the banal, everyday life-story and, through minimalization, has produced a converse blow-up. With *Der Händler der Vier Jahreszeiten* (Merchant of the Four Seasons, 1971), he no longer deals with the parody clichés of the earlier films but with a microscopic exaggeration of the life-story line. He has further extended this exaggeration, using further tightening and minimalization with very strict camera and dialogue situations, in his excellent film *Die Bitteren Tränen der Petra Von Kant* (The Bitter tears of Petra Von Kant, 1972/3).

In his *Neurasia* (1968) Werner Schroeter films some make-believe amateur dramatics seen in the flash-bulb lighting of exaggerated acting. Records of the 'thirties accompany this dramatized parody of a rehearsal for a soap-box opera. Movements are staged to the point where cliché itself becomes a cliché. Technique is destroyed by flat, inadequate lighting, first too dark and then too bright. All this takes place on a real cardboard stage inside a cinema. This distortion of a ritual farce is treated with great sophistication in Schroeter's *Eika Katappa,* with its superstar characters such as Magdalena Montezuma. *Der Tod der Maria Malibran* ('The Death of Maria Malibran') is another example of Schroeter's operatic parodying. *Maria Malibran* is called 'an ecstacy in three acts'. It is complete with gala sound, thunder and triviality overlaid with conscious sentimentality and manneristic stage acting. The film develops its parody out of the life of the opera prima donna Maria Malibran (1808-1836) who sung herself to death in Manchester. The film maintains Schroeter's habit of contrasting shrieking and whispering.

Rosa von Praunheim (an alias) made *Rosa von Praunheim* in 1967.

The colour film *Die Bettwurst* is more comically straight. It is the story of the queen and the middle-class, middle-aged woman who becomes involved in romantic adventures that parody dramatic situations and classic characterization. She sings and poses by a window. She twirls her parasol beside a pier, then gaily wiggles by in light, washed tones. She tries, he tries. The conversation forces them together and they become companions. With her high-pitched voice and his light feminine modulations they embark on the most unlikely parody of a movie love-affair. Our happy, gay hero finally saves Miss Wonderful from an American car driven by two gangsters who kidnap her, shrieking.

The next film that von Praunheim made, *Nicht der Homosexuelle ist Pervers, Sondern die Situation in der er lebt!* (It is not the Homosexual who is Perverse but the Situation he has to live in!), is more honest. A very verbal soundtrack discusses the situation of the homosexual while the images act it out in pantomime, make-believe documentary style. *Leidenschaften* ('Passions') was made by von Praunheim originally in Super-8 which was then blown up to 16mm. The blowing up gives the film an amazing colour rendering which becomes an essential part of this dreamy, romantic, wanderer-of-the-world statement.

Whereas Godard in *A Bout de Souffle* (Breathless) or *Bande à Part* or Truffaut in *Tirez sur le Pianiste* (Shoot the Pianist) simply incorporated characters and styles from the 'grade B' American gangster film, or the cheap 10-cent novel, film-makers such as Fassbinder, von Praunheim or Werner Schroeter do not merely incorporate them, they exaggerate them by isolating them in the context of the film, making visual banality entertaining. The comic-book film becomes an operatic parody, with flamboyant, positively baroque stylization. The combination of comics with traditional opera dramatization creates a feeling of total madness.

Though this operatic madness is a speciality of contemporary German film-makers, the best examples of it that I have seen are the films of the Italian film-maker Carmelo Bene, *Nostra Signora del Turchi* (Our Lady of the Turks), *Cappriccio* or *Don Giovanni*. In *Nostra Signora del Turchi* a cook is involved in an orgiastic frenzy of preparation in what appears to be

P

a castle cellar but looks like a prison kitchen, full of gigantic pots and bub-
bling food. The pitch of frenzy is sustained throughout this film, which is
like a contemporary Arabian Nights gone berserk. The films that come
closest to this beautiful madness are recent Brazilian films such as Joaquim
Pedeo de Andrade's *Macunaima* or *Bang Bang* by Andrea Tonacci.

A problem that arises here is that of financial backing. Obviously, the more
popular and understandable a film the easier it is to get financial backing
for it. A case in point is Fassbinder, who has sufficient backing to introduce
the large cast, sets and elaboration of the commercial cinema. Fassbinder's
films are so popular and so widely accepted that he is no longer classified by
the critics as an 'underground' or 'experimental' film-maker, whereas the
Kuchar brothers are so classified.

In discussing certain films there is a point between structure, story and
technique where content and association become nebulous and impossible
to convey in words; this is the realm of abstracted and subjective associations. With conventional and linear narrative films the story can be retold
and how well its story-meaning is conveyed can be judged. The physical
structure of many films can be described in the same objective manner, and
technical mannerisms can be scrupulously analysed, but such descriptions
become meaningless and powerless in their attempt to capture certain films.
When describing the 'madness' of a Bene film or the outlandish drama
quality of a Schroeter film, there can be no real objective precision because
there are no conventional yardsticks or bases of comparison for this feeling of extreme gesture or behaviour. This is particularly the case when a
gesture represents an action which seems visually familiar but appears in an
unfamiliar way; this speaks to me with a freedom and beauty which I can
associate with, and in a direct confrontation with the film, can experience
through my associations. But, in writing, I can only call it 'madness'; the
madness or outlandishness of poetry.

Cocteau said that film is a 'powerful projection of thought'; 'thought'
being the accumulation of all a person's sensibilities. But this aspect of film
evades words. The fairy-tale, mystery and poetry instilled through Cocteau's
films is moving and meaningful, yet an account of the pictorial events is
useless in trying to understand them, and all the more so when he uses
classical and familiar tales such as *La Belle et la Bête* and *Orphée* as a narrative base. The thoughts Cocteau has imparted to the films are his alone
and it is through them the films achieve their unique expression and feeling,
not just because of the story. Cocteau's films and his 'thoughts' live with me
for ever, though I could never recount the stories step by step. The descent
to hell, the floating bodies, the destroyed buildings, the strange expressions in
Orphée; the tears in the Beast's eyes, the arms emerging out of the walls,
the galloping horses in *La Belle et la Bête*; the muse coming alive from
stone, the body sinking through the mirror and floating along the walls to
the doors in *Le Sang d'un Poete*; all these become meanings by being
absorbed through and with my own sensibilities.

Stories are also important; they are situations in which life can happen. In Phillippe Garrel's *Le Révélateur* I feel the strong flow of a story happening; however, what it is remains abstract. Instead there remains the penetrating starkness of the staring people, who, though fixed in a figurative ground, float in that distance of space belonging often to closeness. The images provide a relationship and that relationship is within the expressions of the beings you see. Their expressions come from their story, whatever it is, and from you, whoever you are. Truth or fiction soon ceases to be important or even a concern.

Shirley Clarke's *Portrait of Jason* shows a man who talks, moves, tells stories, laughs, drinks, thinks, and unfolds himself in front of the camera, in front of us: Shirley Clarke herself calls the film *cinéma vérité* and it is certainly very alive and full of all that Jason has. Jason is a queen, he says, a black queen. He tells of things he has done: of living with this guy, or working as a maid, or picking up someone else and getting paid for such and such sexual perversion. He mimics Mae West. He goes on about things he likes, the sadness and the anger. What kind of film is this? It is a confrontation with another person. Is it a 'documentary'? It is certainly a document. Is Jason acting? Is he real? Jason loves it; he entertains – showbiz baby – but he is real. There before your very eyes is Jason, laughing and crying. Fact or fiction? If he is in fact acting a memorized script what happens to your opinion of Jason? He is still very real, however you define the film.

Another film that takes a direct 'documentary' approach is *Makin' It* by Simon Hartog. Like *Portrait of Jason* it confronts the viewer directly with a person. The viewed person (on camera) takes on a 'first person' quality. Whereas *Portrait of Jason* offers one person having a conversation with the viewers, *Makin' It* confronts you with nine girls who present themselves in a special and limited situation. Each girl is presenting herself for a screen test for a role in a film. They are confronted with a panel of 'testers' or 'inquirers' who ask them to perform and act to see whether they are qualified for the role. As each girl comes forward the camera is moved further away from the scene. Each is filmed in one 10-minute take. At the beginning we merely hear the adjudicators' voices, though by the end we see their silhouettes seated round the area in which each girl must act. The camera remains motionless for each act, so that when, for example, one of them bends down the frame becomes 'empty' white space. Then suddenly her face returns, the white space seeming like a strange punctuation. The girls' actions are directed at the camera, but since the adjudicators often request difficult positions, they have to move their attention away from the camera, to face one or more of the adjudicators. Thus the viewer is at times directly confronted with the action, then pulled away to be only a witness, then is confronted again, and so on.

In *Makin' It* the structure is secondary because the configurations of gestures, expressions, confrontations within the given situation are the essential statement. Each girl reacts, relates, moves and pretends in her own way, using her own gestures and behaviour patterns. The revelation of individual characteristics is what gives the film meaning for the viewer, in much the same way as we feel that we have known Jason personally for some time. The difference is that in *Makin' It* the viewer is also in contact with the adjudicators. At these times he becomes rather like a member of the jury watching the confrontation between the witness in the box and the tricky barrister. One becomes aware not only of the girls' personalities, but of that of the adjudicators, whose egoism is displayed by their urge to test the girls. Yet we never see them as individual personalities (except one for a brief moment): they merely symbolize the position of power. This helps to make us feel sympathetic towards the girls, as we do with Jason.

Before the arrival of the sound film, during the 'silent era' of film-making, the moving image of the human form was the principle mode of expression, (especially as cameras had very little mobility). The image of a person was associated with recognizable events, actions and objects, or these actions and events were made recognizable by their associations with human images. More pointed than the narrative itself was the effectiveness of the image as a way of making thoughts and meanings comprehensible. The narrative really became a body or a frame, as a structure, into which these expressions were put. The essential communication was the recognizing, through an alter-ego experience, of the image representing a living reality. Even though the stories were often 'fictionalized' the confrontation with an image of living reality, in the form of another person, no longer remained 'fictional'. The association with the particular images (and not the narrative) made things become believable, and that association made the image of the person have its own reality. (As a reminder: in magic the image of something and the object made from the image are never sharply differentiated and most things in magic become equalized on the same conceptual plane.)

Since the style of the early commercial films was evolved from the theatrical procedures of the day, when synchronized sound began the theatrical concepts were linked even more closely with literary concepts. Subsequent adoption of theatrical and literary attitudes demanded more technical methods of interpretation. This has led to a greater concern with 'style', with narrative credibility, with technique, with structure. It is significant that the independent films most admired by the critics are those that lay emphasis on structure, ideas, concepts, sequence of events, style, technique and technical achievements.

One 'knows' or one can 'feel' when someone is sad or happy just by looking at them and one can 'know' the many degrees of sadness or happiness by being in a visual presence with that someone. This 'feeling' or 'knowing' is abstract, and though it is a reality it is hard to give it a tangible objective form. One experiences such a reality when one sees an image of a person on film and receives a series of impressions in the same way as when one is confronted with another living being, in the flesh. My own film *Dyn Amo* was to include a girl making a confession about herself. The sequence was shot in two ways. In one the girl recited a scripted confession. In the other she stood in front of the camera without saying anything. The difference was enlightening. Watching both the 'silent' take and the sound take I realized that in the sound take the words formed a sort of mask for her body; as she talked her body became frozen, neutralized, more objective than in the silent take, where she could not verbalize (and therefore intellectualize) her supposed feelings; instead she transmitted her thoughts through her body and facial movements. This is not to say that verbal expression is less powerful than body expression. But since verbal expression seeks more tangible and precise meanings it often obscures the abstract level of thought rising slowly to an intelligible and definable form.

This aspect of expression, the associative reality caused by recognized body and facial gestures in a filmed subject, has been my primary concern in my own films. As a general rule the human organism attempts to make human sense out of general abstraction and uses other human beings to do so. In this way and on this level there is a basic similarity in experience, and in the process of realizing the self a basic agreement is inevitable. Whether I manage to convey this in my own films is another matter, but I am aware of this physiological experience in my life in many ways – with people and things.

Visual representation of time and movement is a way of making thoughts felt. Pictures always hold more than just fascination since each picture has hundreds of different meanings and intrigues. Every image produces an involvement (although I have never stopped to wonder why?). Perhaps Joyce began to scratch the surface of things with *Ulysses*. Degrees of colour like degrees of black and white; like the grain on film; like the moments of waiting; like the twitch of a muscle; like the shape of a shadow; like the length of a note or the change from one octave to another; like the people passing the window; reality itself functions within the basic conception that an image of another human becomes a distinct person. Through such a basic understanding and relationship to the human image the acceptance of its reality is immediate, this is primarily because the image relates to the individual's conception of himself. In film we recognize the reality of another person even though that person is a 'filmed' image – a person who as a distinct and physical body is no longer there.

Recognizable pictorial images are usually assumed to be photographed from a 'live' subject, with which movement is normally associated. When a normally still object is put into motion, the term 'animation' is used. So when Emile Cohl sent Fantoche on a rampage, when Walt Disney made Donald Duck leap, when Alexandre Alexeieff made moving pictures dot half-tones of light (by his 'pinboard' method) and illustrated Mussorgsky's *A Night on a Bare Mountain,* when Al Sens made lines fluff away and appear as if film were a magic eraser and applicator and when Yoji Kuri made lines move to create a bizarre sexual fantasy, animation had begun.

The 'animated' film follows the path of the so-called 'live' film: from narrative to abstract forms and rhythms to optical kinaesthetics to computer films and conceptual structures. Only the assumed 'live' action (normally associated with 'realistically' photographed forms that are theoretically 'alive' when filmed) is now replaced by more graphic, stylized, symbolic or abstract objects. The 'live action' film has developed an aura of mystical romance that is rarely associated with the animated film, perhaps because film-makers' concern with the animated films comes closer to the more concentrated aspects of movements and rhythms, whereas the 'live action' film is primarily realized in a form that alludes to physical reality. Even in the cartoon or dramatic animated film, the drawn image that represents figurative forms still has a stylized and generalized feeling rather than attempting photographic naturalism.

In the world of independent film, animation is better integrated into the overall scheme of personal film expression than in the commercial cinema. For many film-makers indeed it represents a way of getting down to direct and basic statements. It is also important to note that animation allows the film-maker to work much more on his own, without the problems of dealing with other people; this is clearly an advantage for the personal film. It also of course often means less expense.

Oskar Fischinger has produced some of the most beautiful and visually exciting film experiences ever seen. His *Optical Poem* (1937) or *Composition in Blue* (1933) convey such abstract visual excitement with their rhythmic use of moving lines, shapes and colours that they are totally engrossing.

Though a description of them makes them sound over-simplified, these films are made with painstaking care and great sensitivity.

Another film-maker who is involved with movement is Len Lye, with his *Trade Tattoo* (1937) and *Night Mail* (1936). The brilliant interplay of colours, textures, lines and shapes gives the viewer a personal sense of movement and the use of hard painting on the film enhances this effect.

Without knowing anything of Len Lye's work, Harry Smith in the late 'thirties pursued the freedom of painting on film, in a series with the title of *Early Abstractions*. This includes a group of films identified by number. Some of the catalogue description ran as follows: 'No. 1: hand-drawn animation of dirty shapes – the history of the geologic period reduced to orgasm length; No. 2: Batiked animation.' The different periods of Harry Smith's film activity brought to completion three film entities. The first is called *Early Abstractions*, the second *Heaven and Earth Magic* (1957-62) and the third *Late Superimpositions*. The first period was completely devoted to the process of painting on film. The process for the first films (No. 1 and No. 2) has been described by Smith as follows:

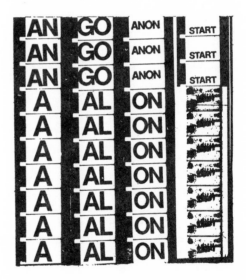

My first film was made by imprinting of the cork of an ink bottle and all that sort of thing. . . . The second one was made with come-clean gum dots, automatic adhesive dots that Dick Foster got for me. It's like a paper dot with gum on the back. The film was painted over with a brush to make it wet, then with a mouth-type spray gun, dye was sprayed onto the film. When that dried the whole film was greased with vaseline. Of course, this was in short sections – maybe six foot long sections. Anyway they would be tacked down, with a pair of tweezers the dots were pulled off. That's where those coloured balls drop and that sort of stuff. Being as it was pulled off, it was naturally dry where the dot had been and that part which had been coloured was protected by the vaseline coating at this point. Then colour was sprayed into where the dot had been. After that dried, the whole film was cleaned with carbon tetrachloride.[20]

The process of applying materials to film is an endless one, offering any number of visual possibilities. Naomi Levine, for example, has used dyes almost exclusively, while scratching and burning have been used by a very large number of film-makers, including Brakhage or Frampton, as well as animators such as McLaren or Lye. Special paints and dyes are now being manufactured for use on film, and materials such as Letraset will also adhere to film. (One difficulty here is that many laboratories will not handle painted film because they claim that it will dirty their equipment.)

The second stage of Harry Smith's *Heaven and Earth Magic* departs from the painting on film method and becomes what we might call collage animation (not to be confused with what I have called the collage film). Collage animation involves making a collage image within each single frame, and making it seem to move by altering the collage with each subsequent frame. The single image is visually related to the traditional static collage. Of his film No. 12 (part of *Heaven and Earth Magic*) Smith said:

> It is incredible that I had enough energy to do it. Most of my mind was pushed aside into some sort of theoretical sorting of the pieces, mainly on the basis that I have described: First, I collected the pieces out of an old catalogue and books and whatever. Then made up file cards of all possible combinations of them. Then I spent maybe a few months trying to sort out the cards into logical order. . . . What actually happens at the end of the film is everybody's put in a teacup, because all kind of horrible monsters come out of the graveyard, like animals that folded into one another. Then everyone gets thrown in a teacup, which is made out of a head, and stirred up. This is the Trip to Heaven and the Return, then the Noah's Ark, then The Raising of the Dead, and finally the Stirring of Everyone in a Teacup. . . .[21]

Thus fantasy and dreams turn into film magic, though few films made in this way have reached the eloquence of Harry Smith's. Other examples of brilliantly inventive dream fantasy on film can be found in the work of Walerian Borowczyk (*The Theatre of Madam Kabal*) or Yoji Kuri.

For Robert Breer the notion of absolute formal visual values came into conflict with the number of variations surrounding each single notion he had. Each frame of his film became a 'painting' of each of these variations and he assembled them to form a single composition under the title *Form Phases* (1952). Breer's films are related to those of Fischinger in that the majority of the forms seen are abstract shapes in movement, though Breer is more of a formal painter with his concern for the two-dimensional plane. Breer extends the formal painting attitude into the constantly changing aspects of the statement, in the same manner in which a painting is subjectively modified during viewing. Breer's attitude also gives a new note to abstract movement, as with, say, Norman McLaren's films. Breer's movement is non-rational awareness being more important than association. *Blazes* (1961) is a single frame-by-frame assembly of a hundred basic images, but the notion of continuity is disrupted. The single-frame accumulation results in the viewer receiving impressions without retaining any one single image. Although *Blazes* is made up of abstract forms it is related to Werner Nekes's *Spacecut*, which uses photographed natural images.

Breer has said: 'My own approach to film is that of a painter – that is, I try to present a total image right away, and the images following are merely other aspects of and equivalent to the first and final image. Thus, the whole work is constantly presented from beginning to end and, though in constant transformation, is at all times its total self.'[22] Breer's approach involves laying down a form, building round it, adding, taking and transforming the image in the process. The film itself, representing a capturing of the process, is the finished piece. Discussing his film *A Man and His Dog out for Air* (1957) Breer said that it was 'constructed from the middle towards the ends. I started with an image which evoked a feeling and I expanded this feeling in several directions.'[23] Breer's films not only display a sensitivity to pure visual shapes and freedom of movement and colour, they also illustrate the need for unrestricted thought about images. Thus *Form Phases I* shows the evolution of the abstract forms in space; *Form Phases II and III* (1953) is made up of collage, drips, washes and lines; in *Form Phases IV* (1954) movement becomes an integral part of the total composition; *Images by Images I* (1954) is an endless loop made up entirely of disparate images; *Images by Images III* (1956) a series of disparate images repeated several times with variations; *Motion Pictures* (1956) has forms derived from Breer's paintings; *Recreation I* (1957) is a frame-by-frame rupture of continuity in a follow-up of the endless loop of *Images by Images I; Jamestown Baloos* (1957) is a synthesis of all the earlier techniques; *Inner and Outer Space* (1960) has animation connecting kinaesthetic space with outer space.

Breer's films also introduce 'live' photographic images in the form of collage, as in *Eyewash* (1959). He has also made some completely live 'action' films, notably *Homage to Jean Tinguely's Homage to New York* (1966) and *Pat's Birthday* (1962) which was made in collaboration with Claes Oldenburg.

The animation collage drawn from social content is part of Stan VanDer-Beek's imagery, with its magazine cuttings, fixed movements and juxtaposition with drawings. The use of scale and size offers an array of associations in which people gain tyres and cars rule people. The sacred paradoxes of the American nightmare became the horror of the rest of the West. The film now becomes the 'political cartoon', as with VanDerBeek's anti-war film *Breathdeath* (1964). *Wheels* (four versions made between 1958 and 1965) portray social horror as the machine runs over life. VanDerBeek's many films range from animated collages to mixed-media films, computer films, to the 'expanded cinema'. Examples of his mixture of assemblage and serious and comic political and social satire are *Skullduggery* (1966), *Summit* (1963), *The Life and Death of a Car* (1962-) and *Science Friction* (1958/65). Needless to say, most of the films are brilliant visual experiences. But VanDerBeek's approach also involves an engrossing concern with the medium as a method of communication. He has explored and expanded the potential of film language as a form in itself and with his Movie-Drome he has explored film's potential for environmental expansion, beyond the flat screen into the surrounding space. His involvement with the technology of visual language has also taken him into multiple-screen projection and thus into the area known as the 'expanded cinema', which is the subject of the next chapter.

5 Conclusion: The Expanding Cinema

When we arrive at the point known as the 'expanded cinema' many additional concepts open up that can be argued in many different ways. I could not possibly include all the approaches to film and many films, film-makers and attitudes have been left out; many aspects are covered more thoroughly in other publications. Still, many attitudes, concepts and styles cross-refer, and if one could reapply some of the general concepts and terms from one to the other a broader understanding would be possible. The generic term 'expanded cinema' covers concepts and attitudes that have already been mentioned in the context of specific films. It implies many things, but in general means film material and activities that branch out beyond the familiar single two-dimensional screen in the cinema-theatre, combined with naturalistic photographic recording on film emulsion. Yet this definition is invalid, because one can use kinaesthetics and animation within the conventional two-dimensional cinema situation, and two-dimensional images can be given multi-screen projection in beyond-the-standard-cinema situations, while naturalistically photographed imagery can be projected on to more than one screen. So no real dividing line exists. I shall therefore stick to films that involve kinaesthetics, inter- and multi-media and moving-picture technology. The rest of the definition I shall leave to you.

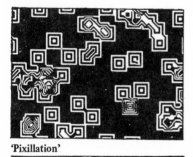

'Pixillation'

When Werner Nekes turned his projector on to an audience while his film was running, we could say that he expanded his cinema. When Lutz Mommartz projected one film through a hole in a screen on to a screen opposite, while a second film was projected through a hole in the opposite screen on to the first screen, he too expanded the cinema. When Stan VanDerBeek or Malcolm Le Grice projected a two-screen film, or like Antonio De Bernardi or Saul Bass, used three or four screens or Charles Eames, eleven screens, they expanded the cinema. When Abel Gance produced his three-screen epic *Napoleon* in the 'twenties (using 360° spinning cameras, cameras on horseback and so on) he expanded the cinema, and so did Takehisa Kosugi when he cut away a movie screen, or James Whitney when he used an analogue computer to make *Lapis*, or Scott Bartlett when he combined video and film colour distortions, or Charles Csuri when he made *Hummingbird* with the aid of a computer. One inevitably ends up describing physical effects and techniques for film *situations*, but a great deal of the personal experience with any presentation is lost in description. Still, in most 'expanded cinema' situations the physical confrontations are exhilarating and stimulating, as if we were stepping into new environments. In most cases – there are exceptions – the physical element itself is the message: the poetry lies in the confrontation between you and it. Allusion to other things, and free association, is diminished (sometimes totally) for the sake of the thing itself, the object.

If we take some of the new imagery that has been put on to film emulsion, we may hit upon something that is often called 'kinaesthetics'. In its fundamental sense it can be taken to mean pure configurations in motion: in other words, motion aesthetics. This imagery and aesthetic can be linked with some of the earlier work of Moholy-Nagy, such as his moving sculpture and his light photographs. Many of these ideas were displayed with light projections during the Bauhaus period, when there was a very strong concern with movement. A more recent light projection activity has involved 'light-shows', which used slide projectors that projected colour patterns moving from the slide position (movement produced by the heat of the lamp, causing the combination of coloured water and oil to change constantly). Marcel Duchamp's 'roto-reliefs' and some of Hans Richter's early films also display an engrossing concern with abstract movement. The growth of technology has facilitated numerous abstract ramifications of motion in film. Among contemporary independent film-makers the major explorers of these techniques have been the Whitneys and Jordan Belson.

John and James Whitney originally called their activity 'motion graphics'. Between 1941 and 1944 the two brothers produced the five films that make up *Film Exercises*. Here we have a concept of image-making that rests on moving patterns, shapes and colours. After 1945 the two brothers worked less often together, at the same time becoming more involved in developing devices to make and control far more elaborate optical light configurations. Thanks to the energy of John Whitney an analogue computer was devised and gradually refined to produce more and more optical patterns. His *Permutations* (1967) and *Catalogue* (1971) use floral and calligraphic patterns as a basis for moving configurations.

While John was developing his analogue computer, James was working by hand on *Yantra* (1950/60), which took ten years to complete. Although he was ostensibly more involved with the myths and concepts of oriental religion, he structured *Yantra* on a specific concentration pattern used to contain psychic forces. He went on to make the beautiful and hypnotic *Lapis* (1963/66), using an analogue computer. This involves subtle radiating dot configurations focused on a centre and unified as a mandala. The colour changes constantly in endlessly fluid movements, producing kaleidoscopic patterns of seemingly infinite richness.

Influenced by the elder Whitneys, the younger brothers, particularly John Jr and Michael, continued to use multiple abstract movements in film, expanding into environmental and multiple-screen presentations, as well as single-screen films such as John Jr's *Byjina Flores*. Michael followed with a more modular film, *Binary Bit Patterns* (1969). In these films we find a growing use of mathematical and computer-controlled configurations. Though many aspects of this were begun by the Whitneys, this whole area of film-making – which overlaps with television – is spreading and developing at a rapid pace and attracting a great deal of interest. Now known as 'cybernetic cinema', it is a method of creating imagery with various types of computers. Here we begin to see the cross-breeding of the artist with the scientist/engineer, to produce a cinema in which technology is an integral part of the content. Films like John Stehura's *Cybernetik 5.3* (1965/9) use computer-based imagery to evolve continuous and vast panoramas of abstract form and space, patterns whose movement and colour offer a newer and larger field for the visual imagination.

These new sources provide not only an array of abstract patterns but also variations on imaginary and concrete figurative forms. Films like Peter Kamnitzer's *City-scape* (1968) use imaginary city-like structures, while Stan VanDerBeek (with Kenneth Knowlton) has produced various computer films such as *Poem Fields* and *Collide-oscope* (1966), which is made up of mosaic-like configurations and images formed by breaking down words. Many of these activities are still in the early stages and most of them are happening in the United States, where various scientists and corporations such as the Bell Telephone Laboratories have collaborated with artists in exploring the field. The number of films being made with the help of computers is growing rapidly.

No discussion of kinaesthetic films can omit the work of Jordan Belson. Originally a painter, he started in 1947 to make single-frame animated films – first with cards, like Robert Breer, and later with animated scrolls. From 1947 to 1953 he made such films as *Mambo* (1952) and *Mandala* (1952/3). His work at the Morrison Planetarium in San Francisco no doubt involved him with space and astronomical forms, with the result that his more recent films have been described by Gene Youngblood as the 'cosmic cinema of Jordan Belson'. With *Allures* (1961), Belson changed from single-frame animation to more organic spatial outbursts and transformations. Personal imagination, ideologies of space and space flight and philosophical concepts drawn from Buddhism and *The Tibetan Book of the Dead* refined Jordan's imagery to the point where it became sensitive non-figuration related only to inner mystical feelings. Amorphic changes and fusions develop into the splendid period which begins with the film *Re-entry* (1964). Launching himself further into 'cosmic' imagery, into some of the most powerful and overwhelming abstract imagery in film, Belson followed with *Phenomena* (1965) and the even stronger *Samadhi* (1966/7). Of the intensity of the latter film Belson himself has said, 'I knew I had achieved the real substance of what I was trying to depict. Natural forces have that intensity: not dreamy but hard, ferocious.'[1] Soon after this he made his sun-bursting film *Momentum*.

New creations are provoked by the growth of new environments. Space and technology are becoming as familiar a frame of reference as trees and comics. From this, and from the personal imagination that they provoke, a continuous attempt is being made to translate, transcribe and restate the newly forming language. Film, with its insistent ability to hold time/motion imagery, has provided the basic medium for containing many of these elements visually. So the cinema expands. Here too we find the varied breed of image-conjurers whose images become a statement all on their own. The technology and the chemistry transform the familiar form into a kind of re-enchantment of that form, and through this transformation a new form is born. The process of the change, like the opening of a flower, has its own fascination; the opening, as well as the flower itself, awes and engrosses. The fascination of the visual tool has become more pronounced as television technology and materials become more accessible, and with the awareness of the potential of colour both in film and in television. Colour alteration has become not merely a technique but almost a visual world in itself, and many films are being made with colour as the dominant principle. Others are made in conjunction with television. Films like Scott Bartlett's *Off/On* or *Moon* have explored the combined language of colour video-tape recording (VTR) and 16mm film. The resulting visual sensation is a cross between kinaesthetics and figurative abstractions. Electronic celluloid is finding a growing corroboration in the increasing number of films being made in this way. The video-to-film imagery represents a new stage in visual thinking – as is shown by the films of Tom De Witt, Jud Yalkut, Lutz Becker, Aldo Tambellini and Loren Sears, among many others. The content still ranges from abstraction to narrative, so we may find anything from pure colour and line patterns to revisualized documentary films – as in Sheldon Rochlin's

Paradise Now, which was originally made on a portable video-tape unit, then put through an electronic colour synthesizer and finally put on to motion-picture film. Rochlin, who also made the crisp film documentary *Vali,* here fused the visual ingredients of optical enchantment with a more explicit story.

The consideration of whether television will replace film, or whether the two will support each other, or whether they will remain separate, can at this point be only a syllogistic argument. Television and VTR are definitely their own medium, producing their own visual sensations. Much of the work of Nam June Paik, for example, who has done an enormous amount of creative work with television, is markedly different from film, although there is some similarity in the concepts and the type of abstract images used. The innate difference between the two media will, however, produce different concepts. Television is far more immediate than film; it is electronic and shows a 'received' image. Film is a more extended process: it is chemical and shows a 'projected' image. Having worked with both television and film, I have found a very different 'feeling' in the way the two work. The imagery produced by them induces completely different sensations, though verbal description might make them sound the same.

For the reason of space I cannot discuss the vast impact that television and video is now having, but we can be sure that its scope and importance as an expressive and communicative medium will increase. Because it is – like film – such a potent medium, political and commercial pressure must undoubtedly affect its creative growth. Many of the personal and independent film-makers' aspirations for exposure and exhibition have theoretically been realized in the possibilities presented by television cassettes, since films can be seen privately, without the controls and limitations implicit in theatrical and commercial distribution. The idea is similar to that of home libraries of 8mm films. However, the monopoly-controlled EVR systems (film cassettes received by television sets) have already placed more emphasis on direct VTR systems, where no transfer to special film is required. This again is another reason for more direct use of video material for personal statement: it avoids interference from certain areas of the commercial cinema industry.

Many film-makers are turning toward a greater emphasis on personal television expression because of the accessibility of small, compact and relatively inexpensive television and video-tape units (some of which are less expensive than some ciné equipment). It is not that television will replace film expression, but merely that television is a new and sometimes more immediate medium in which many people can express themselves and explore new ideas. It also bypasses some of the suffocating attitudes and controls that have gripped film. Because it explores and develops visual time/space sensibilities, television is, in part, an aspect of the expanding cinema.

In film expression one essential expanding device is to thrust outwards beyond the frame. This, at least, gives a literal meaning to the term 'expanding cinema', which is not an addition to cinema, but part of cinema. Consider, for example, that a number of film ideas go back to the evolution of film, when the principles of light and the projection of light were the initial elements from which shadow plays, magic lantern shows, or things like E. G. Robertson's *Le Magasin Pittoresque* developed, projecting illusionistic light images into large rooms. The expanding cinema takes such basic elements of the film concept and restates them. It does not merely use the image on the film emulsion, it is also involved with the projection of light, plus endless variations in time and movement. Then if we think of perspective boxes, mural paintings, mirrors, kaleidoscopes, photo-montages, collages, actions, circuses and theatre, we begin to understand the urge to let film escape from its fixed frame. If we can understand how painters, after 'Action Painting', needed to move the action beyond the canvas, then we can also understand the urge of film-makers to move the frame beyond the screen.

In the expanded cinema the images contained in the moving frames function less as expression and suggested associations and more as actual occurrences. What appears in the frame is important, but the way in which it happens is also essential. The expanded film is more outgoing and conclusive in the form in which it is presented. The contained film is far more ingoing and suggestively inclusive. Both can be highly expressive or evocative.

The first step into expanded film was multiple-screen projection. A two-screen project is a simple step forward from the single screen, with an essential juxtaposition of two actions, movements or images – sometimes counter-movements, sometimes parallel movements, sometimes counter-statements, sometimes simultaneous statements (on stage and backstage at once, or the splitting apart of the superimposed thoughts of a single screen). The parallel development of two strains which, though separate, still fuse is a dual relationship that is soon absorbed by the eye and mind and not consciously remembered. Take such films as Warhol's *Chelsea Girls*, Van-DerBeek's *Walls of the Worlds*, Le Grice's *Little Dog for Roger* or *Love*

Story II, made only of colour changes, or Fred Drummond's *Globestrobe*. Of course we need not stop at two screens, as De Bernardi's three- and four-screen films show; we also have Francis Thompson's six-screen *We are Young* (shown at Expo '67), John Chamberlain's seven-screen *Wide Point* or Charles Eames's eleven-screen *Think,* made for IBM and shown at the New York World Fair in 1964. The multiplicity of screens and moving images can produce clusters, counterpoints, oppositions and parallels in an endless statement, to say nothing of the expanding statement of scale that the commercial film industry explored with Wide-Screen, Cinemascope, Cinerama and 70mm film.

When in 1927 the Dadists showed Picabia's *Relâche* with music by Satie, the ballet included two nudes (one of whom was Duchamp) who were occasionally lit up, actions in among the audience and René Clair's film *Entr'acte* literally between the acts. They expanded the cinema by removing these various elements from their familiar contexts. This was the beginning of the projection of film into the environment and out of the static-projection box-screen relationship. So when Ed Emshwiller (known for his earlier *Relativity* (1963/6) and his stroboscope-imaged film, *Image, Flesh and Voice*) projected his *Body Works* (1965) of dance pieces on to actual dancers, or when John Cage and Ronald Nameth put on *HPSCHD* with eight thousand slide images, a hundred motion picture films and fifty-two loudspeakers, we have an extension of film in which the projected moving and still images are no longer an isolated component of the environment, but an element in a more total situation. Multiple-screen projections create moving relationships of light images falling next to and on top of each other, the element of extension lying in the way the moving image and light relationships themselves form a relationship with moving bodies, and fixed forms combine with sounds as if giant live collages were unfolding.

What Peter Weibel and Valie Export call 'expanded movies' give some idea of film's extension into live action. All the elements used are considered to be the material – film, light, bodies – for a more direct audience relationship that has the sensitivity of live theatre or of 'happenings'. Weibel and Export, both from Vienna, deal with what they called direct art. In Export's *Ping Pong* (1968) (see p. 89) the action is simple, but the integration of the actuality of the live situation is more complex, involving an understanding of the dimensional and sculptural consequences of such an action. The space immediately changes and the film is no longer 'up there' but 'right here'. In the film *Cutting* by Export and Weibel there is a stage by stage transference from the moving film, to the changing screen, to the actual physical body. Part one opens as a documentary. A projected window is cut out of a paper screen and part two is a 'talkie' as a homage to Marshall McLuhan. The main element of this part is the phrase: 'the content of the writing is the speech.' The phrase is cut out of the screen by Valie Export. She shouts the word 'speech'. Part three is in homage to Bazooka Joe and part four is in homage to Greta Garbo. Part five is the full

Q

public action which occurs alongside the paper screen. Valie Export sucks the penis of Peter Weibel in the light of the projector.

The extension of live material in film is further touched on in Weibel's and Export's *Electron Ray TUBE,* which is based on an autogenerating sound screen. The screen is prepared with photo cells, which transform the light waves projected on to the screen into sound waves, each picture having an equivalent sound. In Peter Weibel's *Nivea* an actor stands for one minute (frozen like a still) in front of a screen lit only by the projector light. The soundtrack (on a tape recorder) consists of the sound of a running camera, while the image on the screen is the actor's shadow. This kind of expansion is carried further in Weibel's *Fingerprint* (1968) where fingerprints on celluloid are put on to each 35mm frame. This hand-made film was intended to be projected on to the rather large screen of a 'drive-in' cinema. Weibel's work, like Valie Export's, is evolving not simply into 'direct action' but into what Weibel calls 'expanded communication'. In his *Theater der Thenmaien Perzeption* or his 'Action Lecture' he exposes the interrelationships of the senses, in that he uses as many combinations of intermedia experiences as in an 'actual time' performance. Valie Export, however, produced a symbolic metamorphosis of the actual event and a cinematic concept in her *Tapp und Tast Film* (Touch Film, 1968) (see p. 89).

'*Tapp und Tastkino*' pleads for public sex. In a more esoteric sense the Fluxus 'tactile boxes' invite you to put your hands into closed boxes (through rubber diaphragms) and to touch the different elements in there (powder, earth, metal, water). The *Tapp und Tastkino* states and allows a renewal, or even a discovery of sensations. Unseen elements transform by touch alone – water, for example, can feel solid. The redevelopment of the senses is part of the essential statement of the expanded cinema.

In order to continue this redevelopment the film material itself becomes part of the many other sense media. Film becomes involved as part of the intermedia experience of enclosing and enveloping at the moment of presentation. As with the Cage/Nameth *HPSCHD* or Milton Cohen's Space Theatre or VanDerBeek's Movie-Drome, one finds the total audiovisual sensation making the space an organic fluctuation of changing and moving experiences. The realization of moving scales, light perceptions and encompassing physicality is hard to describe. The whole space in Wolf Vostell's *Electronic Happening Room* is an assemblage of objectives, movements, scales, textures, sounds, colours, confrontation; the viewer himself seems to be changed into a moving piece within it. The film projections, which change and relight, also redefine forms and shapes, and cover and uncover what becomes an overwhelming series of discoveries.

When Hans Scheugl projected his *Sugar Daddies* (1968) on to a lavatory wall he was offering an instance of cinema within an environment (see p. 89). The film extended itself by turning back on itself. The wall was transformed by the projected wall into a wall covered with words from a wall of its own kind. Everything shifted, only to re-establish itself. The wall *per se* was not important, the graffiti themselves were not important, the film itself was not important, but the whole room was, throwing the moving projected image on to the world.

The projection is accompanied by a resurfacing, or as Wolf Vostell calls it a 'decollaging'. The process of breaking down allows space for re-entry. Time is re-presented, and out of the sense of disorder, order is established. The 'happening' that uses film, such as Carolee Schneeman's *Illinois Central* or *Night Crawlers* or Robert Whitman's *The American Moon* or *Prune Flat,* exploits the basic contrast between flat and three-dimensional space and movement. But the two types of space and the two aspects of movement are physically fused by the breakdown, reformed by the complete sensory involvement of the participators. Literal images and real forms move in counterpoint. This live relationship is within the audience, which is constantly shifting.

When in 1967 Jeffrey Shaw projected looped films over his two-storey plastic inflatable inside which forty nude people were floating, the projection made the film images into three-dimensional moving abstractions that were also transparent, moving and growing. They were alternating and reshaping, and the images became multifaceted. VanDerBeek made a multifaceted screen so that the moving image broke apart. I myself worked on a cube screen in which all the component cubes moved into different positions as the moving images were projected over them. The result was that the image (a face) became a multiple of changing pieces. Each piece became a configuration of the other pieces; the distortion gave each piece a greater unity and clarity than if it had been static.

So we have the moving image projected like a blanket, reforming some forms, swallowing up others, renewing others. The moving picture happening. Events of changing light and moving forms. A scale and time constantly altering. Fantasy, thought, and concept. These are the result of thoughts formed, feelings felt and commitments made. Plastic actions become the physical self. Film is thrown out into the environment and its many forms state our own presence. The lists can grow and the blind eye still will see nothing, but the images of experience will flow rhythmically. Film is expanding in all directions.

If the measuring of the film frame or the frame within the frame, or the man walking on the screen is stated as the man walking on the screen, the information presented by film states explicitly what one sees and *is* what one sees. Film will be oscilloscopes and laser beams, and holographic illusionary three-dimensional objects. Film is fantastic because behind each new way and each method lies the basic aim of realizing the inner sensibilities in a given form. Each of us lives in a series of simultaneous relationships and we are each the accumulation of these relationships. As in film, one move, one look produces so many others and in this relentless process there is no return. Change is a thing we absorb and create; it is all around us even if we stand still thinking that we are safe. The points are many, the directions endless. One could lits and label and show but all the things are together.

When feathers are made in plastic we think in plastic terms. Film will be, film is and film was.

Books and Magazines Consulted and for Further Reading

BOOKS

Battcock, Gregory (ed.), *The New American Cinema*, New York: E. P. Dutton & Co., 1967.
—— (ed.), *The New Art*, New York: E. P. Dutton & Co., 1966.
—— (ed.), *Minimal Art*, New York: E. P. Dutton & Co., 1968.
Becker, Jürgen and Vostel, Wolf, *Happenings*, Hamburg: Rowohlt Taschenbuch Verlag, 1965.
Carmen, Ira H., *Movies, Censorship and the Law*, Ann Arbor: The University of Michigan Press, 1967.
Cassirer, Ernst, *The Philosophy of Symbolic Forms*, Connecticut: Yale University Press, 1966.
Cowie, Peter (ed.), *International Film Guide*, London: Tantivy Press; New York: A. S. Barnes; published annually since 1963.
Donner, Jorn, *The Films of Ingmar Bergman*, New York: Dover Publications Inc., 1972; (published by Indiana University Press in 1964 as *The Personal Vision of Ingmar Bergman*).
Duchamp, Marcel, *Dialogues with Marcel Duchamp*, London: Thames and Hudson, 1971.
Durgnat, Raymond, *Eros in the Cinema*, London: Calder and Boyars, 1967.
—— *Films and Feeling*, London: Faber and Faber, 1967.
Eisenstein, Sergei, M., *The Film Sense*, London: Faber and Faber, 1958.
Eisner, L. H., *The Haunted Screen*, London: Thames and Hudson, 1969.
Geduld, Harry M. (ed.), *Film Makers on Film Making*, Bloomington: Indiana University Press; London: Penguin Books, 1970.
Gidal, Peter, *Andy Warhol*, London: Studio Vista, 1971; New York: E. P. Dutton & Co., 1971.
Graham, Peter, *A Dictionary of the Cinema*, London: Zwemmer, 1968; New York: A. S. Barnes, 1968.
Hein, Birgit, *Film im Underground*, Berlin: Verlag Ullstein, 1971.
Huaco, George, A., *The Sociology of Film Art*, New York: Basic Books, 1965.
Jacobs, Lewis, *The Rise of the American Film*, New York: Teachers College Press, 1968.
Kirby, Michael, *Happenings*, New York: E. P. Dutton & Co., 1965.
Klee, Paul, *Pedagogical Sketchbook*, London: Faber and Faber, 1953.
Low, Rachael, *The History of the British Film*, Vols 2, 3 and 4, London: Allen and Unwin.
Manvell, Roger (ed.), *Experiment in the Film*, London: The Grey Walls Press, 1949.
Mekas, Jonas, *Movie Journal: The Rise of the New American Cinema 1959-71*, New York: Collier Books, 1972.
Meyer, Ursula, *Conceptual Art*, New York: E. P. Dutton & Co., 1972.
Miller, Arthur C. and Strenge, Walter, *American Cinematographer's Manual*, Hollywood: American Society of Cinematographers.
Renan, Sheldon, *An Introduction to the American Underground Film*, New York: E. P. Dutton & Co., 1967; (published in London by Studio Vista in 1968 as *The Underground Film*).
Sharps, Wallace C., *Dictionary of Cinematography and Sound Recording*, London: Fountain Press, 1959.
Sitney, P. Adams, *Film Culture Reader*, New York: Praeger, 1970; (published in London by Secker and Warburg in 1971 as *Film Culture*).
Spottiswoode, Raymond, *Film and Its Techniques*, Berkeley: University of California Press, 1963.
Stephenson, Ralph, *Animation in the Cinema*, London: Zwemmer, 1967; New York: A. S. Barnes, 1967.

Tyler, Parker, *Underground Film*, New York: Grove Press, 1970: London: Secker
and Warburg, 1971.
Youngblood, Gene, *Expanded Cinema*, London: Studio Vista, 1970.

MAGAZINES AND JOURNALS

Afterimage
Cinema Rising
Cinematics
Cinim (London Film-makers' Co-operative)
Film Culture
Film Forum
Filmkritik
Film Kunst
Filmmakers Newsletter
Radical Software
Skoop
Take One

Notes

CHAPTER 3

1. *National Film School, Report of a Committee to Consider the Need for a National Film School* (HMSO, 1967).
2. Octavio Getino and Fernando Solanas, 'Toward a Third Cinema', *Tricontinental* (Havana, 1969).
3. *New York Film-makers' Newsletter,* Vol. 1, No. 12 (1968).

CHAPTER 4

1. I owe most of this information to George A. Huaco's *The Sociology of Film Art* (New York: Basic Books, 1965).
2. *The Seamless Web* (Allen Lane, 1970).
3. Ernst Cassirer, *The Philosophy of Symbolic Forms* (Connecticut: Yale University Press, 1966).
4. A statement made in *Film Culture* magazine.
5. *Film Culture* magazine.
6. From a brochure.
7. *Film Culture* magazine.
8. Ibid.
9. A statement made to the author.
10. A statement made to the author.
11. A statement made to the author.
12. From a brochure.
13. Ibid.
14. Quoted in W. N. Whitehead's 'Process and Reality', in *Speculative Philosophy.*
15. Ibid.
16. *Film Culture* magazine.
17. A statement made to the author.
18. *Film Culture* magazine.
19. *Film Culture* magazine.
20. *Film Culture* magazine.
21. Ibid.
22. From a catalogue.
23. *Film Culture* magazine.

CHAPTER 5

1. Quoted in Gene Youngblood, *Expanded Cinema* (Studio Vista, 1970).

Index of Films

Where no date is given, the film has proved impossible to date.

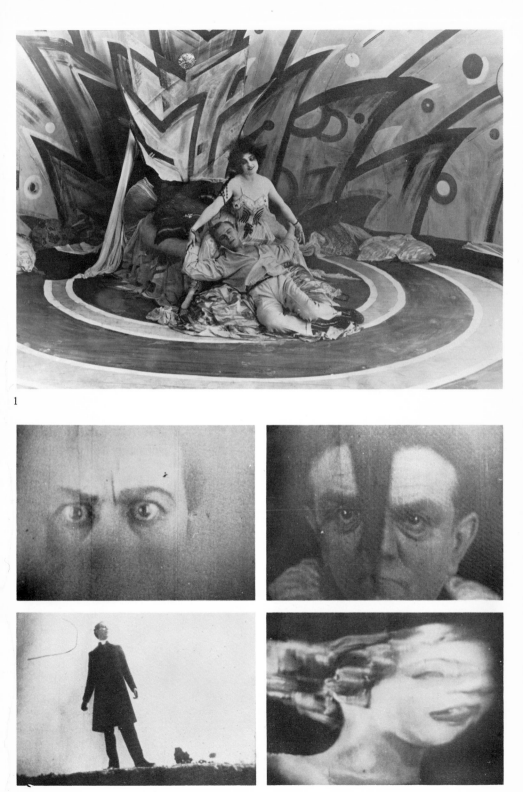

1

2, 3, 4, 5

6

7

8

9

10

11

12

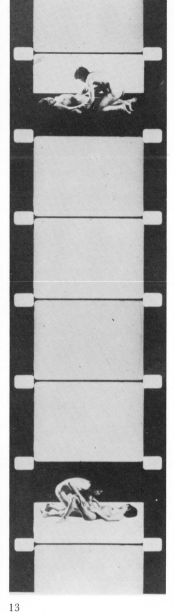

13

14

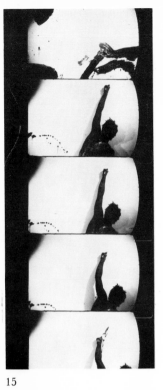

15

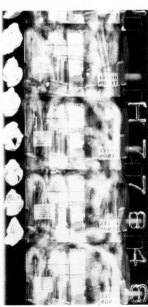

16

17

18

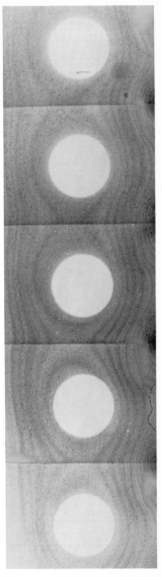

19

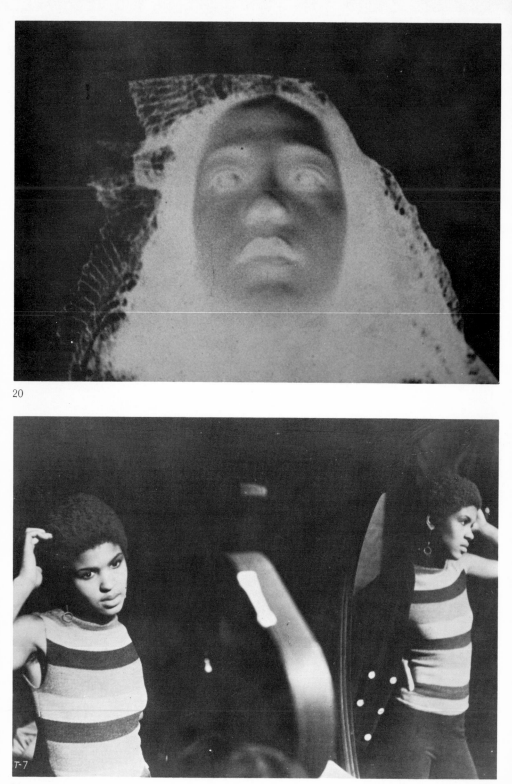

20

21

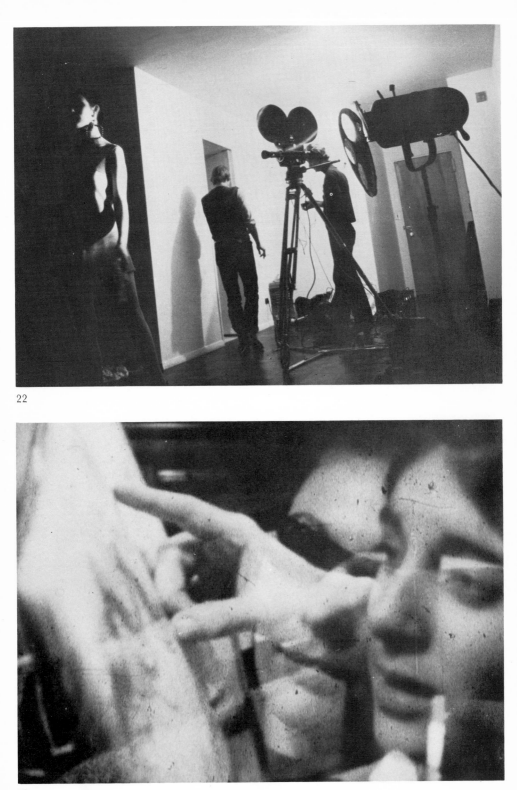

22

23

24

25

26

27

28

29

30

31

32

33, 34   35

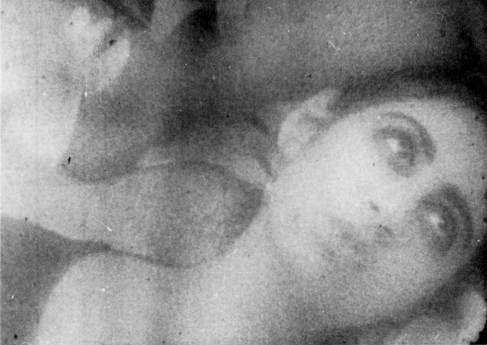

36

37

38

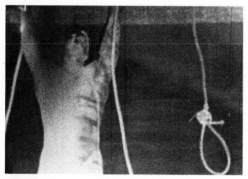

39

40

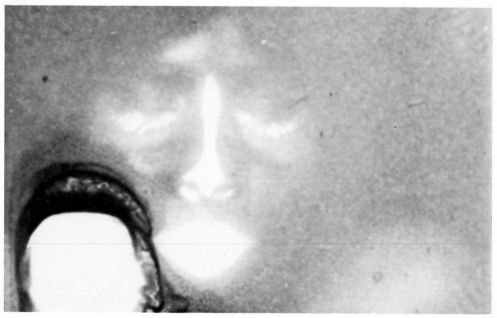

41

42

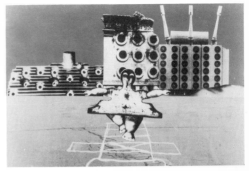

43

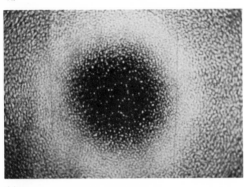

44

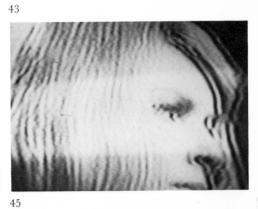

45

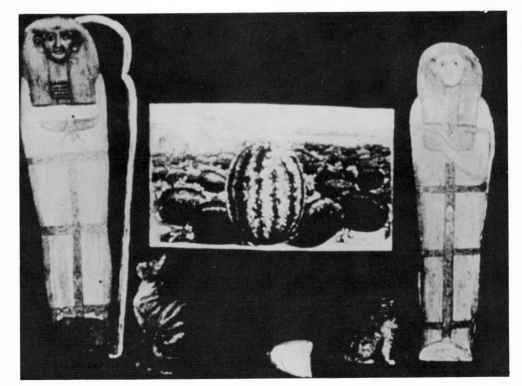

46

47

48

49

50

51

52

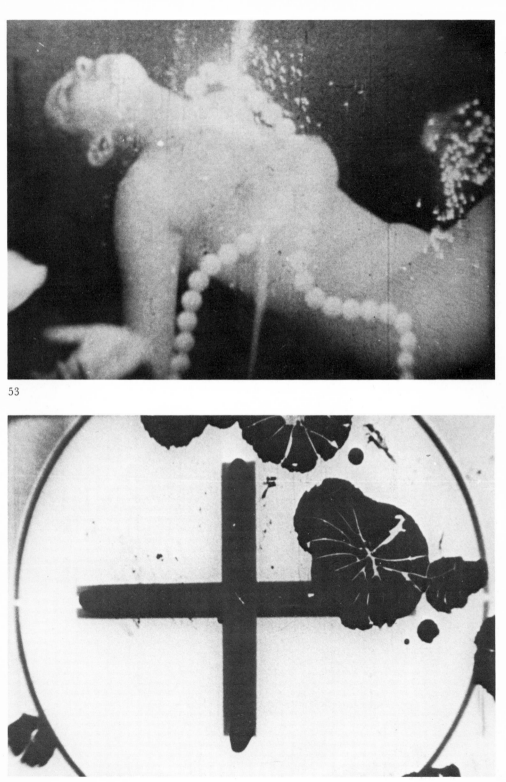

53

54

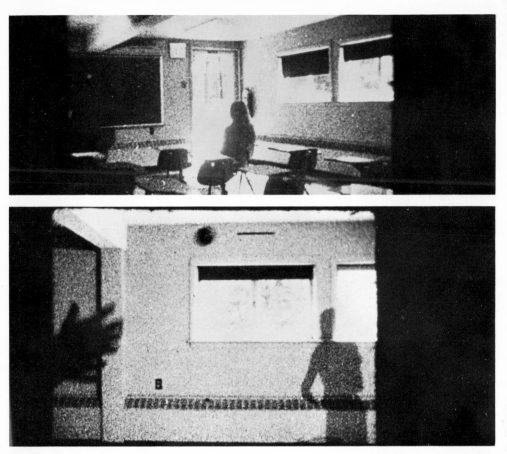

55, 56

58

59

60

61

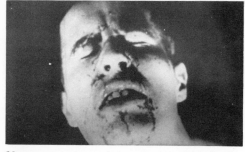

62

63

64

65

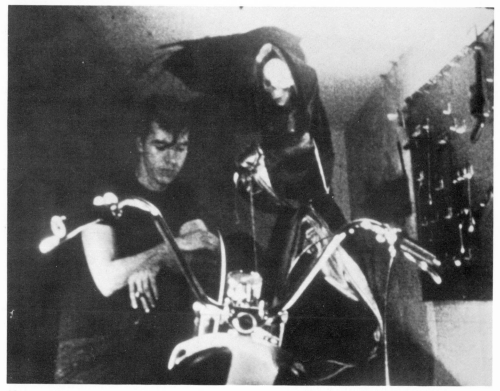

66

67

68

69

70

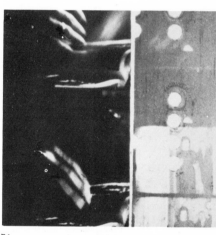

71

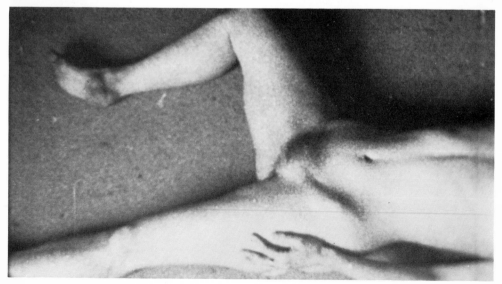

72

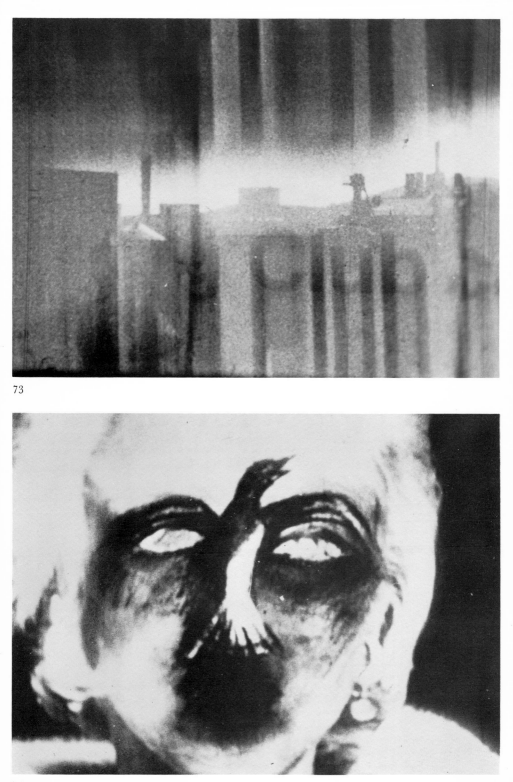

73

74

75

76

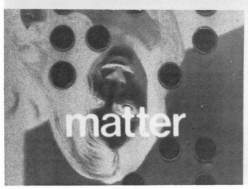

matter

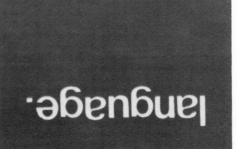

·language

77

79

80

81

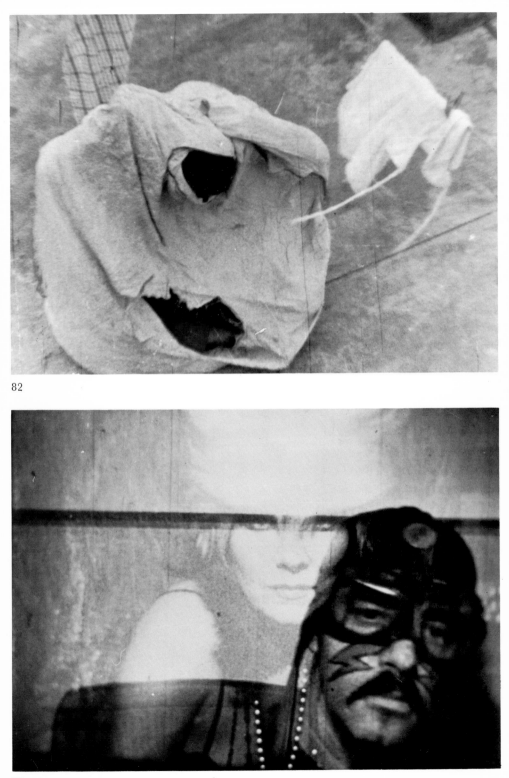

82

83

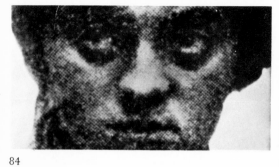

84

85

86

87

88

89

90

91

92

93

94

95

96

97

98

99

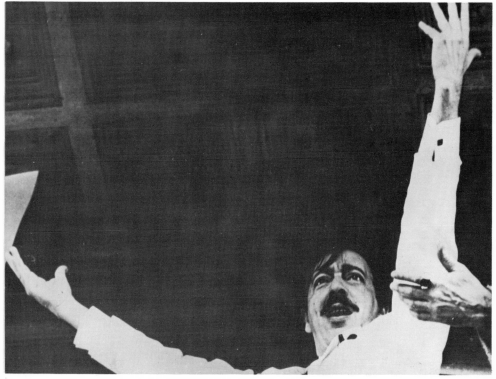

100

101

102

103

104

105

106

107

108

109

110

111

112

113

114

115

116

Illustrations

1 Robert Wiene's *Genuine* (Germany, 1920).

2, 3, 4, and 5 Scenes from Germaine Dulac's *The Seashell and the Clergyman* (France, 1926).

6 Reinosuke Kinugasa's *A Page of Madness* (Japan, 1926);

7 Lev Kulechov's *The Extraordinary Adventures of Mr West in the Land of the Bolshevik* (USSR, 1924) – two newly discovered examples of expressionist film-making outside western Europe.

8 Maya Deren in her *Meshes of the Afternoon* (USA, 1943).

9 *Meshes of the Afternoon.*

10 Jean Cocteau's *Orphée* (France, 1950).

11 Robert Frank and Al Leslie: *Pull My Daisy* (USA, 1958).

12 Fernand Léger: *Le Ballet Mécanique* (France, 1924).

13 Paul Sharits: *Piece Mandala/End War* (USA, 1966).

14 Malcolm Le Grice: *Berlin Horse* (UK, 1970).

15 A sequence from *Ana* (Austria, 1964), one of Kurt Kren's films of a Günter Brus *Materialaktion.*

16 From Kren's *Venezia Kaputt* (Austria, 1968).

17 From a *cinetract* made in Paris in May 1968 by a collective of French film-makers including Jean Luc Godard.

18 Godard's *British Sounds* (France, 1969).

19 David Larcher's *Mare's Tail* (UK, 1969).

20 Maya Deren's *Ritual in Transfigured Time* (USA, 1946).

21 ´ Jonas Mekas's *Guns of the Trees* (USA, 1961).

22 Andy Warhol shooting *Chelsea Girls* (USA, 1966).

23 Afredo Leonardi's *Organum Multiplum* (Italy, 1967).

24 Marie Menken and Gerard Malanga in Andy Warhol's *Chelsea Girls.*

25 Warhol's *Poor Little Rich Girl* (USA, 1965).

26 Warhol's *Kiss* (USA, 1964).

27 Warhol's *Mario Banana* (USA, 1964).

28 Mario Montez, superstar.

29 Andy Warhol and the cast of *Chelsea Girls* in The Factory.

30 Mamma Mekas in Jonas Mekas's *Reminiscences of a Journey to Lithuania* (USA, 1971). The scene also appears in *Going Home* by Adolfas Mekas.

31 Tiny Tim in Ron Rice's *Chumlum* (USA, 1964).

32 Rice's *Senseless* (USA, 1962).

33 and 34 Jack Smith's *Flaming Creatures* (USA, 1962–3).

35 *Normal Love* (USA, 1963) by Jack Smith, an epic that never got completed. Diane Di Prima (as the pregnant woman), Mario Montez, Andy Warhol and Joan Adler on Claes Oldenburg's cake.

36 *Flaming Creatures.*

37 Wim van der Linden's *Hawaiian Lullaby* at Knokke, 1967.

38 Jack Smith and Mario Montez.

39 Ernst Schmidt's *Bodybuilding* (Austria, 1965–6).

40 Carolee Schneemann in her event *Ghost Reu* (USA, 1965).

41 Barbara Rubin's *Cocks and Cunts* (USA, 1966).

42 Robert Breer: *Form Phases I* (USA, 1952).

43 Erling Johansson: *Anima Mundi* (Sweden, 1965–7).

44 James Whitney: *Lapis* (USA, 1963–6).

R

The Author and Publishers are grateful to the following organizations and individuals for the use of illustrations which appear in this book: Bob Adler; The British Film Institute; Film Verlag der Autoren, Munich; Museum of Modern Art, New York; The New York Film-maker's Co-op; The Other Cinema/ Politkino; The Royal Film Archive of Belgium; Andy Warhol's Factory Fotos, and the individual film-makers themselves.

General Index

Adler, Bob, 13
Adler, Joan, 185
After Image, 70
Alexeieff, Alexandre, 29, 230
Alvarez, Santiago, 71
Anderson, Lindsay, 45
Angeli, Franco, 96
Anger, Kenneth, 20, 41, 43, 55, 85, 154–8, 195
animation, 29, 33, 38–9, 41, 42, 102, 230–1, 233–4; and pixillation, 39, 41
Anschütz, Ottomar, 25
Anti-University, Britain, 62
Antonioni, Michelangelo, 63, 92, 108
Antonucci, Emile, 163–5
Apollinaire, Guillaume, 26
Arbetsgruppen för Film (AFF), 80
Arenhill, Ake, 80
Argentina, 61, 71
Argus, The, 23
Aristotle, 118
Armory Show, New York, 1913, 34
Artaud, Antonin, 28, 187
Arts Lab, London, 63–4, 69
Australia, 38, 61, 98–100
Austria, 61, 83, 86, 87–91; and *Materialaktion*, 87–8, 89
Autant-Lara, Claude, 29

Bach, J. S., 30, 33
Bacigalupo, Massimo, 92, 96, 97, 138, 143–5
Baillie, Bruce, 165–7, 195
Bargellini, Pierfrancesco, 96, 97, 138
Barlow, Roger, 37, 55
Bartlett, Scott, 236, 238
Baruchello, Gianfranco, 95, 97, 118, 143, 192, 215
Bass, Saul, 235
Basse, Wilfred, 32
Bauhaus, 187, 236
Beatles, The, 44, 62, 110
'Beats', the, 45, 50–1, 62
Beatty, Talley, 40
Beavers, Robert, 161
Beck, Julian, 56
Becker, Lutz, 238
Belgium, 12, 24, 61, 83, ·103; *and see* International Experimental Film Festival
Belson, Jane, 55
Belson, Jordan, 42, 55, 236, 237–8
Bene, Carmelo, 225–6
Bergamo Film Festival, 97
Bergman, Ingmar, 28, 43
Berkeley Barb, 23
Berlin International Film Festival, 86, 87
Bernard, Sidney, 49
Berne, Joseph, 37

Bierce, Ambrose, 37
Biggs, Ronald, 162
Biguardi, Umberto, 96
Bitzen, G. W. 'Billy', 181
Blomdahl, Karl-Birger, 80
Blue Book, The, 110
Bolivia, 71
Borowczyk, Walerian, 232
Boultenhouse, Charles, 41
Bouchard, Thomas, 38
Bragaglia, Guilio, 26
Brahms, Johannes, 33
Brakhage, Stan, 41, 43, 55, 98, 124, 127, 138, 139, 145–52, 153, 154, 162, 165, 215, 216, 232; *Metaphors on Vision*, 151
Branaman, Bob, 154
Brando, Marlon, 157
Brandt, Bill, 178
Brazil, 61, 71, 226
Breer, Robert, 171, 195, 232–3, 237
'Brighton School', 26, 38, 154
Britain, 26, 33, 83, 86, 102; Arts Council 67; contemporary avant-garde film in, 61–76, 84; development of avant-garde film in, 38–9; 'Free Cinema' documentary, 43, 44–5, 62, 92; and politics, 71–3; social and economic constraints in, 65–7; technical orientation of films, 73–5; visual arts in, 62
British Film Institute, 54, 64, 67–8
Brocani, Franco, 94
Brodie, Bill, 72
Brook, Peter, 185
Brooks, David, 220
Broughton, James, 41, 42
Brown, Kenneth, 56
Brunius, Jacques, 28
Brus, Günter, 87, 88, 196, 197, 198, 199, 200
Brussels, International Congress of Avant-Garde Film-makers at, 33
Bryan, Winifred, 117
Buñuel, Luis, 26, 28, 30, 44, 54, 132, 133, 209
Burckhardt, Rudy, 199
Burnshaw, Stanley, 125–6
Bute, Mary Ellen, 38
Buttenbender, Gisela, 208

Cage, John, 46–7, 121, 128, 241, 242
Calder, Alexander, 33
Canada, 114; contemporary avant-garde film in, 61, 99, 102–103; National Film Board, 39, 102
Canadian Underground Minifestival, 102–103
Cannes Film Festival, 44, 87

261

262

Cantrill, Arthur, 100
Cantrill, Corrinne, 100
Canudo, 26
Capanna, Roberto, 93
Caravaggio, M. A. A., 141
Carracci, 160
Cassavetes, John, 50
Cassirer, Ernst, 136
Cavalcanti, Alberto, 38
censorship in film, 53, 65, 83, 97
Centazzo, E., 96
Centazzo, R., 96
Cézanne, Paul, 93, 114
Chabrol, Claude, 44
Chamberlain, John, 241
Chamberlain, Wyn, 13, 19
Chayevsky, Paddy, 44
Chessa, Mauro, 96, 97
Chicago Seed, 23
Chomette, Henri, 29
Ciné-Club de France, 54
Cineindependent, 69
Cinema, 70
Cinema Action, 68, 72
Cinema Militante, 97
Cinema Rising, 70
Cinema 16, 54–5
Cinemantics, 70
Cinema et Cie, 26
Cinémathèque Français, 29, 44, 54, 81
cinéma vérité, 36, 50, 72, 93, 142, 227;
   and see documentary
Cinim, 64
Cinerama, 29
Clair, René, 27–8, 241
Clarke, Shirley, 207, 227
Clayton, Jack, 45
Clementi, Pierre, 83, 94
Club des Amis du Séptième, 54
Cobbing, Bob, 64
Cocteau, Jean, 132, 155, 156, 166, 167, 226
Cohen, Milton, 242
Cohen-Séat, Gilbert, 26
Cohl, Emile, 26, 230
collage, 192–4, 233–4
computers, 235–6, 237
Conner, Bruce, 55, 192–4, 219
Conrad, Tony, 139, 183–5, 187
Constable, John, 38
Continental Film Review, 69
Cordua, Beatrice, 162
Corso, Gregory, 51
Costard, Hellmuth, 85, 138
Cowan, Bob, 103
Creative Film Foundation, United States, 40, 54
Creative Film Society, 55
Crick, Philip, 64
Csuri, Charles, 236
Cuba, 61, 71, 72
cubism, 23, 90, 114, 161

cummings, e. e., 158
Cunningham, Merce, 47
cybernetics, 75, 237
Czechoslovakia, 103

Daalder, René, 78
Dadaism, 23, 26, 27, 32, 45, 90, 241; neo-, 48, 102
Dali, Salvador, 30, 209
Dante, 132, 146
Daphnis and Chlöe, 201
Davis, Ron, 218
De Andrade, Joaquim Pedeo, 226
De Antonio, Emilio, 72
De Bernardi, Antonio, 94–5, 97, 132–4, 138, 143, 162, 215, 235, 241
De Chirico, Giorgio, 162
De Hirsch, Storm, 153
Déjeuner sur L'herbe, Le, 129
De la Parra, Pim, 77, 78
Delluc, Louis, 26, 44
Denmark, 81, 83
Depression, the, 34, 37
Deren, Maya, 40–1, 43, 54, 153
De Rinaldo, Nicola, 96
De Sica, Vittorio, 92, 108
Deslaw, Eugene, 29
Desnos, Robert, 27
Destruction in Art Symposium, 64, 196, 200
Deutsche Film und Fernsehakademie, Berlin, 83
De Witt, Tom, 238
Dictionary of the Cinema, 207
Dine, Jim, 48
Di Prima, Diane, 19, 21
Disney, Walt, 33, 131, 230
Ditvoorst, Adriaan, 78
documentary, 31, 34, 36, 38, 71, 100, 102;
   and cinéma vérité, 207, 227–8; cinétracts,
   see France; 'Free Cinema', see Britain;
   'newsreel' movement, 71, 82–3, 208; 'pop'
   parodies, see Germany
Doghani, Renato, 96
Domus, 97
Donner, Jorn, 81
Douglas, Bill, 68
Dovzhenko, Alexander, 108, 188
Dramaturgy of Films, 56
Drames de Cinéma, 26
Drummond, Fred, 64, 241
Duchamp, Marcel, 27, 28, 33, 50, 236, 241
Dulac, Germaine, 26–7, 28
Dunford, Mike, 64
Durant, Clovis, 103
Durgnat, Raymond, 196, 205
Dwoskin, Steve, 21, 59, 162, 181, 185, 189, 194, 205, 210–11, 218, 229, 243

Eames, Charles, 235, 241
East Village Other, 23, 154
Edinburgh Festival, 213